Ticket to Ride

the PROMISE *of* AMERICA

a true story

Ticket to Ride

the PROMISE *of* AMERICA

a true story

by

Don Hussey

SEAWALL
BOOKS, INC.

Published by Seawall Books, Inc.

For more information please contact:
Seawall Books, Inc., P.O. Box 194,
North Weymouth, MA 02191
www.Seawallbooks.net

Cover and Interior Design by Kat Massaro
www.BarkingKatDesign.com

Produced by Peapod Press, an imprint of Publishingworks, Exeter, NH
www.publishingworks.com

First Printing
Printed in the United States of America

LCCN: 2010912257

ISBN 978-0-615-37353-9 (paperback)

"Those Were the Days," English lyrics written by Eugene Raskin. Music from traditional Russian folk song. Song was recorded by Mary Hopkin in 1968, and produced by Paul McCartney (Apple Records).

I dedicate this memoir to my wife, Brenda,
who supported and encouraged me to tell my story…
giving her blessing and quietly stepping aside
as I revisited events earlier in my life that challenged
every fiber of my being.

And to my son, Gregory, and my daughter, Jennifer—
my two remarkable children who have left the nest,
armed with resolve and integrity, steeped in the principles
of fair play, determined to find their place in the world.
They have enriched my life beyond measure.

It's past all controversy that what costs dearest is, and ought to be, most valued.

Miguel de Cervantes Saavedra
Don Quixote. Part I. Book iv. Chap xi.

prologue

This memoir began as a letter to my son Gregory dated September 9, 2006—a few weeks before his deployment to Iraq as a field artillery officer with the United States Army. My letter was an attempt to detail for him my life as a young boy growing up on the South Shore in Massachusetts—time and events he knew little about or could never have imagined.

From the time he was a little boy, I would carry my son upstairs when it was time for bed, give him a kiss and set him gently down in his crib. He would pull himself up and stand as soon as I left the room. Most nights I wouldn't make it downstairs before he'd start screaming. During dinner one evening, I turned around in my chair and looked up the stairs at him standing in his crib crying out for me, "Dah…dah!" I said to my wife, "I can't stand this anymore," and I left the table, gathered up some of his books from the other room and went back upstairs.

With his outstretched arms reaching for me, I picked him up and asked, "How about we read some books together. Would you like that?" He nodded in agreement as I wiped his eyes dry, then we settled in next to each other on a bed I'd set up in his room along the opposite wall. He cuddled closer to me as I began reading. And from that night on for the next eight years he went to bed with me at his side. It was always ten books—he'd count them. Some nights, if I didn't fall asleep myself, we'd read all ten a second time through.

* * *

They were all adventurous, exciting and beautifully illustrated children's stories: *Where the Wild Things Are*, by Maurice Sendak;

the Uncle Remus tales of Brer Bear and Brier Fox and Brier Rabbit, by Joel Chandler Harris; several Dr. Seuss books, *The Cat in the Hat* and *How the Grinch Stole Christmas*, by Theodore S. Geisel and Audrey S. Geisel; and *Scuffy, the Tugboat*, by Tibor Gergely, to name a few.

In one of his books there was a fearful-looking, mystical creature from Australian folklore called The Bunyip. It was pictured in colorful detail across two side-by-side pages. I'd ask my son, "Do you want me to turn the page and see what's next? By now he knew what was coming and said, "No...Bunyip." As he got a little older he looked forward to seeing the Bunyip. "I'm not afraid of that Bunyip any more," he announced one night with pride. It wasn't long before I'd read the beginning of a paragraph and he'd finish it from memory. When he was really little, we'd finish the ten books and he would wrap his tiny hand around my right thumb and draw my arm over and around his little body. I'd hold him tight and he'd go off to sleep.

I watched as he grew into a man, playing high school football, baseball and basketball. After high school he went on to Fairfield University and Brown University, where he majored in Chemistry. He was named Captain of the Fairfield Ski Team and Captain of the Fairfield Karate Team—he became a piano player, a skater and subsequently a chemical engineer.

Following the never to be forgotten events of September 11, 2001, he came to my wife and me said with complete resolve, "Dad, Mom, I can't stand on the sidelines with this any longer, I've got to do something."

Weeks later he kissed his wife and two small children goodbye, and left the quiet comfort of his home to become a United States Army officer. I acknowledged his decision, and then followed with, "At some point a young man moves out from under the shadow of his father and takes his own place on the stage. This is your life, not mine. You've put together a plan and are now executing that plan...I admire that. I'm with you, boy. I'll always be with you, and you can count on that."

I dropped him off at the Holiday Inn in Somerville, Massachusetts on a cold February morning in 2003 to join the other enlistees as they left for basic training and OCS (Officer Candidate School) at Ft. Benning, Georgia. After several months of intensive training and a year in Korea, my son received orders to deploy to the deadly and unforgiving Anbar Province in Western Iraq.

I had realized all along that if this day ever came I might never see my son again, so I figured it was time to answer the many questions he must have had for me throughout our time together, but had never asked. I wrote what I could given the constraints of time and handed it to him as he exited the briefing room with his M-16, his armored vest, and his loving heart. On December 3rd at 0600, I watched as my son's flight, heavy with soldiers and weapons of war, lumbered down the runway at Fort Hood, Texas, lifting off into the early morning haze, bound for Iraq.

ONE

Stolen Youth

We moved too many times when I was young and growing up. Brockton, Brookville, Abington, Hanson, Bryantville, Rockland, Marshfield, and Hanover. Except for the city of Brockton, these were small, rural towns south of Boston, not far from the coast. There were eleven or twelve moves and seven different school systems. Most of the time these moves were planned somewhat in advance, but not always. On at least two occasions the local authorities paid us a visit with their papers and badges to serve us a notice to vacate. Sometimes we wouldn't wait for their knock at the door. We'd slip out on the weekend or in the middle of the night. I never got used to being called "the new kid," especially later on when I was in junior high and high school.

All my belongings, clothes included, would fit in a couple of cardboard boxes. It never took my brother Peter and me very long to pack. Paying the rent on time every month became a constant challenge and was often the cause of bitter fights between my mother and stepfather. It got so bad once that my stepfather, who hadn't shaved or been out of the house in three days, opened the front door, snapped his cigarette to the ground, got into our black two-door '4I Buick, and backed it up to the front steps. Then he stepped out, slammed the door, opened the trunk, and with me helping, loaded our old white refrigerator onto the rear bumper of the car. I watched and never said a word as he strung ropes through the rear windows securing the refrigerator to the car. He was always ready with a "backhander" if I questioned him or asked what he was doing. He filled the back seat with a small table, a couple of lamps and some other items.

I

With the refrigerator poised straight up in the air, we drove off to a Saturday morning auction site in Hanover. For fifteen miles the front wheels skipped along, barely touching the ground.

We arrived at the auction site, unloaded the refrigerator, removed the table and other items, and placed them next to each other on the lawn. The auctioneer looked everything over and asked about the refrigerator, "Does it work?" My stepfather assured him it worked perfectly. The auctioneer assigned a number to "the lot," and when it came up for bid, tapped his gavel to the podium and said, "Sold." He collected the money and handed my stepfather $35. It wasn't much, but it was enough to pay the rent and buy his goddamn beer.

My stepfather's name was Charlton Welch. Everyone, including my mother, called him "Bud." It was always Bud Welch. He was a short, balding man who walked with a noticeable limp. He had been in an elevator accident many years before. I never knew the details, but apparently his left leg had been caught between the elevator floor and the approaching platform. It was never right after that.

Bud could whistle like a songbird and knew some fancy rope tricks, but beyond that, he had nothing to offer. He was a mean and abusive man who, when he was drunk, would curl the left side of his upper lip, revealing his hateful, arrogant nature. I always reminded myself that I was not genetically connected to him, and that was all right with me. I never intended to be like him anyway. He never showed much respect for anyone or anything, including himself. He was a sorry character with little moral substance who took out much of his miserable life on me. What little respect I had for him came from knowing he served with the Army's 3rd Infantry Division during the landing at Anzio, Italy in January of 1944.

* * *

I had inherited asthma from my father. Sometimes during the seasonal changes I'd have to take suppositories, which burned like hell, and then lay in bed for hours until the burning and asthma settled down. Sometimes I'd boil some water and pour it into a bowl with a tablespoon of Vicks VapoRub. I'd put a towel over my head and lean over the bowl and breathe in the vapors trying to clear my lungs. I eventually graduated to a medicated inhaler, which usually relieved the tightness in my chest within minutes.

My little brother Peter was born a hemophiliac, a "bleeder." He was very often laid up with towels packed with ice, wrapped around one of his ankles or one of his knees or an elbow as he struggled with the swelling and pain from frequent internal bleeding episodes. He looked to me for love and guidance throughout his childhood, especially as he tried to hold back the tears from the intense pain. When he was born the doctors asked my mother to sign a release giving them permission to perform a circumcision, a normal procedure following the birth of a male child. Although she didn't know it at the time, she suspected that Peter might be a hemophiliac, just like her father. Her father had passed along the carrier gene to my mother. She had been lucky with me, but she wouldn't take the chance again. Against the heavy-handed objections of my father and his family, she refused to give her consent. Had they gone ahead with the procedure despite her objections, Peter would have bled to death.

When Peter bumped himself or fell down, enormous bruises would appear. Even biting his tongue would send him to the hospital for a lengthy stay, and this happened several times when he was a young boy. Peter was always very active, always trying to be like the other kids. But when he was hurt, it was usually pretty serious.

* * *

In early November 1959, I walked out of Marshfield High School and bid farewell to the tormenting shackles of a hopeless future. My mother, stepfather, my younger brother and I were living in a rented, three-room summer cottage on 6th Road in the Rexhame section of Marshfield, Massachusetts. It was a converted cottage, which simply meant there was heat and running water throughout the year. Like most of the cottages nearby, the kitchen cabinets and walls were made of knotty pine wood, and the floors were covered with drab green, worn-through linoleum. Marshfield was a quaint and rather unique mid-sized New England town consisting of seven separate villages: Marshfield Center, Fieldston, Ocean Bluff, Rexhame, Brant Rock, Green Harbor, and Marshfield Hills. Rexhame and Brant Rock were considered the poorest sections of town, mostly unheated summer cottages that were now vacant and boarded up for the winter. Our place was located just a few yards from the Atlantic Ocean which, on a high tide with nor'east winds, would drive ten-foot waves into the rocks below and hammer the concrete retaining wall, sending a soaking sea spray high into the air and out across the road.

It was a Monday morning in early November. My mind was racing as I zipped up my coat, opened the side door and walked down to the end of the road to catch the approaching school bus. The windy, biting chill off the ocean was at my back, pushing me along. Thanksgiving was two weeks away.

The bus stopped to pick me up, and two others who lived nearby. We followed the usual route taking us north along Ocean Street to the center of town, then turning right onto Forest Street, and finally a quick left to the high school. When we pulled into the semi-circular driveway in front of the building, I stepped out, walked along with the others through the main entrance, and started down the hallway. I was in no rush. The others hustled passed me, off to their respective homerooms. Along the wall to my left was the school bulletin board. I had never paid much attention to it in the past, but this was my last day, and for some reason it caught my eye. Enclosed in the glass case were beautifully decorated pictures and drawings of autumn scenes with colored leaves and Indian corn, a traditional New England Thanksgiving display. I stayed out in the hall as the principal began his morning announcements over the sound system: band practice in the auditorium after school, the Thanksgiving Day football game and the homecoming dance, something about the yearbook, and then the Pledge of Allegiance. I wasn't part of anything going on here. The yearbook meant nothing to me. And I wasn't going to the dance.

This was the beginning of my junior year. It had been another move—another new school—six schools in five years.

I was living enough hell at home to fill a book. I was losing my grip in school, and it haunted me. I slipped into the boys' room and remained out of sight while the principal concluded his announcements. When he was finished, I left the boys' room, walked down the empty hallway to my locker, cleaned it out, and headed around the corner to my homeroom. I had done all the thinking about this over the weekend, but never spoke a word of it to anyone. Now I just wanted to do this quietly and with the least amount of interference or discussion. I was leaving and no one was going to stop me.

I entered my homeroom, walked over to my desk and, without sitting down, lifted the desk lid and gathered up my books and whatever else was in there. As I walked past my homeroom teacher on the way out, I said, "I'm leaving. Sorry, but I have no choice." She stood with her mouth open and watched as I swung the door open and headed down the hall to the principal's office.

* * *

When I arrived at the office, I walked through the open door, set my books up on the counter and explained to the secretary what I was doing. "I've had enough. Here are my books. I'm leaving." As I turned and started for the front door the principal, who was watching me from his inner office, came charging out. "Come back here, come in here," he demanded. "Do you know what you're doing?"

I stopped and turned around, and watched as he went back into his office. He reached behind his desk and grabbed a shiny chrome-plated shovel that must have been used in some ceremony days before. He brought it out and held it up for me to see and said, "Take a good look at this. If you leave school, walk out that door, this is all you'll be able to do for the rest of your life, dig ditches!"

I thought to myself, If you only knew what I was dealing with, you might understand. But how could he possibly know? And I was not about to tell him; that was my business. I looked at him and his secretary, who was sitting quietly pretending not to listen, and walked out.

Though I really wanted to stay and make some friends and succeed in school, and maybe find a girlfriend, my mind was made up. There would be no class ring, no junior prom, no senior prom, and no high school diploma. I felt as though I was the only person who ever had to deal with this. The chip on my shoulder was a permanent fixture.

I figured that from that moment on I'd be known as "a high school dropout." The label and the implication would be hard enough, but the lost youth could never be fixed or replaced. I didn't have many friends at Marshfield High School; I had only been there a few weeks. My first day set me on a collision course with the inevitable. I had checked into the office for a brief orientation. The secretary had handed me a copy of the school floor plan and confirmed my class assignments. Then I headed for my new homeroom. I was late, and when I arrived everyone was seated awaiting the first bell.

I walked through the door and headed over to the teacher who was sitting at her desk to the right, in front of the chalkboard. The students were all seated in rows to my left. The guy in the front seat of the second row pointed his finger at me saying, "Ohhh, look at the new kid. What do we have here? And he's got pimples." There were snickers throughout the room.

I stopped—a dead stop—then turned to my left and walked over to him and pointed my finger in his face. I fixed my eyes on his and said, "Watch your mouth!"

"Oooooo, I'm scared," he said. The whole class was involved now, everyone giggling and whispering. All eyes were on me, waiting to see what would happen next. I don't think he realized what he was dealing with or how much heat I brought with me into that room. I was ready to bloody his cocky, self-assured, smart-ass face.

The homeroom teacher jumped out of her seat, hurried over to me and demanded to know my name. I told her who I was, and without further discussion, she instructed me to "Go over there and take a seat." I threw my papers on her desk and headed across the room to the last row of seats on the far right, then sat down and stared out the window to my left.

I was lost from the beginning. I tried to get a handle on things, but my classes were more advanced than Rockland High School, where I'd spent my sophomore year. I fell behind and figured I'd never catch up, and I'm not sure at that point if I even cared. I was overwhelmed with the nonstop fighting, the drinking and the name calling at home. I was sixteen now and could get the hell out if I wanted...and I wanted.

The weekend before I quit school, my stepfather grabbed me by the arm and told me to come with him. We walked about a half mile along Ocean Street to the local market, a small mom and pop grocery store. He barked at me in his usual sarcastic manner, "Now listen, pinhead, I'll get some milk and talk to the clerk. You grab some cans of tuna…stuff 'em in your pockets." It suddenly occurred to me that this was one of the rare moments we did anything together. There had been no milk in the house for cereal that Saturday morning; my brother and I had had our cereal with water. There hadn't been much to eat the night before, either. I had whispered to my brother, "Hey, try sleeping on your stomach. It won't bother you so much."

* * *

Route #139, better known as Plain Street, was the main road connecting Hanover to Duxbury, and it ran right past the front entrance of Marshfield High School. After the principal had finished his lecture with the shovel, I turned and walked out the front door without saying a word. I headed out across the lawn to the edge of the road and stood on the curb looking for a ride. I glanced over my left shoulder for one last look at the building and wondered whether I would come to regret this day. Then I tilted my head up to the sky, watched the billowy clouds move rapidly overhead and said out loud, "Okay…here I come, world!"

My plan was to hitchhike to Rockland, about fifteen miles north of Marshfield, to talk with the manager at Tedeschi's Supermarket and ask him if I could have my old job back. I had worked there the summer before when I lived in Rockland. I could work full time now; nothing was stopping me. While standing at the edge of the road, I let my guard down for a few seconds and an empty feeling began rumbling through me, a feeling that reminded me of the day my dog Susie was killed by a car. I lost a close friend that day, and walking out that door gave me the same sickening feeling. I was alone now. It was all up to me, and that was just fine. The moment of insecurity quickly passed. I had things to do and was fired up, determined to succeed—determined to make something out of the one life I had been given.

They took me back at Tedeschi's and assured me I could work full time; in fact I could start right then. The manager handed me a white apron and a time card and sent me to the meat department to learn how to cut and package chicken.

I would be late getting back home that day, really late. My mother would be worried. I called her from the pay phone at Tedeschi's to tell her I had turned in my books and left school and that I would be late getting in. Then I gave her the good news. "Mom, I'm working full time at Tedeschi's."

A week later I was stocking shelves and bagging groceries. I told my boss that I was game for anything, just "give me the hours. I won't disappoint you."

After a couple of weeks, I made my way to Brockton to meet with an Air Force recruiter. The job at Tedeschi's was good, but I couldn't see myself working there for a lifetime hoping to make manager someday. I wanted more, much more. I wanted to become an Air Force pilot.

Ever since I was five or six years old I had dreamed of the day I would fly planes. Even though I was under age, the recruiter let me fill out and sign all the papers that day. He said they couldn't take me until I turned seventeen. I had known that before I went, but I also knew what I wanted. I had a plan and was setting it in motion.

After enlisting I found out that to be accepted for flight school, you had to have a college degree. No one had ever told me that. It really didn't matter at that point. I was grateful for the chance to get away from this going-nowhere life. I figured three squares, clothing, and a roof over my head was a hell of a lot better than what I left behind.

The night after I returned from the recruiter's office, I had a long talk with my mother about my future. "Mom, I've got to get out of here and start my own life," I said. "I'm going to stay with the job at Tedeschi's and help out until you and Peter can get settled somewhere else, but after I turn seventeen, I'll be leaving."

With a resigned voice and a distant look, she said softly, "I know," and then started to cry.

TWO

Endless Circle

Following my mother's divorce from my father, and her subsequent marriage to Bud, we had moved into a small apartment attached to the rear of Faxon's General Store in Brookville Center, a section of a larger town known as Holbrook. After a short stay at the rear of Faxon's, we moved down the street to number 43 South Street, beyond the Brookville elementary school. In those days there was a small one-bay firehouse next to the school and I would stop there on my way home to look at the big red fire truck. I'm going to be a fireman when I grow up, I assured myself.

The small firehouse and the school are gone now, razed and replaced by a modern two-story fire station with multiple bays. The school was never rebuilt.

I completed first, second and third grades there before moving to Abington. One bitterly cold morning while in the second grade, I began having empty feelings, like I didn't belong. Something wasn't right. I had a tough time reading and was pretty much considered a non-reader. There were three reading groups in my class, each named after a bird. I was in the crows, and that said it all. We'd sit around in a small circle with the teacher asking each of us to read out loud. When it was my turn, I'd manage to stumble my way through some of the pages of a "Dick and Jane" book. I can still see the pictures of the little boy and girl in the story, kids with happy faces going off to school. Warm and charming little stories about nothing in particular, but warm and charming nonetheless.

But it was more than my poor reading that made me feel the way I did. I sensed that the teacher didn't have the same regard for me as she had for the other children. I came from a "broken home." That's what they called it in those days when your parents were divorced. I felt she didn't like or have much respect for my mother because her last name was now Welch, different from mine—a bad woman for being divorced and living with another man. Nothing was ever actually said, but that didn't matter; I felt it.

I tried to avoid walking home with the boy who lived across the street from me. He was a big kid, at least bigger than me. "Biffy" Benson was his name. I never knew his real name—we all called him Biffy. He would push me down or beat me up most every day. One day he grabbed my art paper, crumpled it up and threw it in the street. Then he laughed and walked away. I was proud of my paper and was going to show it to my mother. I arrived home, opened the front porch door and showed Bud my wrinkled art paper.

"Look what Biffy did," I said, looking for support. Biffy stood at the edge of the road with his hands on his hips and a grin on his face. Bud responded in his typically nasty manner. "Get the hell out there and beat him up, and don't come back into this house until you do. I'm tired of all this belly-aching!" Bud threw my art paper on the floor, spun me around and shoved me out the door.

So there I was standing in my yard with Biffy in front of me, and Bud behind me, sneering at me through the screen door. Biffy walked up to me and was about to push me down again when I grabbed his left arm and bit him on the shoulder so damn hard that he screamed bloody murder and ran off across the street.

Bud came charging out, grabbed me by my left ear, and dragged me into the house. Then he gave me a backhander across my face and sent me upstairs to my room in the unfinished attic. Punishment for what he called "fighting like a girl and always hiding behind your mother's apron-strings." Maybe if he had taken some time to show me how to fight…but he never did. Biffy never bothered me again.

The move from Brookville to Abington was a step up—our own house in a settled neighborhood, lots of kids and no Biffy Benson. Things were pretty good in Abington for quite a while. Most of my earlier years, my happier years, were centered around my time there. We lived for about three years at number 62 Linda Street, one of the short interconnecting streets in a section of town referred to as the Green Street projects. I passed through grades four, five and six while living there. I was well liked, played little league baseball, had a girlfriend and felt pretty good about myself. Everyone needs a hometown and Abington was mine.

It seems I lived for baseball. I played the outfield, first base and even pitched a couple of games. And I had a batting average of 410. School was no problem. I always had good grades and was well liked by almost everyone.

Then it all began to fall apart. The real mess was just beginning, a series of converging and cascading events that ended when we finally hit bottom. Bud lost his job and my mother, who taught tap, ballet and ballroom dancing, began losing students. Square dancing was becoming popular and enrollment in her classes began to dwindle. Money was tight. We lost our house on Linda Street and moved into a rented house across town at 561 Oak Street. I attended Abington Junior High School while living there and was finishing up my seventh grade class when it was time to move again. This was the defining move, the move that triggered the toughest period of instability and chaos. Our next stop would be Hanson.

God, how I hated leaving Abington. There went my hometown and all my friends, including my girlfriend. For the first time in my young life, I wished I was on my own; I was barely thirteen. I figured when I was finally free to do what I wanted, I would move to Florida where there were no heating bills, no need for boots or warm clothing, no winter expenses at all, and you could pick fruit right from the trees.

What mattered to me—what and how I felt, or what my brother felt, or what effect this would have on either of us—didn't seem to matter to anyone else. No one was listening. They could have found another place in Abington, a cheaper place, perhaps an apartment. But they didn't. So there I was—there we were—living in Hanson on Route # 58, Washington Street, a second-floor apartment at Mrs. Howe's place.

I settled into the Indian Head Junior High School and completed what was left of the seventh grade. I made a lot of friends right from the beginning, joined the basketball program on Saturdays, went to the junior high dances, and successfully completed eighth grade.

I started my own paper route business while in Hanson, delivering fifty-two Brockton Enterprise papers every day except Sunday. The route took me into three different towns. I would get off the bus from school, grab the papers, which had been dropped off an hour or so earlier, load them into my cloth "Brockton Enterprise" shoulder bag, wrap the bag across the handlebars, and ride through the towns of Hanson, Pembroke and Hanover. I wouldn't get back for several hours, and in the winter, I wouldn't get back until well after dark.

At the end of each week, I would make my deliveries, collect the money from my customers, and when I got home, I'd buy some cupcakes and ice cream—a pint of vanilla, chocolate and strawberry—and share it with Peter.

One Friday afternoon, after making my rounds and collecting my money, I counted out what I owed the deliveryman and put it in the envelope he had provided. I tucked it under the doormat outside the front door to be picked up when he dropped off the Saturday papers. But when Saturday came, the money was gone.

He knocked at the door to inquire about the weekly collections. I told him I didn't know. "I left it right here as usual," I said. Later, when I asked my mother about it, she told me that Bud must have taken it. I asked, "Well, what am I going to tell Mr. O'Brien when he comes next week? He'll be collecting for two weeks then." She gave me some of her pay, and with what I had collected, including tips, I was able to pay him. There was nothing left for the cake and ice cream that week.

After that I changed the "usual spot." Now nobody knew where the money was hidden except Mr. O'Brien and me.

* * *

The principal and teachers at the Indian Head School in Hanson made a big deal out of eighth grade graduation. They called a full student assembly together in the auditorium with the graduating class seated up on stage ready to receive their certificates. The principal gave an inspirational speech to the seventh grade students in the audience and then presented certificates to each of us as we exited the stage. It seemed a little odd that they would go to all that trouble for eighth grade, but it made us feel important, which I guess was the whole point.

Summer was soon upon us and, along with the paper route, I found a job working at a blueberry and strawberry farm up the street about a mile away. They had a farm stand set up out front, along Washington Street, and acres of fruit bushes out back. I was paid seven cents to pick a box of strawberries and fifteen cents for blueberries. I was doing pretty well. I saved enough to buy myself a new bike, one with a saddlebag in the back.

Then one afternoon there was a knock at the front door downstairs. It was Mrs. Howe and her son Arthur. The rent had not been paid in months. It was time to move.

This time we were off to Bryantville, a small village in the town of Pembroke. We would be living in a converted summer cottage down at the end of a dirt road, across from a lake that everyone called Little Sandy.

I was fourteen and would begin my freshman year at Silver Lake Regional High School in Kingston. Bryantville was one of the towns included in the regional system. I seemed to fit in pretty well, earned some good grades and made lots of friends. I began reading everything in the school library about flight, from multi-engine propeller planes, to jets, to rockets and even space travel—books by Wernher von Braun and Robert Goddard. Even articles on the dimensions of space and time by Albert Einstein fascinated me.

One day, after the usual long and boring ride home on the bus, I began gathering up some materials to build a glider. I was going to fly. If the Wright Brothers could do it, why couldn't I?

I told Peter what I was up to and not to say anything to anyone, especially Bud. Peter was eager to help. It took us several days to put it together. We'd haul the materials into the woods out back near the power lines so nobody would see us. The wingspan measured eighteen feet when it was completed. The glider was made out of wood strapping, nails and rope, and covered with cloth, old sheets and a blanket.

When our makeshift project was ready for flight, Peter and I carried it out of the woods and up the end of the dirt road to "Leo's garage." The garage didn't belong to Leo. He lived in there by himself in a separate freestanding building about fifty feet from the main house.

Leo was a skinny, scruffy-looking old hermit with short white whiskers and no teeth. I don't know if he ever took a bath, but if he did, he didn't take it in that garage. There was no bathroom, just a small sink. The main house and garage were located directly on Main Street, about a half mile from Bryantville Center. The uneven, hand-painted lettering on the old wooden door simply read, "Leo's Bicycle Shop."

A wood-burning potbelly stove, a small fold-up cot, and a table with a couple of chairs were all the furniture Leo had, along with some tools and several dirty, thread-bare rugs, which were scattered all over the floor to keep in the heat. It wasn't much, but Leo called it home. Many of the kids in the neighborhood, including myself, visited Leo often, and he loved the company.

When I told Leo about the glider, he tilted his head to the left and gave me a puzzled grin. When Leo grinned, his broad toothless hollow cheeks would fill with air and his eyes would shut tight. I'd never seen anyone scrunch up his face like that. The first time I saw him, I burst out laughing. "Sorry, Leo," I said. "I didn't mean to laugh." Leo just grinned again and told me not to worry about it. "Comes with age, plenty of experience and some good whiskey once in a while."

I explained to Leo what I had in mind, asking him if it was all right if we launched our glider off his roof, our first test flight. He had no objections and was even eager to help. Peter and I stepped out of the garage and Leo followed close behind. There were three or four other friends waiting in the yard who had come to watch the historic event, but they kept their distance, not knowing what would happen and just a little afraid of Leo. Peter helped me raise the thirty-foot wooden ladder, which was lying on the ground next to the garage, and we leaned it against the roof. He steadied it as I slammed my right foot down on the bottom rungs to stabilize the footings. When I was sure it was straight and would hold me, I began my climb. Once on the roof, I kept my center of gravity low, crawled like a cat the rest of the way to the peak and steadied myself on the roofline. I figured I better take my time and think this through…no mistakes!

I began pulling the glider up with the long rope I'd slung over my shoulder, inching it slowly along the ladder and onto the roof, and resting it next to me. I stood up slowly, balancing myself across the roofline, and began a quick survey of the landscape looking for the best place to land. I figured the open field in the backyard was the safest and would provide the softest landing.

I reached down and lifted the glider up over my head and locked my hands in a white-knuckle grip around the two main supports. All of my friends, including Leo and my brother, were as excited as I was to watch me sail off the roof into the open field below. I wasn't scared at all. I figured if this didn't work out, the only downside would be a twisted ankle, no big deal. I thought to myself, How great is this! Look at me…just like the Wright Brothers.

There was a barroom directly across the street from Leo's, and all of a sudden my stepfather appeared at the front door with his hands on his hips and started screaming. "What the hell's going on over there?" He scared me half to death and frightened away my friends, who quickly scattered through the backyard and into the woods behind the main house. Leo and Peter scrambled inside the garage and slammed the door. I wobbled like a dog running on a frozen pond and damn near fell.

"Get the hell down from there," he yelled.

The hell with him, I decided; I'll send the glider off the roof anyway, to see how far it will fly. I wasn't listening to him. I blocked out the screaming and reached back with all my strength and launched my glider up into the clear sunlit sky.

Almost immediately it banked off to the left and struck the electrical lines coming from the main house to the garage. The live wires were ripped from the side of the garage, sending sparks snapping and dancing like a snake across the lawn, back and forth and everywhere, triggering a grass fire.

"Ohhh no," I said out loud. "I'm in big trouble now." I glanced down at the fire and then turned to my left, nearly losing my balance again, trying to keep an eye on Bud. He was still standing across the street in the barroom doorway, glaring up at me. Then he started crossing the street. I figured I had enough time to make it down the ladder before he caught up to me, so I sat down and inched my way off the peak, then turned around and put my foot on the top rung and began my descent.

The ladder began slipping off the roofline toward the backyard. I went down one more step and then jumped, landing with my knees bent like a paratrooper. I rolled when I landed, got up and beat it down the dirt road back to my house.

Later that night, I heard Bud come in. I was in my room, a room I shared with my brother who hadn't come home yet. Bud opened the front door, slamming it behind him. I heard him bellow, "Now you're really going to get it, you no good little bastard!"

He came to my room and tried to force the door open. I was braced up against it from the other side, trying to stop him from getting in. He was grunting and farting and swearing, calling me all the rotten, familiar names: fucking sonofabitch, no-good bastard...he was pushing with all he had. My heart was pounding. I pushed back as hard as I could, surprised I could hold him off, but I knew what was coming. I decided that on the next hard push, I would pull the door open wide and send him flying across the room. And that's exactly what happened. He staggered and stumbled through the doorway, landing with a thud on the floor between the two beds. I slipped around the open door, shut it behind me, and ran like hell up the dirt road to the bar where I knew my mother and her friends, Lorraine and Ray Meade, were sitting having drinks.

Running at full tilt and out of breath, I burst into the bar and quickly slid into the booth next to Mrs. Meade. My mother was across from me, next to Peter, who had left Leo's after Bud took off after me. Mr. Meade sat in a separate chair at the end of the table.

Still trying to catch my breath, I explained what had just happened. "I think he might have hurt himself when he fell. He really landed hard, head first on the floor. I'm afraid of him. I think he's going to give it to me tonight when I get home."

My mother told me not to worry. "He'll probably be passed out by the time we get home."

Two Bryantville fire trucks had arrived earlier in the day to put out the grass fire. It wasn't much of a fire but with the sirens blaring, you'd think the whole damn town was going up. They were all laughing about it at the bar. My mother and the Meades finished up and paid for their drinks and piled into Mr. Meade's car for the short ride across the street and down the dirt road, back to my house. I thought it would be better to take my time getting home, so Peter and I walked. Maybe they could reason with him before I got home.

As they had predicted, he was asleep on the couch—his mouth wide open, left arm hanging down touching the floor—passed out. The right side of his forehead was red and bruised from hitting the floor. That night, before going to bed, I shut the door to my room and leaned a chair up against the inside doorknob. I didn't want him coming in after me in the middle of the night.

On Saturdays I worked with Leo and another local character named Marty Flynn. I would get up early on Saturday mornings and walk up the road from my house to Leo's Garage, where we met up with Mr. Flynn. Mr. Flynn had a small business picking up trash and garbage. The three of us jammed into the front seat of his old, battered Chevy dump truck. Sections of the left rear quarter-panel had been painted red with a paintbrush, and his front windshield was badly cracked on the passenger side. I think the muffler was missing; it made one hell of a racket.

I sat in the middle, between the two of them. As soon as we pulled away from Leo's, Mr. Flynn would reach into the breast pocket of his red flannel shirt and pull out one of his rotten smelling cigars. I nearly gagged every time he lit one up in the close quarters of that cab. I never said anything, but I hated it. I also hated it when he would turn off the engine at each stop along his route. That meant it was time to pick up the trash and awful-smelling, maggot-infested garbage. I was only fourteen at the time, but I was strong; so they let me do much of the heavy work.

Mr. Flynn handed me two dollars at the end of each Saturday. One week, after we finished up the day and returned to Leo's place, Mr. Flynn turned to me and said, "Can I pay you next Saturday? I'm a little short today."

I was disappointed but said, "Sure." I worked with him for several Saturdays after that, but he never paid me for that day, and I never brought it up.

One Saturday afternoon I finished up with Mr. Flynn, he paid me my two dollars and dropped me off at Leo's place as usual, and I walked home. Waiting for me in the front yard was Bud. He was especially friendly toward me that day. He handed me a small Tootsie Roll candy, which looked as though it had been in his pocket for years. When he turned his back I threw it in the woods. I thought it might be rotten or maybe it was some dirty trick of his. He smiled at me and said, "You get paid today?"

"Yeah, two dollars," I said.

"Well," he said, "if you give me your two dollars, I'll give you the keys to the car and you can go drive around. You know, you need the practice before going for your license."

I knew he didn't give a shit if I ever got my license and it obviously didn't matter to him that I didn't even have a permit. I knew I shouldn't be driving without an adult in the car, but I decided to take the chance. After all, I reasoned, it cost me my two dollars, so I was going to make the most of it. It would be worth it. I could drive all around town if I wanted. He pocketed my two dollars, handed me the keys and then walked up the dirt road to the bar.

After my little jaunt around town, I turned left at Leo's, drove down the dirt road to our place, pulled onto the front yard and turned off the key. When I got out and shut the door, I realized the back passenger-side tire was almost flat. I looked in the trunk, but there was no spare, which didn't surprise me. I figured I'd catch hell for causing a flat tire, so before Bud came home, I jacked up the car, removed the bolts with the tire iron and maneuvered the tire off the car. I learned how to do all this when I worked at my Uncle Joe's junkyard in Rock-land, two summers before.

I laid the tire on the ground and jumped up and down on the edge of the tire to "break it" from the rim. Then with the tire iron and hammer I lifted the tire enough to reach in and pull out the inner tube. I took a good look inside the tire trying to find the nail. I ran my hand around the inside of the tire and found the problem. It was a small, silver screw. I removed the screw with the claw end of the hammer and took the inner tube up the road to the gas station which was right next door to the bar where Bud was drinking up my day's pay.

The owner sold me a black rubber patch for the tire and another one for the inner tube. He asked if I knew where the hole was. I told him no but I'd find it.

"Well," he said, "let me help you. Watch this." He filled the inner tube with air and dipped it into a metal trough filled with water. "See the bubbles?" he asked. "There's your hole."

He wiped off the tube with a towel and drew a circle around the hole with a marker. I thanked him very much and paid him fifty cents for the two patches and then walked home.

I stuck a patch on the inside of the tire where I'd pulled the screw out earlier, then patched the inner tube and put it back inside the tire. Now the hard part: fitting the tire back onto the rim and lining up the air stem. Using the tire iron and the hammer, I pounded and pounded around the edges of the tire until it finally cleared the rim, then I dragged it back to the gas station for some air.

The mechanic filled it with air until it popped into place around the rim. He checked to make sure the air pressure was correct and sent me on my way. I thanked him again and rolled the tire past the bar, across the street and back down the dirt road. When I got home I mounted it over the bolts, tightened them down with the tire iron and lowered the jack. As soon as I put the jack and the tire iron back in the trunk, the tire began hissing again. "Can you believe it?" I said out loud.I opened the trunk, pulled out the jack and tire iron, and went through the same motions as before, jacking up the car, etc. None of this bothered me very much. It was a challenge and I wasn't going to give up until it was fixed. I took my time, looked the tire over more carefully and found the problem. The tire had been punctured by not one, but two screws, and of course the screws kept puncturing the inner tube.

I went back to the gas station, bought two more patches, and when I got back, I pulled the second screw out of the tire with some pliers and stuck the patch over the second hole. Then I carried the inner tube back to the gas station to find the other hole. The man at the gas station gave me a smile when I returned and said, "Don't tell me you got another flat? I hope this time it's fixed for good."

I smiled back at him and said, "Yeah, me too." He found the second hole for me and I patched over it, then walked back down the road once again and stuffed the inner tube inside the tire and pounded the tire over the rim, then dragged the tire back to the gas station for air.

I figured it was a good experience to work through this pain-in-the-ass flat tire, and finally succeed. I was proud of myself.

This whole exercise lasted most of the afternoon. Bud stayed at the bar drinking his ten-cent drafts and never knew what was going on, right under his nose.

* * *

I found an after school job working in the local town cemetery, cutting the grass, trimming the stones and raking the leaves. I worked there every afternoon, until the winter settled in. It was spooky in that cemetery, especially in the late fall when it was dark. I would put the wheelbarrow and tools away in the old shed down back near the woods, padlock the door and run like hell up the path alongside the gravestones and out on to the road and then walk home.

They paid me $14 a week, the most money I'd ever made at one time. It was enough to buy lunches at school and help pay for some of my clothes.

I was always up to something, and most of the something I was up to took place at Leo's garage. A group of us showed up there one Sunday morning to assemble and test my latest project. I knocked on Leo's door and it slowly swung open. Leo was still in his bed. I didn't want to embarrass him, so I remained outside and hollered in, "Hey, Leo, you in there? Don't want to bother you, but do you mind if we come in and show you something?"

Leo got right up, splashed some cold water on his face, and with a raspy, half asleep voice, said, "Yeah, come on in." He sat down in his worn-through wicker rocking chair and watched us as we brought in a small piece of plywood and set it down on the floor. What we had this time really amazed him. We had the parts and the chemical compounds for a solid-fuel, single-stage rocket. I opened my paper bag and began arranging various rocket parts and jars of powdered chemicals along the plywood in some remotely logical order. Then, just as quickly, and with much anticipation, I began to build the rocket.

My rocket was the fourteen-inch steel pipe that I had muscled out from the inside of my locker at school. The pipe was connected horizontally to both sides of my locker and used to hang up my jacket. I eyed it for a week or so before taking it. I capped one end of it with a quarter and some black electrical tape and steadied it on the plywood in an upright position. Then I began combining the chemicals to make ready the fuel that would send it high into the sky. The mixture of chemicals, when combined, made gunpowder: charcoal, saltpeter, and sulfur. We added—no measuring, just added—some potassium chlorate, which I had found in a jar in the science lab at school. I read about this in science books from the school library. Potassium chlorate would act as a catalyst. It would interact with and accelerate the explosive power of the gunpowder, and increase the needed thrust for a successful launch.

We sat down on Leo's floor, spread out a small piece of cloth on the plywood, and mixed it all in together, rolling it into a fine powder with a foot long, one-inch diameter wooden dowel. After it seemed ready, we funneled the black solid-fuel propellant into the rocket, filling it to the top. I began packing it in, a little at a time, with the end of a metal chisel that Leo gave me from his toolbox. I thought to myself that I shouldn't pack it too firmly or strike the chisel too hard. I was sure the chemical reaction had already begun and I started to wonder if it might explode and maybe blow my head off.

After loading in the fuel, I wedged a wooden nosecone firmly into the open end. Leo was wide-eyed and grinning like a child. "You kids know what you're doing?" he chuckled.

I motioned for him to stay away. "Better stay back, Leo, this thing might blow up." He put his hands up over his head and said, "I do believe you're right. I'll just stay back here, out of the way!"

I held the fully-loaded solid-fuel rocket in my hands as we all left Leo's place and walked out back to the woods near the power lines. Leo said, "I'll wait here. Come back and tell me what happened... and good luck." When we arrived at the sand pit, I stopped for a moment and told the others, "I think we should do a test fire first, see how much fire power this thing has." This was our first attempt at building a rocket and I wanted see what kind of thrust it would produce. Maybe it would fizzle out or maybe it would blow up; none of us really knew for sure. I told everyone to scatter and find a safe place to hide behind the mounds of sand. Then I walked into the center of the pit and jammed the nosecone deep into the sand. Then came the big moment. I struck a match and lit the long gas-soaked piece of string that served as a fuse, then ran to the edge of the sandpit, ducked down behind a large mound of sand...and waited.

When the lit fuse reached the rocket, there was no hesitation; it roared to life. The quarter flew off, followed by a deafening and beautiful display of power. I yelled out loud, "Did you see that? Wow!" The solid-fuel rocket propellant ignited with such force that flames shot out from the point of ignition, a distance of three or four feet.

It ended as quickly as it began—a burn of about six seconds—then nothing. We all ran over to get a good look as the trailing smoke died down. There was so much excitement; everyone was clapping and jumping around. I now knew for sure it would fly. All that was needed were fins and wings, and maybe a gyroscope for guidance, and then we could do it again. I told everyone, "Next time we'll set up a launching pad and do a countdown. Maybe we can even get Leo to come and watch!"

There was one problem. I had used all of the potassium chlorate from the jar at school for the first launch. I had searched for more at school but had no luck. One of my friends spoke up and told me his father was a doctor and that he could write out a "script" and order some at the drug store. So he wrote the 'script for potassium chlorate from his father's pad and brought it to the drugstore across the street from his father's office and handed it to the pharmacist. I stood there with him as he made his presentation to the pharmacist. With a serious grown-up face, he explained, "My father sent me over here with this note for potassium chlorate." The pharmacist said he'd have to call his father to confirm the order, and when he did, we both caught hell from the pharmacist and bolted out the door. It really didn't matter much anyway. We were packing up and moving again…leaving Bryantville and leaving my new-found friends.

Two weeks after completing my freshman year at Silver Lake High School, my mother sent Peter and me to the local grocery store to pick up some cardboard boxes, informing us, "We're moving to Rockland, and Bud won't be coming." Bud had disappeared a few weeks earlier. I didn't know where he was, and I never asked too many questions. Peter and I walked down to the store, brought back some boxes, packed our belongings and left Bryantville that afternoon in the old '41 Buick for a two-room, second-floor apartment on West Water Street, near the center of town. Ferguson's place. The Fergusons had converted a portion of their upstairs into a small apartment, and that's where we stayed for about a year. This endless, disruptive cycle of moving from one town to another had now brought us back to the beginning. When I was a baby, I had lived in Rockland with my parents in a rented second-floor apartment on North Avenue. My grandmother rented the apartment below us on the first floor. I was too young to remember much of that, but I knew my mother and father had roots in Rockland. It was home to both of them when they were growing up.

During her Rockland High School days, my mother became a dancing teacher and established her own school: The Wyman School of Dance. She had been schooled in dance and loved every minute of it, and she loved the trappings of the stage. She was a small-town success story at eighteen. There were often thirty or forty young children in some of her beginner classes. Students came from Rockland and many of the surrounding towns. You name it and she could dance it and teach it—tap, ballet and even ballroom dancing—and now that she was back in Rockland, she figured maybe she could give it another go.

My father had left for Michigan after their divorce when I was four years old; he was gone before I really knew him. He walked away from his job, his wife and his children and headed west. He was a welder by trade and there were plenty of good paying jobs for weld-ers in Detroit, the auto capital of the world. My father's two brothers remained in Rockland and lived next door to one another in their own homes on Norman Street. Donald was now a Rockland police offi-cer and William, or Bill, worked for Wyman's Nursery (no relation to my mother) in Abington. Their mother, Kate, my grandmother, was still living in the same old house on North Avenue in the first-floor apartment that I remembered as a young boy. I thought maybe this move back to Rockland would work out, but I hated moving again. I had made some friends in Bryantville and was, despite the turmoil at home, doing well in school. Now I'd have to start all over. New friends, new surroundings, new this, and new that. I was getting pretty damn tired of it.

My uncle Donald served as the off-duty traffic cop at Tedeschi's on Saturdays, and he helped me land my first job there. I worked most afternoons after school, and weekends. My mother worked as a waitress in a small restaurant in Hanover and began teaching dance classes in a local hall on Church Street in Rockland.

I never saw my stepfather during the entire time we were in Rock-land. I was a little puzzled by this, but it was all right with me; we were doing just fine without him. I did find out one day that my fa-ther, who was home from Michigan that summer, beat the shit out of him one night behind a barroom in Abington called The Central Club.

Each year, my father would come back to Rockland to visit with his mother and his brothers and friends. He'd drive the eight hundred miles straight through with his new wife, Jane, and his two new sons, Jimmy and Paul. Once in a while he'd come by to see us, but not often. Peter and I pretty much gave up looking for him each summer. I never tried to understand it or accept it. It was obvious he valued his time with his brothers and their families more than any time he might have spent with us.

I'd hear stories about how they would all go fishing and hunting together while he was home from Michigan. After a long day at the lake and trekking through the woods, he'd stop by his mother's place, get cleaned up and then hit the bars in downtown Rockland, just like the old days.

My cousin John, my Uncle Donald's second son, once told me, "Your father, my Uncle Pete, is the funniest guy I ever met...just like Jackie Gleason. One day, he gathered us all around the picnic table outside to show us how to cut open a watermelon, and he had us all in stitches! He had a unique way of doing most everything, but the way he'd cut open a watermelon was really something to see. Now, whenever I bring home a watermelon for my own kids, I always open it up just like my Uncle Pete."

It was just another story about my father that didn't include me or Peter. We had never seen him do his watermelon trick.

There was a Chinese food factory down a side street off of West Water Street, almost across the street from where we were living. Somehow I wandered in there one afternoon after school and the manager of the factory asked if I wanted some food, some chop suey. I told him, "Sure I do." So he gave me a three-quart tin container full of chicken and noodles. It looked like watered down paste, but it tasted pretty good. I ate that chop suey for lunch every day until it started going bad.

And then there was Charlie Danforth. Charlie had once been a pillar of Rockland society, a respected man who lived in a beautiful home on lower Union Street. Charlie was at least seventy years old, maybe older, when we arrived back in Rockland. He was a broad-shouldered, good-looking man, always well dressed with a white shirt, bow tie and soft top hat.

Charlie had played the organ during the Sunday masses at the Holy Family Catholic Church on Union Street, and he had played the piano for my mother at all her dance classes, rehearsals and recit-als. She had known or been associated with Charlie for most of her adult life. By this time, however, he had become a public disgrace, drinking too much and stumbling his way all around town. Late at night, he would walk from his house, up Union Street to West Water Street, turn left and walk about two blocks to our place. He would open our downstairs door, step onto the landing, turn left and stagger his way up the six stairs to the mid-landing, then turn right and climb the remaining six stairs to the top. Then he'd bang on the door that opened into our bedroom. There was only one bedroom, so my broth-er and I slept together. My mother slept alongside us in a smaller bed. The kitchen/living room was on the other side of two wooden bi-fold doors. Charlie would knock on our bedroom door and mumble some drunken gibberish and wake us all up. My mother would get up and let him in, and they would go into the living room to talk. It was loud talk and it always kept me awake.

Apparently my mother owed Charlie some money for playing the piano during several of her afternoon classes, but I didn't think money was the reason for his late night visits. I figured whatever was going on between them was none of my business, except that I would find it hard to get back to sleep after he left.

Charlie's familiar drunken rant was in full swing one particu-lar night. The longer he went on, the louder he became. My mother couldn't shut him up. In a tight-lipped, controlled voice, she implored him to leave. "Please, Charlie, you'll have to go. The kids have school in the morning and I have to go to work." My mother always seemed to handle outrageous behavior with a sense of detached calm…go along to get along. I'm sure it took its toll.

Trying not to wake Peter, I slipped out of bed and watched through the opening between the bi-fold doors as Charlie wrestled my mother down on to the couch. I heard him call her a "goddamn whore." That was enough for me. I threw open the doors and stormed across the room and stuck my finger in his beet-red, sweaty face. "Get up!" I told him. "I've had enough of this shit! Now get up on your feet and shut your filthy mouth and get the hell outta here!"

Peter, now twelve years old, finally woke up. Like our father, he had a quick, explosive temper. Any threat to our mother or me sent him into an unstoppable rage. Peter came bursting through the opened doors, bumped me aside and smashed Charlie in the face, breaking his glasses and sending his hat across the room. Peter told him never to speak to my mother like that ever again, and then he hit him again to make sure he got the message.

A screaming match broke out between Peter and Charlie. My mother, now trying to settle everyone down, started yelling and crying, and demanding that Charlie leave. "Just leave! Damn it, Charlie, leave!"

It never occurred to me to call the cops. It wouldn't have mattered if it had; we didn't have a phone. But I knew if I could reach him, my uncle Donald would take care of Charlie. This was the third or fourth time he had pulled this shit and it would be the last.

I told him if he ever showed up here again, I'd shove him back down the stairs. "I don't care how old you are," I said. He glared at me, turned around, reached down and picked up his hat, then grabbed what was left of his glasses and mumbled some obscenities before bracing himself against the wall and stumbling down the stairs.

Two weeks later, my mother handed me an envelope with some money inside. She asked me to walk down to Charlie's house and hand it to him. She said, "This is the money I owe Charlie. Tell him that's it, he's paid in full." When I knocked at his door, Charlie's daughter answered. As I handed her the envelope, I told her it was from my mother. She grabbed it without saying a word, then shut the door in my face.

I never knew what happened to him, but that long night upstairs in our apartment was the last time I ever saw Charlie Danforth.

THREE

No Back Door

What little security we had continued to slip away during our time in Rockland. I was a sophomore in high school and Peter was in junior high.

Bud continued to be a mystery. I went to work and so did my mother. Peter wasn't going to be left out. He decided to pitch in as well. He and one of his friends hatched this "brilliant idea," as my mother later called it, for making money. They thumbed their way down the coast to Marshfield with a plan to stop at every house and collect donations for the Hemophilia Fund. I don't know if there was ever a legitimate Hemophilia Fund, but Peter was collecting for it anyway.

It must have sounded like a good idea to him at the time, and knowing him, it was all well-intentioned—ten percent for him and ninety percent for the fund, sort of. After catching a ride to Marshfield, Peter, hobbling on crutches from a swollen knee, walked for miles with his friend, knocking on doors in each of the neighborhoods. He became excited while telling me the story. "Don, we had a lot of money. We even stopped for a clam dinner lunch in Brant Rock before heading over the marshes to Green Harbor."

It was in Green Harbor that they knocked on the wrong door. The man who opened it was the Chief of Police for the Town of Marshfield. After they left his house, the Chief called the station and they were soon picked up. The two of them handed over what money they had left and the next day wound up in front of a judge.

Both of them were placed on probation for a year. "If you stay out of trouble for one year, the records will be sealed. There will be no further action and no record," said the judge.

Peter's friend got into some trouble before the year was up and ended up in the Shirley House of Correction, one of the Massachusetts state run institutions for juvenile offenders. Peter stayed straight, and after a year the incident was forgotten.

The Fergusons charged us $75 a month for rent, and we always had a tough time coming up with it. We'd pool our money every week so by the time the rent was due we'd have enough. Christmas that year was all about the three of us. We had one another and not much else. "Count your blessings," my mother would say.

My mother was always emotional around the holidays, especially at Christmas. She'd cry at the drop of a hat. Because of our meager circumstances, this Christmas was going to be especially tough on her. So Peter and I decided we'd make a real Christmas out of it, no matter what. He went out one morning and later that day, well after dark, opened the downstairs door and struggled up the stairs with a huge Christmas tree that barely made it through the door at the top of the landing.

He had been working at the church for the past week or so, helping sell Christmas trees, and they must have given him one to take home. "Don," he said excitedly, "I dragged that tree all the way across town, down Union Street from the parking lot at Holy Family Church. What do you think? Pretty nice, eh?" It was a beauty.

For my part, I managed to slip out the back of Tedeschi's Market with a large smoked ham and a four-stick package of real butter. I had it all planned out so I wouldn't get caught. I knew if I lost my job at Tedeschi's, I'd embarrass myself and my Uncle Donald and, perhaps more importantly, I'd be out of work, but I had to chance it. We were going to have a decent meal at Christmas, just like everyone else in town.

I'm pretty sure the manager spotted me when I pushed the cart out the side door and around to the rear of the building, but for some reason he looked the other way. He never mentioned it to me either, even when I went back to work after Christmas. I think he understood more than he let on.

I carried that ham and butter in a paper bag all the way from Market Street to the Holy Family Church at the top of Rockland Hill, a couple of miles away. I walked into the front door of the empty church, which was beautifully decorated for Christmas, flowers neatly arranged down front. I sat in the first pew to my right and placed my bag of groceries next to me, then knelt down and stared up at the altar. I began talking to God. I told him I was sorry and asked him to forgive me. My confession was directly to God, nobody else's business. And although I told him I was sorry, I also told him I wasn't taking it back. I told him I felt like Robin Hood, robbing from the rich and giving to me.

My mother just shook her head when Peter showed up with the tree. Peter could tell she was happy…surprised and happy. When I opened the refrigerator to show her the food, she asked, "How'd you pay for all that?" I figured I'd tell her a "little white lie." (A white lie wasn't a real lie, so it wouldn't count.) I told her they gave it to me at Tedeschi's.

The night before Christmas, the three of us put up the tree and decorated it with some ornaments my mother managed to save over the years, and on Christmas Day we sat down to a home cooked dinner: ham, carrots, potatoes and cabbage that had been boiling away on the stove for hours and making the place smell like Christmas. My mother looked across at the two of us and just shook her head, and with a sad but knowing smile said, "I know we're going to make it."

Nobody in my family, including my aunts, uncles and cousins, all of whom lived just a few miles away, and even my father out in Michigan, ever knew any of this. And I wasn't going to tell them. Nor was my mother or my brother; it was none of their business. We weren't living in a car and we weren't beggars. No handouts accepted, thank you! I made the junior varsity baseball team at Rockland High School that year; playing baseball was the one good thing I looked forward to in those days. I could forget about all the other shit that was going on around me when I was on the field. I would have played baseball every minute of every day if I could.

We traveled around the South Shore playing schools in our district division. One game stands out in my mind, among the many. It was the final game of the season. My team members and I had been called out of class early in the afternoon to board the bus for a game with

East Bridgewater. The game began with a flurry of runs in the bottom of the first inning—all from East Bridgewater. Inning after inning, they kept racking up the runs. When we were up it was "three up and three down." Nobody could hit that East Bridgewater pitcher.

At the top of the ninth inning, with two outs and down eleven to nothing, I reached into the canvas bag and picked out a thirty-four-inch bat. It was a heavy bat for me. I usually chose a thirty-two. I stepped into the batter's box and swung through the first pitch on a late swing, a high inside fastball. I was always a sucker for a high inside pitch. On the next pitch, I smashed an eye-level, over-the-plate, hanging curveball. It sailed out over the head of the right fielder and I took off. I rounded first and without hesitating headed for second. I was on my way to third when I realized I might not make it. The right fielder had caught up with the ball and threw a one-hop strike to second, a great throw. I skidded to a stop and lunged safely back to second. On the very next pitch, I grabbed a wide lead and broke for third. The catcher made a quick throw to third and I slid headfirst extending my hands through the sand and under the bag, and under the tag. Safe at third!

I jumped to my feet, dusted myself off and readied myself for a run at the plate. The next batter ran the count to two balls and two strikes. I can still see it. The game was nearly over and we were getting shut out eleven to zip, and I'm ninety feet away. I began razzle-dazzling the pitcher from my position at third, trying to get him to throw a wild pitch so I could make a dash for home. I ran down the base line toward home, distracting him, then quickly scrambled back. Down and back, two or three times, waving my arms and yelling at him. I kept this up until the ump threw his hands in the air, walked over to the mound, pointed to the pitcher and called a balk, then turned and motioned for me to come home. I smiled and walked into home about as proud of myself as I could be. We lost that game with East Bridgewater, eleven to one, but we didn't get shut out.

I had one close friend in my sophomore class at Rockland High School. We were in English class together. His mother and my mother had known each other years ago, before either one of us was born.

They worked together at the Brockton Hospital; she was a nurse, my mother a nurses' aide.

Tom Condon was his name. Tommy and I palled around quite a bit when I wasn't working or playing baseball, or keeping an eye on Peter. Tommy's father, George, managed the lunch counter at Tedeschi's and I would see him most every day. You couldn't tell with George if he liked you or not. He was a no-nonsense type of guy who rarely smiled, but I think he liked me. Every once in a while I'd say something funny and he'd crack a half smile. Sometimes I ate at his lunch counter, and when I did he always gave me extra chips.

One frigid, snowy winter's night, Tommy wracked up George's new car, a brand new black, four-door Buick. He slid on an icy road on a side street in Rockland and slammed into a tree. There would be hell to pay. I walked over to Tommy's house the next day and George was still ranting and raging, pacing back and forth in the kitchen. Tommy was never allowed to drive his father's car again, never. Tommy tried to explain and apologize but George would have none of it. One of the Rockland police officers drove over to Tedeschi's to speak with George to try and settle him down. He told him, "There was nothing he could do, George; the road was just too icy." But George wasn't listening and he was never, ever going to forget it. This one car accident with no injuries became the talk of the town. It's all George talked about for weeks at the lunch counter. Tommy's relationship with his father was never the same.

In the summer of 1958, I walked home as usual from Tedeschi's after work and found the door to our apartment on West Water Street locked. Not locked with a key, but tightly roped off from the inside. No matter how I tried or what I did, I couldn't get it open.

The Fergusons had deliberately locked us out. I couldn't figure it out. We always paid the rent on time, so what was going on?

The Fergusons weren't home when I arrived, so I walked around to the front of the house and waited for them. It was getting dark and I was getting hungry, and I was pretty damn upset at them for doing this. I wandered into the barn, which was to the left of the main house, and sat down upstairs next to the workbench. After awhile I got up, cleared the tools off the workbench and lay down to get some rest until they returned.

I finally heard them pull into the barn down below in their light blue Ford station wagon. When they got out of the car and went into the house, I came down the stairs from the attic and walked around back. There was a walkway that ran along the rear of the house between the barn and the back door. I knocked on the outside screen door to find out what was going on, and immediately Mrs. Ferguson swung it open wide, nearly smacking me in the face. I could tell she was ready and expecting a confrontation. She was a difficult, high-strung woman with a fat, nasty face and a personality to match. Her husband was useless from what I could tell. He just stood there, as frightened of her as she must have thought I was.

I told her I couldn't get in and I needed to eat and get some sleep. "What's going on?" I asked. "I have to work in the morning."

She gave no explanation as she turned to her husband and told him to remove the ropes. "Let him in," she barked. Neither one of them mentioned or even hinted that this would be the last night we'd ever be allowed back into our apartment. She stepped back into the house and slammed the door behind her, catching her wide, oversized dress in the doorway.

I figured she was pissed off at my mother for Charlie Danforth's late night antics. I was sure they could hear the foul language, the drunken advances made on my mother, and the general mayhem from the second-floor door in our living room, which opened into their upstairs hallway. It was from that door that Ferguson was able to enter our apartment and string his ropes through the house and down the stairs to the doorknob of our front door. They obviously let themselves in whenever we weren't around.

My mother and Peter didn't come home that night. I didn't know where they were or where they stayed. In the morning I went to work, and when I returned I still couldn't get in. The place had been, once again, roped off. I sat down on the curb on West Water Street and waited for my mother and Peter to return. About an hour later, I looked up and spotted the old '41 Buick chugging up the street. "Hey

Mom, where you guys been? You know what's going on here? They've locked us out!"

Peter told me they had been down in Norwell visiting my aunts and had decided to stay the night. When I told my mother we had been locked out, she went over and knocked on Mrs. Ferguson's front door, but Ferguson refused to answer. Ferguson raised the front window a crack and hollered out that her lawyer would be sending a letter. She said, "It's addressed to your sister, go talk to her. Now get off my property…all of you." Then she slammed the window down and closed the curtains.

My mother wasn't much of a fighter; she said to Peter and me, "Come on, we've got to find a place, at least for tonight." We drove around for hours, but couldn't find a place to stay. It was after dark and getting late, so we pulled into the parking lot behind Tedeschi's and curled up for the night in the car. She refused to go back to Norwell. She'd be too embarrassed and there'd be too many questions. The next morning, I got out of the car and went to work. I was early. The sun was just coming up. I wanted to get inside and clean up before my shift, so I walked over to the side door on Howard Street and pulled on the entrance door, and it set off the burglar alarm. I covered my ears trying to drown out the wails of pulsating noise bouncing off the nearby buildings and throughout the neighborhood. Suddenly an early morning cleaning company employee threw open the door and I explained what happened. I told him that I worked there and needed to punch in. "Can you turn off that damn alarm?" I shouted. He called in the false alarm and the system shut down. I said, "Thanks. Sorry for the commotion. I've got to get ready for work. Thanks again."

So I went to work and my mother and Peter went looking for a place to stay. She picked me up at the end of the day and I asked her if she had found a place. She said, "Yes, it's in Whitman, nothing special, and it's just temporary…any port in a storm."

We settled into a rooming house on a side street off Route 14 in Whitman. It was a large, four-story building just beyond the Venus Café. After three nights in that place, we left for a back-alley, four-story, brick hotel off Main Street in the center of Brockton. It was right around the corner from the dimly lit late night bars, the street-walkers, the pool hall, and the police sirens that sounded throughout the night. There was one large bed in our room on the third floor, so the three of us slept together. As we settled ourselves into the bed, my mother, trying to put a light touch on the moment, said, "Pretty tight quarters, hey?" We all laughed. It relieved the tension for a moment, but there was nothing funny about the fix we were in. I don't know how she found these places. The blinking red neon sign, attached to three rusted, metal brackets just outside our window, kept me awake most of the night. It flashed in my face through the faded window shade and tattered lace curtains that hung from the only window in the room. "Pizza," every three seconds, all night long.

I finally fell asleep, convincing myself that nothing lasts forever. This string of bad luck, which seemed to come in waves and without warning, had to run out of steam someday. Most of the time I'd just laughed it off. I could handle it. But this time, this was bad...a new low for us.

My mother was worried; she always worried. It didn't seem to trouble my brother, though. As young as he was, he was pretty damn tough. Peter was on an adventure. He had no trouble sleeping. I wondered where we would go from there.

My mother contacted a lawyer who, for a small fee, would file a suit against the Fergusons to recover our belongings. The Fergusons hired their own lawyer, who sent off a letter to my mother, in care of her sister, Betty Smith. About two months later, we all ended up in court in front of a judge. I sat there glaring at Mrs. Ferguson and her lanky, spineless husband, hoping the judge would order them to return our belongings. Peter sat beside me in the row behind my mother and her lawyer. The proceedings took place in a court building in Abington on Route 18, just before the Whitman town line.

Ferguson's lawyer cross-examined my mother, asking her if she had left any garbage out on the kitchen counter when she went to work that day. My mother was the cleanest person I ever knew, and although it was unlikely that any garbage was left out, she said, "Well, there might have been some; I couldn't say for sure."

That's it, I thought. The reason...the excuse Mrs. Ferguson used to justify what she had done. I looked down at the floor and shook my head. I knew there was no garbage left anywhere. I was the one who usually took it out and I wasn't about to leave garbage hanging around.

My mother's idea of telling the truth was to tell everything she knew or thought she knew. She gave the court enough "reasonable cause" to find in favor of the Fergusons. She had given away the store.

That was that. The judge decided that the Fergusons were law-fully exercising their rights. "They had every reason to do what they did, given the circumstances." The judge did, however, order them to pay my mother $300. The Fergusons were never ordered to return any of our belongings.

They stole everything we had, everything except what we were wearing. A new baseball glove I had just bought, a new pair of shoes and a new erector set I bought for Peter. My mother lost all her jew-elry, all her clothing and everything else. It was all packed in the bed-room closet. Many items from her mother, who had just passed away, were stored in there as well.

I've always regretted not standing up and saying something. I was only fifteen and figured I'd somehow screw it up and make things worse, or maybe get myself in trouble. It was over before I had enough time or courage to speak up. I knew the whole damn thing was a pack of lies.

We stayed for the remainder of the week in the third-floor, back-alley hotel in downtown Brockton before leaving in the middle of the night for a small motel in Green Harbor, a section of Marshfield, some twenty-five miles to the south of Brockton. Green Harbor was directly on the ocean and was populated with mostly summer peo-ple vacationing in their summer homes or cottages. We moved into a one-room L-shaped apartment in the back of a small motel on Beach Street, just around the corner from Careswell Street, the main road into Green Harbor from Brant Rock. Beach Street was aptly named: a narrow, half-mile stretch of poorly paved road that ran past the lo-cal shops and one-room post office and straight down to the beach, then turned right and ran along a stretch of waterfront homes, then another right at the end, then back out onto Careswell Street. A two-mile, U-shaped roadway that brought you into Green Harbor and back out again.

Bud reappeared from wherever he had been and stayed with us for the remainder of the summer and into the fall of '59. I never asked any questions and there was never any discussion, but I figured he had been staying at the VA Hospital in Brockton or living in a VA-sponsored home, somewhere on the South Shore.

Bud found a job at a local restaurant on Casewell Street, washing dishes. My mother volunteered to do the housekeeping chores at the motel to offset the rent, and I began working full time at Tedeschi's in Rockland. My mother would drive me most of the time, but frequently I'd thumb back and forth. Peter spent most of the summer wandering around with friends at the beach.

We had only been in the motel a short time when a woman pulled up in her official-looking state car, walked around back and knocked at our door. She was from the Brockton office of the AFPCC, the Association for the Prevention of Cruelty to Children.

When my mother opened the door, she said, "We have received a complaint and I'm here to gather some information and make a report. May I come in?"

My mother and Peter both assumed the complaint must have been filed by Mrs. Ferguson. Who else could it be? They figured she was now "turning my mother in" for abusing my brother. Peter was in a great deal of pain that day, lying on the couch, sweating from the oppressive heat and icing down a swollen ankle.

Apparently there was a brief and somewhat contentious exchange at the door before my mother agreed to let the woman in. With Peter lying on the couch and listening in, my mother explained the details of Peter's condition, the reason for his bruises and his disability. She explained that Peter had been born a hemophiliac. He was missing "Factor Eight" in his blood composition, the factor responsible for coagulation and clotting. Peter had inherited this condition, passed on by her, the genetic carrier, from her hemophiliac father. Daughters of hemophiliac fathers would not be affected, but would serve as carriers to their own male children.

My mother started to tear up. Peter was having severe pains in his left ankle and was becoming increasingly upset by the tone of the implied accusations. Suddenly he blurted out an expression we'd heard many times from Bud. "Listen here, sister," he said. "You're barking up the wrong tree. And you can tell Mrs. Ferguson to mind her own damn business. She can stick her complaint up her ass."

Neither of them knew for sure that the abuse complaint had been filed by Mrs. Ferguson, but she was the likely suspect. Peter was giving this AFPCC woman both barrels. My mother tried to calm him down, but he was not going to clam down. He tried to get up but couldn't. He couldn't stand. If he could, he would have thrown her through the screen door. As far as he was concerned, the interrogation was over. He told her to get the hell out. As young as he was, he wasn't going to take any shit from her or Mrs. Ferguson.

The women from the AFPCC finally realized this had been a terrible mistake; there was no legitimate abuse complaint here. It was simply a misunderstanding. Peter saw it differently. He told her, "This is nothing less than a dirty trick leveled at my mother by that bitch, Ferguson." For whatever reason, Mrs. Ferguson had it in for my mother. By now the tenor of the meeting had changed considerably. The woman became sincerely apologetic, not only to my mother, but to Peter as well, and focused her attention and concern on Peter's well-being. "I know of a place where we might be able to get some help for Peter," she said. "I'd like for you and Peter to consider taking a ride with me to New Hampshire and visit Crotchet Mountain, a highly regarded rehabilitative live-in facility for crippled children. Would you be willing to take a look?"

Although my mother wasn't sure this would be the answer for Peter, she and Peter agreed to the trip. Maybe there was something there for him, something to make his life easier. The plans were made, and they left for New Hampshire the following week and stayed at the facility for nearly two weeks. All expenses were paid by the AFPCC. During the visit, my mother began looking around for work, figuring she could stay up there and be close to Peter. After several evaluations and subsequent meetings, the counselors at Crotchet Mountain determined that although Peter had frequent and severe periodic medical episodes, he was not permanently crippled and therefore did not qualify.

It was revealed that Mrs. Ferguson had indeed filed the complaint and was advised that her concerns had been addressed and she need not pursue it any further. In other words, as Peter put it, "She should mind her own goddamn business."

Labor Day passed, signaling the end of summer. The motel owner would soon be turning off the water and boarding up the place for winter. It was time to move. In late September we left Green Harbor, Marshfield and moved across the marshes to a small side street off Ocean Street, still in Marshfield, called Sixth Road. There were twelve short roads off Ocean Street, numbered one through twelve, all of which ran about a hundred yards in length, straight in from the road, and ending at the concrete seawall. My stepfather remained with us during this time and tagged along to Sixth Road. His dishwashing job ended when the restaurant closed after Labor Day. After that he pretty much gave up looking for another job. I couldn't understand how or why my mother ever took him back in the first place. I think she felt sorry for him, and by now he was obviously lost and sadly dependent on her. Neither one of them ever seemed to pay enough attention to the future. Whenever my mother would manage to save a little money, she would become fearful that something would happen, and it always did. So they focused, as best they could, on the here and now.

Sixth Road was another tough time for my mother, another tough time for all of us. She was struggling to keep us together as a family, working to pay the rent and dealing with two kids, one a hemophiliac and the other an asthmatic. Having Bud around wasn't helping matters either. I figured she was hoping in vain that he would eventually contribute a little stability and perhaps a little money. He'd spend most of the day drinking his beer and smoking cigarettes...and staring off into the distance.

A soon as I turned sixteen, my mother took me to the Registry of Motor Vehicles to apply for my driver's license. She let me drive once in a while for practice, and more than once I'd wake up early on Saturday mornings, grab the keys to the '41 Buick and drive off around town by myself. I was always back before anyone noticed. When I went for my license I was ready. I passed the written and practical tests without a hitch.

My mother started working as a waitress at a local restaurant in the center of Brant Rock, about two miles away. On her days off she would drive me to Rockland and pick me up after work. Sometimes I would drive myself. She worked with another lady who would pick her up twice a week and that would free up the car for me.

The old '41 Buick would always make it, bald tires and always on empty. We used to laugh about the "E" on the gas gauge. I told her it must stand for "enough." I talked the owner at the nearby gas station into giving me some drain oil for the car. Drain oil was the used oil drained from cars before adding new oil during an oil change. He was kind enough not to charge me. It was of no use to him anyway, so he was glad to get rid of it. I'd bring along a couple of empty oil cans and he'd fill them up for me. I must have been his only drain oil customer. The Buick went through a lot of oil, almost as much as gas it seemed.

My first full-time paycheck from Tedeschi's was for fifty-two hours—lots of money. I bought bags and bags of food, filled the gas tank all the way to full and bought myself a winter jacket.

Bud worked odd jobs here and there, trying to make something out of nothing. I spotted him outside a barroom in Hanover one day, while on my way to work. He was sweeping the parking lot with a broom in front of the building. I pulled over to the side of the road to get a better look. He didn't see me. I was sure he'd made a deal with the owner to sweep the lot in exchange for a few drinks. What a waste, I said to myself.

When I came home that first payday, he was sitting in a chair at the kitchen table having a beer and a smoke. As soon as he saw me he asked me for some money. I knew he wanted it for his beer, and I figured it was easier to give it to him than put up a fight.

We were putting it together, paying the rent, keeping the car running, and eating every day, but I knew this would be the last stop for me on this train without tracks. I was going nowhere and felt trapped, like spinning inside a round room looking for the door.

I would be leaving soon. My daily hitchhiking routine to Tedeschi's Market was coming to an end. I would be leaving to join the military, a four-year enlistment in the U.S. Air Force. I would stay with my mother and Peter long enough to help out with the bills and get them settled somewhere, and away from Bud. I would be seventeen in February and it couldn't come fast enough.

One day, out of nowhere, my Aunt Betty called. I was surprised; she never called. Someone died, I figured. Betty was my mother's younger sister. She and her husband Joe lived on Webster Street in Rockland. Apparently Betty had been talking with my Aunt Patricia, my Uncle Donald's wife. Betty would get all "the dirt" about us from Pat. My Aunt Pat seemed to know much of our business, and I could never figure that out.

When we lived in Rockland, Peter would cut through the high school parking lot on his way over to North Avenue to visit with my grandmother, my father's mother. She would pump Peter for information and he'd usually tell her whatever she wanted to know. Then, presumably, she'd pass it along to Pat and Donald, and then on to my father in Michigan. Then Pat would call Betty to fill her in. Sounds complicated, but that's what I figured happened and that's how Betty seemed to know everything. But now, we were living way down in Marshfield, so this really baffled me.

Pat must have called my father's place in Michigan to speak with Jane, his second wife. It wouldn't be like my father to do the calling. Jane and Pat would talk frequently and exchange information about their families and what was happening with Peter and me. After speaking with Jane, Pat called Betty to see if Betty could arrange for me to travel to Michigan and visit with my father. Betty and her husband Joe had a scrap metal business in Rockland and could afford to pay my way. Apparently my father wanted to spend some time with me before I went off to the military.

My mother and Betty never got along and I never knew why. Maybe it was their age difference. My mother was nine years older and was the center of attention before Betty came along. Peter and I had lived with Betty and Joe for a brief time following my mother's divorce. Betty insisted that my mother pay her to take care of us; otherwise she would have refused. At the time, my mother was trying to put her life back together, living in a one-room apartment behind the Brockton Hospital.

I've always thought my parents' divorce, though clearly justifiable, resulted in Peter and me becoming outcasts in the family. It had been a nasty, bitter divorce, and from that time on, there was very little interaction between us and our cousins, aunts, uncles or anyone else on my father's side. My uncle Donald went into the divorce court to defend his brother, my father, and to damn my mother. In those days, proof of wrongdoing had to be established before a divorce could be granted, and as a result of the findings, one parent or the other would be awarded custody of the minor children. Someone would always get hurt in the process.

Betty never had any children of her own. Everyone figured she didn't have children because she was most likely a carrier of hemophilia as well. I thought that Betty's motivation to send me out to see my father was not so much to benefit me, or to accommodate my father's wishes, but as some sort of vindictive payback aimed at my mother for something between them years ago that never healed. They were always at odds over something. My mother was the gentle one, gentle and reasonable. Betty, on the other hand, was unwaveringly stubborn—heels dug in deep. She admitted to me one day that she "wouldn't hesitate to pick a fight with the devil." Why my father agreed to my visit after all these years was a mystery to me. He'd stopped making the court-ordered $17-a-week child support payments years ago. Seventeen dollars to support two children. It sounds like nothing today, but it would have made a difference to my mother and to us in those days. She had brought us up and had kept us together. He was rarely in the picture.

The last time I had seen him was in the summer of 1957. He had arrived with his family from Michigan in his brand new, two-tone green Oldsmobile. They pulled into the parking lot at Tedeschi's one warm and sunny Saturday morning. I was working, hauling groceries for customers out to their cars. I finished loading bags into the trunk for one customer and began wheeling the empty carriage back into the store. Suddenly I heard a series of loud beeps from a car, and when I turned, I saw my father waving and calling out for me from several spaces away. I stopped and looked over at them. I didn't realize who they were at first, and then I knew. I could feel my face turning red with excitement. I flashed a big smile and hurried over to his car. His new, charming and very attractive wife, Jane, was sitting up front next to him. She reached through the open window, grabbed my arm, and said, "Hi Don, it's so nice to finally meet you." The two boys, my half-brothers, were in the back, smiling and bouncing on the seat, eager to meet me as well.

They didn't step out of the car; they were in a rush. So we spoke through the open windows. Jane turned around in her seat and introduced me to Jimmy and Paul. I reached in and shook their hands. "I've heard a lot about you guys, nice to meet you," I said.

I never revealed it, but I was jealous as hell of them; they seemed like a very close family. We chatted for a few minutes and then they drove out of the parking lot, exiting to the right on to Market Street, and out of sight. The visit was over before it began.

Betty asked my mother for permission to follow through with her plans to send me out to Michigan. After she hung up the phone, my mother asked me if I wanted to go. I asked her, "Why? And for how long? And will you and Peter be all right? What about Bud? I'm going in the Air Force soon, does he know that? And how am I going to get there?"

We had a brief conversation about the trip. She told me it would be all right. "If you want to go, don't worry, we'll be fine. And as for Bud, he's going to the VA. They can take care of him."

I went to Michigan, and Betty paid the airfare. I flew out of Boston on a twin prop DC-3 and sat next to a pretty stewardess in the back row of seats. I'd never flown before and was thrilled as the plane

44

taxied across the ramps and over to the assigned runway, stopping just long enough to run the engines up, release the brakes and start the roll. I watched as the runway markers passed the lift-off point, and with ground speeds approaching one hundred miles an hour, we lifted cleanly off the runway into the warm, sunny, mid-morning sky. I was loving it.

When we landed at Willow Run Airport just outside Detroit, my father and Jane were waiting for me as I exited the plane. I walked down the portable staircase and across the tarmac to the open door leading into the terminal. It was nice to see my father. I felt a sense of belonging when I was around him—something I remembered from when I was really young, and something I missed most of my life. He came up to me, wrapped his arms around me and planted a wet kiss on my cheek. Jane said hello, extended her hand and gave me a loving hug. I put my suitcase in the trunk and sat in the back seat of their shiny new Oldsmobile. Jane sat up front and my father drove. We left the airport grounds and headed for the expressway. My father was driving much too fast for Jane. He took his eyes off the road, looking at something to our right, and drifted over, nearly hitting the curb. Jane spoke up saying, "Pete, look out, and for heaven's sake, please slow down."

They lived on a corner lot at number 13212 Superior Street in Wyandotte. The house was a small, white, cape-style home with an attic dormer and a detached one-car garage. The backyard was completely fenced in to keep their well-trained English hunting dog, Bell, from running out into the road. Jimmy, the oldest at twelve, and Paul, who was nine, were waiting outside in the driveway when we arrived. I jumped out of the back seat and greeted them with enthusiasm. They were both very excited to see me, especially Paul it seemed. Paul reminded me of myself at his age. He had a full head of curly, reddish-blond hair, blue eyes, plenty of freckles, and a warm, outgoing personality. Jimmy was more like Jane, good looking, dark brown hair, and a reserved, but friendly disposition. Jane took my small light green suitcase into the house while Jimmy, Paul and I played touch football on the snow covered front yard.

One freezing Saturday at four in the morning, my father took me out hunting with a group of his pals. We rushed through a hasty breakfast that Jane had prepared, bundled up, and walked out to his car. He opened the trunk, unlocked the gate to the backyard and whistled for Bell to come. She came running out and without a word from my father, jumped up and into the opened trunk and lay down. He closed the trunk and we drove through the dark, crisp, snowy morning to somewhere north of Detroit. I was concerned about the dog being locked in the trunk, but I figured they'd done this together hundreds of times. I didn't say anything. I didn't want to upset my renewed relationship with my father. My father was as rough and demanding with his dog as he was with everything and everyone else in his life. I just sat there quietly.

We stopped at a gun shop along the way to buy some ammunition. My father walked over to the counter and told the clerk he wanted a box of .22 "short." His leftover Boston accent made it sound like he wanted a box of .22 "shot." A near argument broke out over what he wanted. The clerk couldn't understand him and my father's quick temper only made it worse. The clerk finally figured out what he wanted after lining up several boxes of ammo on the glass counter. He bought two boxes of .22 shorts, and we left. Several hours later, we arrived at an old abandoned farmhouse deep in the snow-packed woods of northern Michigan. As soon as we arrived, my father opened the truck and Bell jumped out, barking, wagging her tail and jumping around in circles...ready for the hunt. My father's buddies had arrived before us and were sitting around a table in the kitchen across from a roaring fire having some breakfast. After a few shots of scotch, which they called "eye-openers" (I turned down the offer of an eye-opener. I said I was too young and they all laughed), we headed out on foot through the snow with loaded shotguns and rifles in search of deer or pheasant or anything else that moved.

The six-man hunting party, with me tagging along beside my father, tracked through the open fields of snow for well over an hour before reaching a flat plateau up on a hill, a good place to scan the terrain. As we headed down from the plateau to follow some tracks in the deep snow, someone spotted a rabbit over to our right. It had run into the underbrush. My father, using hand signals like a field commander, motioned for the others to spread out and circle around. I thought to myself, Here was a group of grown, half-lit men, gathering around a clump of bushes waiting to blast a frightened rabbit as soon as he made his move.

Suddenly the rabbit jumped in the air over the low lying brush and bolted between my father and the guy to his right, and they all opened fire. I figured that someone was going to get killed, maybe me. I was in the middle of a goddamn war. I took a few steps back, away from the madness, as they continued to shatter the morning stillness with their gunfire. Chunks of snow and twigs were flying everywhere as the small, wily jackrabbit dashed right past them and out across the field. How they missed him, and how they missed one another, was beyond me.

After a long, cold day of hiking and hunting, we made it back to the farmhouse. There was little to show for the day's effort. We all went inside to warm up and shake off the snow, and have a few drinks. After tossing back a couple of shots of scotch, my father announced he was going outside to do some target shooting and wanted everyone including me to come out and watch. We all followed him outside as he positioned himself several yards from the barn. He reached into his right-hand coat pocket, pulled out a .22-caliber pistol and held it up for all to see. It was a small, single shot pistol that looked like a Derringer. He broke open the barrel, put a shell in the chamber, locked the barrel in place, and took careful aim at the hand-painted target attached to the side of the barn.

I was standing behind him, watching to see if he could hit the target. He squeezed off the round and it missed everything. I don't think it even hit the barn. After a brief pause, he mumbled something, reloaded, and took aim once again.

Three of his buddies who were standing off to the right hollered out, "Hey, Pete, hold up…wait a minute!" Where the hell did that shot go? Nobody knew. They all gathered in behind him and stood next to me. He closed one eye, took aim and slowly squeezed off the second round. The shot rang out, ricocheted off the stone column next to the barn and shattered the glass panel above the side door of the farmhouse. "For Jesus Chrissake, you see that?" bellowed my father. I could see he was aiming straight for the target, but the pistol was firing off to the right. Angry, impatient, and obviously embarrassed, he brought the pistol up to his disbelieving face to get a closer look and then threw it into a trash barrel to his right. "Goddamn thing's got a crooked barrel," he muttered. Everyone thought the whole thing was pretty amazing and pretty damn funny. Everyone except him. Someone, trying to keep it going, hollered out, "Hey, Pete, bet you can't do that again!"

"Hey, cut the shit," he said flatly. "Help me find something to cover the goddamn window!"

That was it for me. I had had enough and just wanted to get the hell out of there.

After an anxious and exhausting day plowing through the snow and wondering what would happen next, we packed up the gear and the firearms to begin the long ride home. It was late and getting dark. My father turned to me and said, "You drive. You know how to drive? You got a driver's license?" I told him I could drive and had a driver's license. He handed me the keys and I opened the driver's side door and settled in behind the wheel. We were joined by two others who had decided to ride with us instead of riding home with the guys who drove them earlier in the morning. I was glad my father wanted me to drive because by now none of them, including my father, could tie their shoes. For all of its comradeship, its anticipation, its fun and glory, I figured hunting was not for me.

Every day after work, my father would come home, open the back door, turn to the right and walk up the two steps into the kitchen. Except for the area around his eyes, his face was completely black from coal dust. He told me he worked underground in the "salt mines." I never knew if he worked mining salt or mining coal, or maybe both, but I knew he worked hard.

Thursday was payday. He'd come home from work, clean himself up, hand Jane enough money to run the house and head out to Chauncy's for a night of drinking. Chauncy's was a small neighborhood bar-room about three blocks from his house, down the end of his street. It was like clockwork, every week. Thursdays, Fridays and all day Saturday he'd drink. I only got a taste of his antics after he'd been drinking, but I knew from talking with Jimmy and Paul he was a troublemaker, always in a brawl at Chauncy's. Always tearing the place apart. Jane had to call the police on several occasions to settle him down when he'd come home from a night out. He used to scare the hell out of my mother when I was a little boy; now it was Jane's turn.

My father was a fast-driving, hardworking, hard-living man who looked and acted a lot like the Jackie Gleason character "Ralph Cramden," a funny guy who was always going to make it big with one scheme or another. He was often the life of the party. But, if you lived with him, he had a nasty and often unpredictable temper that frightened everyone around him.

I had only been out there about a week when the three of us, Jimmy, Paul and myself, began horsing around in the living room. Paul slid off the armrest of the chair I was sitting in and banged his elbow on the heating register. He began to cry, more scared than hurt. My father came into the room from the kitchen where he'd been sipping a beer and wanted to know what had happened. "Did you push him?" he asked me.

I told him that we were fooling around and Paul had slipped. Without a moment's hesitation, he smashed me in the face, a hard open-handed slap. It hurt me more emotionally than physically. I could usually take a shot and shake it off. The physical stuff never really hurt. But I never saw it coming. I was used to this shit coming from Bud, but from him? He turned and walked back to the kitchen without saying a word and sat back down at the table to finish his beer. Jimmy and Paul ran upstairs to their rooms and I sat there wondering what I would do.

A minute or so later, I got up and slowly walked into the kitchen and sat at the table across from him, tears streaming down my face. I planted my elbows on the table and buried my red face in my hands. I told him about Bud and what he had done to me and said, "Now you." He never said he was sorry. He never said anything. It was as if I was sitting there talking to myself.

Later that evening, Paul told me he felt bad about what happened. "That's the way he is," he said apologetically. I thought about packing up and leaving that night—grab a bus for home. But I decided to stick around and talk with Jane in the morning.

Jane said, "Don, I'm sure he regrets what he did; he's always regretful after the fact. I've had to call the police on him a number of times for slapping me around and the boys, especially when he comes home drunk. If you want to leave, I'll take you to the bus, but I think it would be better to stay the whole month and leave on better terms."

I did stay for the remainder of the month, and during this time my father made an attempt to find me a job at an automotive supply house affiliated with the Ford Motor Company, but that never materialized. I wouldn't have taken the job anyway. There was no future for me out there, and besides, I was committed to a four-year hitch in the Air Force and needed to get back home. Two weeks later, Jane and my father and the boys drove me to Willow Run Airport, where we hugged and shook hands before I boarded another DC-3 for the flight home to Boston.

My Aunt Betty picked me up at the airport and dropped me off at Ken's Cabins in Norwell. Peter and my mother had left Sixth Road in Marshfield and moved into one of these cabins along Washington Street.

There were twenty or more small one-room cabins in this complex, lined up side-by-side in three rows separated by dirt paths that served as roads. The complex was set down in a hollow and was littered with rusted cars, tires, auto parts, broken toys and bicycles and other pieces of discarded or abandoned junk—a really depressing spot.

Betty pulled in and drove down the short dirt driveway, turned left and stopped next to the second cabin on the right. She never turned the car engine off. She just motioned with her finger and said, "They're in there." I thanked her for paying for my trip and for picking me up at the airport. She didn't want to stay and chat or even turn off the car, and I could tell she didn't want to be around when they opened the cabin door. I stepped out of the car, grabbed my suit-case from the back seat, and walked twenty feet or so down to the cabin she had pointed out. It was a small, faded red cabin on a low, square cinderblock foundation. I hesitated before knocking on the door. Betty backed up, turned around and drove out onto Washington Street and out of sight. I stood there for a moment glancing around and wondering why or how in hell they wound up here.

Peter opened the door when I knocked. He was so excited to see me and I was happy to see him. My mother came to the door and gave me a hug, saying, "We've really missed you." Then I spotted Bud. What the hell is he doing here? I thought. We had a plan to get rid of him. She had promised me that after I left for Michigan, she would take him to the veteran's hospital in Brockton and let them take care of him.

Bud spoke right up; the first words out of his mouth were, "There's no room for you. Look around here. There's hardly room for us." I felt like saying, There's no room for you, you worthless shit, but I didn't.

I never spent one night there. I had my own money, money left over from working at Tedeschi's and twenty bucks my father had given me when I left Michigan. I told my mother and Peter that I'd be back in the morning and we'd figure things out then. I grabbed my suitcase and walked two miles down Washington Street to the Route 3 Motel in Hanover, where I rented a small room on the end overlook-ing the backyard.

The next morning I walked back to Ken's Cabins. Bud wasn't there when I arrived. He was out getting his cigarettes and beer. I sat down and had a long talk with my mother and Peter. They told me what had happened while I was away. They had been thrown out of Sixth Road because they couldn't pay the rent. I'd heard this all before—many times before. Bud was a financial and emotional drag on everything in my mother's life. In those days, public welfare didn't exist, so you either did it or it didn't get done. I told her she needed to be rid of him, somehow. He was no good to himself and no good to anyone around him.

My mother and Peter were in a tough spot. She had never asked her sister or any of her family for help with money or anything else. I'm not sure why, but she never did. There was nowhere to go but up from here. Ken's Cabins was a desperate last stop for transients and drunks, and others who were down on their luck. I figured that sometimes in life you've got to hit the bottom to get the bounce.

Peter began describing in detail the events leading up to the repossession of the car. "Don, while you were gone, two guys from the Norfolk County Trust Company pulled in off the road and stopped right behind our car, just as we were about to leave. Bud spotted them in the rear view mirror and quickly figured out who they were and why they were there. Don, he floored it, kicking up dust and dirt all over their car. He drove down to the end, spun around, and nearly sideswiped them as we went hell-bent up the hill and out on to Washington Street. They quickly spun around too and started chasing us up Washington Street. We ran right through the red lights at Grove Street, turned right on Grove and left them in the dust. Don, the tires were screeching. I think we went up on two wheels, going like hell. I ducked down on the floor thinking we were going to flip over. Mom kept screaming for Bud to slow down, but he was frozen to the wheel, dead set on outrunning them. We flew around a sharp turn in the road and Bud cut the wheel to the left and slid sideways into a long driveway that ended at the top of a hill. He slammed on the brakes and we skidded to a stop. Then he turned off the key and told us all to get down. The guys from the bank went racing past the driveway and out of sight. Don, it was just like in the movies. I started laughing out loud. Bud had really outsmarted them; they must have felt like fools."

I found out later that they had traded in the old '41 Buick and signed a loan for a newer car, a '53 Ford, and only made one payment on the loan. That's when the bank sent the "repo" guys to grab the car. They came back three nights later and snatched it.

I was standing next to my mother for support when Bud returned from the store. She held up her hand and stopped him from coming in, then looked him square in the eye and told him, flat out, he had to leave. "You can come in and get your things and then I want you out of here. Peter and I will manage on our own. I mean it this time, Bud. Now leave and don't come back!" He glared at me with one of his mean-spirited, lip-curling, nasty snarls, grabbed his beer and a few other things, and left without uttering a sound.

He must have made his way to the Veterans Administration Hospital in Brockton where I'm sure he'd spent much of his time away from us in the past. Weeks later, Peter found out he was living in a private home with other veterans on Hingham Street in Rockland, a place he'd stayed several times over the years.

My mother finally woke up and faced the madness head on, and vowed not to spend another night in that godforsaken place. Now, nearly in tears, she turned to me and asked if I had any coins. "I'm going to make a call," she said. I gave her what I had and asked if she wanted me to come along. She said, "No, I've got to do this myself." She walked to the pay phone up the street and made a call to some old friends in Abington, the Martins. The Martins had lived three houses from us on Linda Street in the old Green Street neighborhood years ago. At the time, my mother had been a close friend of Mrs. Martin, and their son, Alfred, and I went to school and played together as young boys. Helen Martin and her husband Ben told my mother that she was welcome to stay with them, along with Peter, until she could get a steady job and find a place of her own. The Martins, however, made it clear that Bud would not be welcome. They had seen what a miserable bastard he had been to me years before. My mother assured them that she "didn't want to see him, ever again."

Ben Martin told my mother he'd be right along. "Just give me twenty minutes or so, I'll leave now. Are you ready? Do you need more time?" Grateful and crying like a hurt child, she said, "No, I'm ready now and…and thank you!" The burden had been lifted. Bud was gone and the Martins were taking them in. For the first time in a long time, thanks to the Martins, she could smile and maybe be happy again.

Before I left for the Air Force, I took the Brockton bus to the Abington stop and walked over to the Martins' place to see my mother and Peter, and say hello to the Martins. I was surprised to hear that Alfred had also joined the Air Force and was away in Basic Training.

I stayed at the motel in Hanover for a couple of weeks awaiting my military orders. The line on my DD-214 military discharge papers simply says, "residence at time of enlistment: Colonial Motel, Route 3, Hanover, Massachusetts." The motel is long gone, torn down years ago as part of a master plan to build several attached retail shops and restaurants.

My commitment to the U.S. Air Force was just days away, and I felt as though I was abandoning my mother and brother. I'd be leaving them to make it without me. Thank God for the Martins. My mother had hit bottom. No car, no food, little or no money, and no place to live. Thanks to the Martins, she could work her way out of this mess and that's what she did. I felt as though I could have done more, but my time was up; I had to leave.

At four in the morning the Air Force recruiter knocked on my door in the rear of the motel. I was up, dressed and ready. After stopping along the way to pick up two other recruits, he dropped us off at Logan Airport in Boston, where we were joined by several others who were already lined up to board the same flight bound for Basic Training at Lackland Air Force Base, San Antonio, Texas. The only thing I had with me was a small zippered bag of personal items, along with a few dollars I had managed to save. It was May 5, 1960.

FOUR

Flight 471

We landed at Lackland Air Force Base around 11:30 in the morning and were immediately hustled over to a waiting 1950s-style faded blue school bus, which took us to the chow hall for lunch and then to the barracks and training center. I was a little anxious but fully prepared and excited to begin this adventure, this next phase of my life.

The warm Texas weather was a sharp contrast to the damp and dreary skies that had hung over Boston earlier in the day. Little did I know about the suffocating Texas heat that awaited me.

I had everything riding on this—everything. At seventeen, I was the youngest recruit assigned to Flight 471, Squad 3726, and I was lockjaw determined to fight my way through this and graduate. Nothing they could throw at me would be tougher than the bullshit back home. If I failed here, failed at this, I would be lost. There was nowhere else to go, no back door, no fall back position.

When the bus dropped us off at the barracks, we roamed around inside the building waiting for the sergeant to arrive. Without warning and for no reason, one of the other recruits came up to me and started giving me some shit. Maybe he noticed the chip on my shoulder and figured I'd be an easy target. After some words, he shoved me back against the wall. I was all through getting pushed around. I came off that wall and shoved him as hard as he had shoved me. I wasn't a big kid, but I wasn't afraid and he must have sensed that. It ended as quickly as it started when two other recruits came over and separated us, but that taught me to sharpen my wits, keep my eyes and ears open wide, and trust no one.

Right from the beginning the drill sergeants treated us like junk-yard dogs. I glanced around at the wide-eyed group of guys, still in civilian clothes, that I would be training and living with over the next six weeks. Multicolored and checkered shirts, scuffed-up boots and shoes of all types, tattoos stretched across well-developed muscles, long hair, greasy hair and bushy hair. Each of us had our own reason for being there. All of us had volunteered—perhaps the only common thread.

For some of them, volunteering was the lesser of two evils. The courts had frequently given them a choice to either spend time in jail or enlist in the military. Some had completed high school and couldn't find a job, and some, like me, had quit high school and were looking for a chance to start a new life.

The drill sergeants referred to us as "rainbows," mainly because of our multiethnic mix and our multicolored clothing. We were told to "fall in" outside and form a line out on the sidewalk, shortest to tallest. The drill sergeant came out, brought us to attention and began marching us up and down several streets before commanding us to "Halt...halt...halt, goddamnit!" Like dominos, each of us crashed into the guy next in line, trying to come to a stop. He called us to attention. "I said, *attention*, goddamnit!" He was infuriated. "This has to be the sorriest looking group of goddamn rainbows in the goddamn history of the goddamn United States Air Force!" I glanced around at several squads of young recruits marching past us in close disciplined formation. He was right; we were an embarrassment.

The senior drill sergeant came over and called us to attention, then marched us down the sidewalk, around the corner and up four steps onto a concrete platform, which led into the gray, two-story "Clothing Supply Depot." The long counter to my left was manned by four enlisted Airmen, 2nd class. Behind them were rows of metal racks neatly stacked with military clothing, everything arranged according to size. As we moved along slowly, side to side and shoulder to shoulder, they threw plastic bags of socks and underwear at us. Next were the towels, bed sheets, blankets, and a pillow, and then boots, belts, brass belt buckles, and finally uniforms.

One of the airmen behind the counter, the one in charge, was yelling at each of us to speak up as we passed through the clothing stations. When he came to me, he barked, "What's your shoe size?" I told him I didn't know. "What the...? You don't know your own shoe size?" He turned his head and laughed to one of his buddies behind the counter. "Hey Jimmy, this one doesn't even know his own shoe size." He threw some boots at me and told me to move along. The boots fit fine; I wasn't going to complain.

Nothing else fit very well. The uniforms, or fatigues, as they were called, were all too big for me. I stood off to the side and tried on the pants and shirts. The airman in charge told me to take them off. "Here, try these on. You look ridiculous. When's the last time you ate, for chrissake?" They fit fine and everything else was good enough.

I thought to myself, free clothes and free boots; not bad. I'd never worn boxer shorts before, but figured I'd get used to them, along with everything else. I just wanted to follow along, do what the others did. I didn't want to stand out or bring any unnecessary attention to myself.

We had arrived in Texas on a Thursday morning dressed as civilians. By Monday it was all military. Civilian clothes were packed away for the remainder of Basic.

Our next stop was the barbershop. We walked outside the clothing depot and stacked all our gear in neat piles along the walkway, then formed up and marched down the street for the fastest haircut of our young lives. As of yet, there was nothing "uniform" about us. Still rainbows—still misfits. That all changed in a New York minute.

There were six barber chairs lined up next to each other inside the barbershop. In a matter of seconds the barbers hustled us into the chairs and ran electric shavers through our hair, like mowing grass, starting at the forehead, then sweeping over the top and down the back, four swipes. Then a little trimming around the ears and done—bald!

Now we looked alike. Now we were uniform. All the wavy, straight, curly, black, red, blond, and greasy hair covered the floor. Seventy-five guys, shaved clean in less time than you could say the Pledge of Allegiance. When I was finished, I left the chair and headed outside. On the way, I glanced to my right and looked in the full-length mirror hanging on the wall next to the door. A wide, full-toothed grin burst out all over my boyish face. I looked like a ten year old!

Another drill sergeant was standing just outside the door, watching as we exited the barbershop. He spotted me looking at myself in the mirror. He grabbed my arm and screamed at me, "Get your silly ass over here and wipe that goddamn grin off your face, Airman." He scared the hell out of me. I quickly stopped the grinning and attempted to look serious. I couldn't figure out what in hell I had done wrong, but he was really pissed. "I told you to wipe that goddamn grin off your face, now do it!" he demanded. With my right hand, I motioned across my face like I was wiping off my grin. Then I made a fist and held it up in the air for him to see my grin was securely inside. Everyone, now standing in formation and waiting for me, was watching the show. He continued: "Now, throw that goddamn grin of yours on the ground and stomp on it."

I threw my grin with full force on the ground, lifted my right leg and slammed my boot down on top of it. I'm sure I wasn't the only guy to walk out of there with a grin. They all must have felt silly when they looked in the mirror on the way out, but I was the one who got caught. Anyway, the entire scene was ridiculous, and I felt like a damn fool.

After the hair razing, we milled around on the sidewalk anxiously awaiting further instructions. One of the drill sergeants screamed out, "Atten…hut! Now form a line; stand shoulder to shoulder to the man next to you. Now spread out. Stretch your right arm out until it touches the man to your right, then drop it at your side." He then proceeded to get a closer look at each of us, a personal up-close inspection, nose to nose. When he came to me, he looked at my young, pale face and asked, "Did you shave this morning, Airman? You know *how* to shave, boy? You need a goddamn shave, you know that! I better not see you unshaven again. Do you hear me?" I roared back in an automatic response, "*Yes, Sir!*" He examined me from the right side, then the left. My eyes followed him until he screamed squarely in my face, "Keep your goddamn eyes straight ahead. Don't you goddamn *dare* look at me! *You understand me, Airman?*" He continued bellowing, spitting out his words. "You're a goddamn sorry excuse for a man. Do you know that?" I didn't know what he wanted me to say, so I shot back, "Yes, Sir. Yes, Sir!" I said it twice.

Thankfully, he'd had enough of me and moved on to the next guy, and when he was finished humiliating each of us, he looked down at the ground and shook his head in apparent disgust, then announced, "Now we're going to march over to your new home." He ordered us to attention and we marched down several streets before stopping in front of our barracks, our home for the duration.

The drab gray, two-story, wooden, rectangular building was about sixty feet long and thirty feet wide and filled with rows and rows of metal-framed, double-bunk beds lined up on both sides of the room, from front to back. Resting on each bunk, top and bottom, was a thin, gray, worn-out mattress. There were two footlockers assigned to each set of bunks, one on the floor at the head of the bunks and one in the rear. We were told to pick out a bunk and a footlocker and pack our gear neatly inside, leaving the lid open for inspection.

I walked down to the next to last bunk on the left, next to the rear door, and lay my bag and clothes on the lower bunk. I was about to start packing my footlocker when the highest ranking of the three drill sergeants came charging through the front door and screamed for us to come to attention. He said, "Stop everything and stand at attention in front of your bunks." His voice began to settle down to a surprisingly friendly tone as he continued. "Now, boys, listen up. Before we get started, I think it would be a nice idea if we had a party—what we call here in the Air Force a G.I. party."

I remember thinking (and this is how naïve I was), Hey, not bad. We're going to have a party. I wonder if they're going to have music. When we had first arrived, earlier in the day, we were dropped off at a chow hall on the far side of the base for some lunch. While we were going through the chow line, someone went over to a jukebox nestled in the corner and began playing some great music, and I thought, What's so tough about this?

The G.I. "party" was no party at all. The three drill sergeants walked through the barracks throwing mattresses all over the floor and tipping over the bunks. Since these were all double bunks, most of the frames split open, sending the metal dividers rolling everywhere. Crash bang thud and crash bang thud again. Metal frames and end pieces flying across the open area. What a racket. The three of them worked up a dripping sweat, heaving anything and everything across the room. We stood in silence watching and wondering why in hell they were doing this.

When they finished wrecking the place, the ranking sergeant, now out of breath, turned and looked at each of us standing around the room, and with an air of hard-nosed sarcasm, said, "Now, boys, we can have that party I promised you." He began raising his voice, leaving nothing to the imagination…a well-rehearsed script. The more he spoke the louder he became…louder and louder until he was out of control and screaming like a madman. "I want you maggots to clean this goddamn place up, wash the floor and straighten everything out, and don't forget the latrine. We'll be back in an hour for a complete inspection and this place better be spotless. Do you hear me?"

"Yes, Sir," we responded with little enthusiasm.

"I said…Do you hear me?" he roared.

"Yes, Sir!" we shouted in unison.

But he wasn't through.

"And another thing, I want those bed sheets drawn as tight as your ass. I'm going to drop a quarter on your sheets and I better get a bounce!" Then he and the others turned and left the building, slamming the door so hard it bounced back open.

After they left, there was stunned silence. Then a fight broke out. Someone said to one of the guys who was obviously scared to death and wanted to go home, "Hey, you little pussy, shut the fuck up."

Holy shit, I thought, We've only got an hour to put this place back together and there's a brawl going on down by the back door. Four guys ran over and grabbed the two who were rolling around the floor locked in combat. I heard one guy say, "Knock it off. Cut the shit. We're in enough trouble."

Everything settled down as we organized ourselves into teams and began re-setting the bunks and mattresses, sweeping and mopping, and cleaning the sink, toilets, and showers in the latrine. When the sergeants burst through the front door, we scrambled back to our bunks and came to attention. They split up, walked over to each bunk and began their bouncing-the-quarter routine, testing the "tight-ass" sheets. The quarter didn't bounce for anyone except the guy directly across from me. The sergeant made a big deal out of him. "You should all learn a lesson from this man. Out of seventy-five men, he's the only one who did it right." And he was the only one who didn't get a demerit, a "gig-slip," as it was called. Demerits were the last thing anyone wanted. Five demerits and we'd be shipped back to join the group behind us, adding another three weeks to Basic.

Reveille was at 04:00. A record player must have been wired to a series of loud speakers somewhere nearby. The sound of the bugle wouldn't begin right away; the sound of a scratching needle would come first, then the unmistakable sound of a bugle announcing reveille. As soon as that scratching needle sound began, I jumped to my feet, grabbed my towel and headed for the showers. Most of the time I was in there first.

On the third day of Basic, before we were told to "fall out," the same three sergeants came thundering through the front door, demanding we stop everything and come to attention in front of our bunks.

One of them stood in the middle of the room and announced, "This is a surprise inspection. Dump everything you've got—everything you brought with you—dump it out onto your bunks. Clear out your foot-lockers. We want to inspect everything, and I mean everything!"

Oh shit, I said to myself. I had brought my asthma medication. Up until now, I had kept it well hidden. It was a plastic inhaler and a bottle of liquid medicine that went with it. I had it tucked away in a small blue zippered pouch. I thought about hiding it under my bed but I figured they'd see it or someone would rat me out, so I decided to lay the case, with the contents zippered inside, on my bunk along with the rest of my stuff. I knew that if they opened my little blue case and discovered that I had smuggled in medication for asthma, I'd be thrown out and probably court marshaled with a General or Dishonorable Discharge for entering the service under false pretenses.

As I was standing at attention, I glanced at the ceiling and whispered, "Okay, God, this is in your hands. It's all up to you. I'll be thrown out if they open that case." I kept praying that they wouldn't. I stood at attention at the front of my bunk. One of the sergeants came up to me and stared me in the eye and spouted off, "Did you shave this morning?" I said, "*Sir, Yes, Sir!*" It must have been obvious to him that I had shaved because I always cut myself pretty good. My face was a mess with acne and there was no getting around cutting myself. A slight grin appeared on his face when he questioned me. "I don't think you're old enough to shave, boy! What do you think?" I reassured him. "I'm old enough, Sir, Yes, Sir!" While I was being interrogated, the others went through all my stuff scattered across my bunk. They never said a word. It was as if the little blue case wasn't even there.

The plain truth was that they had me so damn scared most of the time that my adrenaline was always high enough to ward off any problems with asthma. Only once did I need to use the inhaler. It was the middle of the night and for some reason I woke up wheezing. Thankfully, I slept in the lower bunk and was able to slither out of bed and crawl around the corner to my locker. I silently lifted the lid, fished around in the dark for the case, unzipped it, poured the solution into the inhaler, and puffed it into my lungs several times. Everyone was dead asleep. I kept my eye trained on the guard at the front door; he never moved and he never saw me.

I liked the rhythmic cadence of all seventy-five boots hitting the pavement in unison. It was thunderous and I felt a blushing sense of pride. I was proud of the worn-down heels of my boots, a clear sign for anyone to see that I was putting in the effort. I'd slam them with deliberate force into the pavement while marching, and we were always marching. We'd yell out phrases to the beat of the march: "I don't know, but I've been told…." Made-up phrases aimed at badmouthing other branches of the service, the Army or the Marines or the Navy, and instilling a sense of Air Force pride. A little *esprit de corps.*

Late one morning, after a three-mile run, the drill sergeants lined us up on the concrete area just outside our barracks. We formed up in four separate rows, all facing forward, one row behind the other. The drill instructor stood out front facing us. He told us to spread out at arms length, side step at arms length, away from each other. "Now, keep both arms outstretched to the sides and pretend you're holding a bucket of water in each hand."

We stood there for a long time with our arms fully extended. It was hot that day—really hot. I began feeling light-headed. We were all hungry and soaking wet from the run. I said to myself, If the guy next to me can do this, if he can last, then I can last. I'm not going to quit and I'm not going to keel over.

Suddenly, to my right, at the far end of the row behind me, the last guy passed out while still standing at attention. He went forward onto the pavement, smashing his nose and his forehead. He was out before he went down. I heard the noise and glanced over my shoulder. The drill sergeant screamed to the rest of us, "At ease! And keep your goddamn eyes straight ahead!" He didn't want anyone else going down and he didn't want any of us watching as they hauled him away.

I never saw how badly he looked after falling. The sergeant shouted out again, demanding, "Keep your goddamn eyes straight ahead!" The others behind me saw the whole thing. His face was covered with blood. I knew he must have been seriously hurt, a broken nose and a concussion maybe. He never came back; one of the twenty-one guys from our flight that didn't make it through Basic Training.

The Texas heat, the midnight marches, swinging from ropes over water, crawling under barbed wire with live explosives, the miserable tear gas experience, and the sleepless nights: It was all part of a program to transform us from undisciplined civilians into men who could take orders, work as a team and work with a purpose—making men out of boys.

Then the rifle range...the much anticipated rifle range. We all looked forward to the firing exercises, a chance to fire off some live rounds.

That morning we lined up outside the barracks and marched two miles to the range. They were ready for us as we entered the firing grounds and proceeded past the guard tower to our left. We were ordered to halt in front of our pre-assigned firing positions. Once in position, we were handed over to the commanding officer, who began a series of instructions from his position in the tower. He called out, "Right face, and stand at attention looking down range." Our weapons and loaded magazines (clips) rested on the rubber pad at our feet at positions in front of each of us. These were weapons—not guns. Semi-automatic carbine, 30-caliber M-I weapons.

Another booming voice from the control tower instructed, "Reach down, pick up your cardboard target, walk down range to your posting position and affix your target to the numbered station." Posting positions were straight ahead, one hundred yards down range. Stenciled on the cardboard target was the outline of a man.

When we returned from posting our targets, we were brought to attention and then instructed, "Slowly bend down and pick up your weapon, keeping it pointing down. Now check the safety switch. Make sure it is in the 'on' position." Each movement along the firing line was monitored by the instructors who paced back and forth responding to the commands from the tower.

We were then instructed to pick up the magazine, the ammunition clip, sometimes referred to as the "metal jacket." Each magazine had been previously loaded with ten live rounds.

Once again from the tower: "Now check the safety, make sure it's in the 'on' position, now load and lock the magazine, then drop down and assume the prone position. Now adjust your sight, take aim at your target, turn your safety off, and upon my command, fire one round at your target." I held the weapon tightly with the stock jammed against my right shoulder and the barrel propped up and held steady in my left hand. I slowly squeezed off the round and felt the recoil jolt my shoulder. Following the round, we were instructed to adjust, if necessary, the sight, up, down, left or right. Then came the command we had been waiting for. I had sighted in my weapon and was ready; my heart was pounding: "Now, ready on the left, ready on the right, ready on the firing line. Commence firing!" As instructed, we took aim and slowly squeezed off the first five rounds. Then, as the tower counted down the remaining time, we were told, "You have five seconds to empty all remaining rounds." It was thunderous. I was tearing up my target. It sounded like we were in the middle of a god-damn war. At that moment, I was troubled by the thought of having to kill someone, someday; I didn't want to think about it.

Following the announced cease fire I switched the safety on, set my weapon down and, on command, walked along with everyone else, down range to retrieve my bullet-riddled target. While I was removing what was left of my target, the guy to my right said something that puzzled me. "What the hell?" His target didn't have a single hole in it, not one. Mine was in shreds. He had been shooting at my target. When we returned and handed in our targets, the firing instructor didn't know what to do. He counted up the points on my card and gave me a score of 248, which meant I was a "sharpshooter." Then he turned to the guy who had been firing at my target and began blasting him out. "You dumb-ass shit. Drop and give me fifty pushups for being so goddamn stupid...*stupid!*"

On the fourteenth of May, I received my first letter from home:

5/11/60
Dear Don,
   Helen and I got your letters today and were we ever glad to hear from you.
   I was worried about that darn sprayer and hoping there would be no trouble from it.
   I have been staying at Martins' and Peter is staying up the street at Jake's house until I can find and afford three rooms for him and me.
   I am taking a physical at the Brockton Hospital tomorrow morning to take a job as nurse's aide. It pays a little over a dollar an hour which isn't bad. If everything goes all right, I hope to start work by Monday.
   I suppose you are pretty tired by now, and have you had your hair cut yet?

The time will go by fast dear and before you know it, you will be coming home to rest up awhile.

Helen will tell you all about Alfred's trip. He had quite a time.

Jake's mother is taking Peter down to Abington School tomorrow so he can finish the year there. He doesn't know what to do with himself while the kids are in school.

Honey, be sure to pick your pals and don't get involved with playing cards.

Inquire about saving some of your money for transportation back home on your leave. The time will go faster than you think.

Be sure and write me as often as you can and take care of yourself, dear.

Lots of Love,

Mother

* * *

We were finally approaching the final days of Basic; only one week remained. On the Sunday before graduating, we were issued a Base Pass. The pass was our first reward. It was intended to give us a break from the routine, and for some reason I thought of the guys who had phased out—the ones who were sent home because they couldn't handle it. They had missed out on this moment.

A bunch of us wound up at the patio for some shade and a coke. I went inside the recreation center next to the patio and played the pinball machines. Then we took a walk to the Base Exchange (BX) and bought some supplies and souvenirs. I gathered up a fistful of change and made a call back home to my mother from the pay phone just outside the BX. She and Peter had left the Martins' place and were living in Brockton. The phone I called was the pay phone out in the hallway of the downtown apartment building. Someone answered it, and when I explained who I was and where I was calling from, he knocked at my mother's door and she came running. She was so happy to hear from me. I'd been gone nearly six weeks now and, although I'd written to her, she was worried about me, hoping I'd make it through.

During our conversation she told me she had applied for some help down at the welfare office in Brockton, a program called ADC—Aid to Dependent Children. I had been sending her most of my pay, but it wasn't much. She told me that when she went into the refrigerator that Friday morning, the only food in there was two hot dogs, nothing else. "So," she went on to explain, "I put my pride in my pocket and went down to their office to ask for help. They weren't at all nice about it, either. They wanted to know all my business and everything about Peter and where his father was."

They gave her emergency assistance right away so she could buy some food, and said she could come back once a week, fill out a form, and they would continue to help her out. The program would end when Peter turned eighteen, three years from then. I was relieved that she was getting some help, and she was very grateful to have it.

After my phone call, the three of us who had spent the morning together on our Base Pass went to the chow hall to check in for lunch. We decided to flip a coin to see who would report to the sergeants sitting at the check-in table that we were ready for lunch. I lost the toss, so I said, "You guys wait here, I'll be right back."

I opened the screen door, marched in, made a ninety degree turn to my left and approached the table. With a snappy salute to the sergeants, I said, "Three members of Flight 471 reporting for chow, *Sir!*"

Without saying a word, the highest ranking sergeant, the one sitting in the middle, dropped his pencil, slowly rose to his feet, stepped around the table, and approached me as I stood there still at attention. Oh shit, I said to myself, Something's wrong.

He came up to me, looked me in the eye, and with both hands, grabbed my class A hat and pulled it down over my ears, crushing the bridge of my nose. I thought he was going to break my damn nose, or rip off my right ear, or both. Then he began screaming in my face, "Don't you ever come in here again with your hat on. Do you understand me?" I think everyone in the chow hall was enjoying the show, watching me get my ass chewed out. "Now get the hell out of here and do it again, and this time without the hat!"

"*Yes, Sir,*" I said, and walked outside to meet up with my buddies, who were wondering why it was taking so long. I told them what had happened. They both started laughing, doubled over laughing. My bruised and scratched red nose and my watery eyes attested to my story.

"Hey, man," I barked. "Take a look at my damn nose and my ears! That really hurt. Now I gotta go back in there and do it all over again."

One of my buddies offered up some smart-ass advice, "Good luck, Hussey, and oh, why don't you just tell him to go to hell."

"Sure," I shot back. I turned, took off my damn hat, tucked it neatly under my left arm and opened the screen door to the chow hall. I marched in like all was well, made another snappy left turn, approached the table and reported for chow. The sergeant, looking at me like I was a complete idiot, said, "That's better! Now get the hell out of my sight!"

The all-day bivouac, which included another late night march, would be the final push, the final obstacle before graduation. After morning exercises that day we were told to "fall out!" The rumors were that this would be the toughest twenty-four hours of Basic Training. I was geared up and ready for a long day and a long night, anxious to get it behind me and finally graduate.

The drill sergeant advised in his now familiar, nasty voice, "The last one out of the barracks will pull guard duty from midnight to 03:00 in the morning." It was the worst possible time for guard duty, especially since we'd be out all day and into the night being pushed to extremes.

There were sixty-five of us now—ten others had been discharged for one reason or another and sent home. Out of sixty-five guys in the barracks that morning, I was the first one out. I quickly stood at my position awaiting the others, pleased with myself for being first. There was a logjam at the door; everyone was pushing and shoving their way out. No one wanted that damn, midnight-to-three-in-the-morning guard duty. As I was standing there ready to go, I realized that I had forgotten my helmet. I muttered to myself, "Damn," and ran back in as the last guy was running out.

The first event of the day was the obstacle course, and the first challenge was the rope-swinging exercise. A heavy rope with a knot tied at the end was suspended from an overhead truss and dangled above a body of water, a drop of about twenty feet. The drill sergeant, standing on the other side of the ravine, would hold the rope and then let it go for each of us to grab. If you didn't get it on the first swing, it would sway back and forth until it came to a rest in the middle, completely out of reach. He explained, "This is a favorite of mine. You better grab it on the first swing or you're going to get wet. If you let it swing until it stops, just jump in, 'cause you're not getting another chance."

The guy in front of me let out a groan as he leapt off the ledge, lunging for the rope. He grabbed it in a one-handed catch, but couldn't hold on. I watched him tumble over and land face first in the muddy water below. (He spent the rest of the day and night in heavy, wet, muddy clothes. By the end of the bivouac he was a miserable looking sight.)

Now it was my turn. The rope swung over to me from its preset position. I knew if I didn't go after it on the first swing, I'd have no chance of reaching it when it came back again. I timed my jump and with everything in me, caught the knot with my left hand and quickly reached up and held on with my right, then swung across and landed safely on the other side, relieved that I wasn't wet and proud that I had completed the first obstacle successfully.

The barricade was next—a twenty-foot wall with ropes hanging over the side. Each of us had to work our way over the barricade using one of the ropes. The drill sergeant screamed in my left ear, "Grab the rope and climb your ass up and over that wall...let's go, faster, faster!" It was always faster, and they were always screaming. Next was the forward crawl—lying face down on the ground and inching forward with my elbows, wiggling from side to side in the dusty dirt with my weapon cradled across my forearms. Inches above my head was a honeycombed mesh of barbed wire. Live explosions threw chunks of dirt and rocks and dust in my face and all over me. I snagged the back of my shirt on one of the barbs but ripped it free and continued on. I thought about how tough this would be if I had landed in the water earlier in the morning. I thought about pictures I'd seen years ago of

U.S. soldiers in World War I being shot to death while caught up in rows of barbed wire, trying to advance their position.

On and on it went throughout the day in rapid succession, one obstacle after another.

We stopped around noon, just long enough for a bagged lunch—a dry bologna sandwich, apple, some chips, and a long drink of water from my canteen. Then came the gas house. The small, wood-shingled gas house was tucked away in the woods off the main trail. We marched in and formed a circle around the inside perimeter of this one-room structure. Each of us was issued a gas mask while the instructor demonstrated its proper use. He was standing in the center of the room, rotating and fixing his eyes on each of us as he explained what he wanted and expected. In a clear, crisp and demanding voice he said, "This is how I want you to put your mask on, and don't put it on until I say so. Not 'til I give the order. I don't care how you feel. Do you understand?"

He wanted us to feel the effects of the odorless gas as it entered our lungs and burned our skin—so that we would be as miserable as possible before he gave the order. He put on his mask and tightened the straps. Then, with his right hand, he reached down and released the gas from a canister sitting on a small table next to him. The gas began burning me up, my lungs, my eyes, and my exposed skin. Everyone in that room was soon suffocating—choking and gagging with tears falling like rain. Finally, he gave the muffled order through his mask. "Okay, now, put your masks on!"

I don't know how or why he noticed me, but I didn't put the damn gas mask on the way he wanted. Instead of pulling the mask and the straps down over the top of my head, I placed the mask over my mouth and nose and pulled the straps up and over the back of my head. He made me take it off. I was already sick from the first exposure; now I was nearly panicking. I couldn't breathe. He finally let me try again and this time I did it correctly. Then he gave the order I was pleading for: "All right, now everyone get the hell out of here!"

I raced for the door and stumbled outside and threw up my lunch. I slugged down the rest of the water in my canteen and threw up again. My lungs were burning, my eyes were stinging, and my skin felt like it was on fire. One of my buddies shared his water with me, pouring a handful into my cupped hands so I could cool off my face.

The bivouac came to an end around 23:00 hours (11:00 p.m.). We marched in ragged formation back to the barracks, and everyone staggered into the showers and then fell into bed. Everyone except me. I had goddamn guard duty.

There I was, standing on the inside of the barracks' front door, guarding. Guarding what? I asked myself. At about 01:00, one of the sergeants showed up and began quizzing me, asking me to recite the enlisted man's "Code of Conduct." These were ten statements written in the Code of Conduct manual. We were expected to memorize them and live by them while serving in the U.S. Air Force. They were printed in a small, dark blue pamphlet and handed out to each of us on the first day of Basic. They were numbered one to ten and began with, "I will" or "I shall."

I rattled off the Code of Conduct rules, enough to satisfy him, and he slipped back away from the door and into the night. I figured he was gone—gone for good—so I sat down to get off my feet and fell dead asleep, propped up against the inside wall next to the door.

He came back, of course, and started pushing the door open, knocking me over and waking me up. He scared the hell out of me as he started ranting and raving. "You're in deep shit, Airman. I'm writing you up for falling asleep on guard duty! You're going to be sent back or thrown out. You're in deep shit!" I wanted to smash him in the face.

My guard duty ended at 03:00. Two hours later I was jarred out of a deep sleep with the familiar scratching sound that preceded revelry. I scrambled to the showers, got dressed and hustled outside with the rest of the guys. The drill sergeant was looking for me, calling me out of formation. I stood in front of him at attention as he rammed his clipboard into my stomach. "You're a real fuck-up. The old man wants to see you upstairs in his office, *NOW!*" He made it sound like I was about to be executed.

I gave him the usual salute and the obligatory "Yes, Sir." Then I left the formation and climbed the outside wooden staircase to the second floor, two steps at a time. Whatever was going to happen was out of my control. I just wanted to get it over with.

I rapped on the door. "Enter!" came the voice of the executioner. I knew I was about to catch hell, holy hell. The "old man" turned out to be the same smart-ass sonofabitch who pulled my hat down over my ears in the chow hall a few days earlier. I'm really in trouble now, I figured.

He started in right away. "If you ever fell asleep while on duty in a combat zone, you'd be court-marshaled or shot! Do you understand me, Airman?"

"*Yes, Sir. Yes, Sir.*" It was all I could say. I was scared to shit, but I stood there ramrod straight, expecting the worst. "You're now on probation; from this moment on, you're on probation. One more fuck-up from you and you'll be sent back...sent back three weeks with the flight behind us. And if you fuck-up there, you'll be out. You're lucky I'm not throwing your ass out right now! You understand me?" He was screaming and spitting with every word. I could see the vein in his forehead bulging. "You volunteered for this. Nobody twisted your goddamn arm. You're not fit to serve in the Air Force. Do you hear me? Do you know the Airman's Code of Conduct, all ten of 'em?"

"Yes, Sir," I said with confidence. I'd been through this before. He began demanding answers.

"Give me number six! Now number ten!"

He asked me all ten of them. I had them memorized. I think he was surprised, maybe even impressed. I didn't stumble once. He said, "All right, now get the hell back down those stairs and fall in, and remember you're on probation!"

I saluted him and bolted down the stairs to re-join my squad. They were still lined up in formation waiting for me. Somebody behind me whispered, "How'd it go?"

I didn't respond. I was in enough goddamn trouble for one day, and I sure as hell didn't want to go through another three weeks of this shit.

I knew I would and could stick it out, if they let me. I was not going to quit or give up or give in. My whole goddamn future was riding on this.

A week later, I received another letter from home:

5/24/60
Dear Don,

I was so thrilled to hear your voice Sunday. I only wish I could have talked with you longer. I got your picture in the mail today. The one the Air Force took. It is very good dear, you look so much older.

I went apartment hunting last night over to Brockton. I have found one on the corner of Warren Ave. and West Elm St. It is right next to the hairdressing school.

Mr. Martin is going to move my things Thursday nite. It is furnished with a ref. and small gas stove in it. I will be able to cook and the bus is just down the street.

I have four days off this weekend but will have to work the next two weekends to make up for it. Peter will be with me most of the time, and since I am going on the 7:00 to 3:30 shift starting next week, he can finish school in Abington by taking the bus with me in the morning and going home with me after work.

Honey, please save all you can so as to be sure of getting home and back. I will be able to help you by then, I hope, but not too much. I would like to save enough to buy a cheap car for myself before you get home.

Mr. and Mrs. Martin and I just came back from Brockton. They went over to look at the apartment and thought it was all right.

Bud is living down in Scituate Harbor in a room. He calls once in a while and he was going to come up to pick up his clothes, but we haven't seen him.

By the way dear, the letter you wrote telling me about reporting for chow and having your hat on causing the Sgt. to chew you out was the funniest thing I ever read. Helen and Mr. Martin almost split a rib laughing. We all know that it wasn't a bit funny to you and I bet it will never happen again.

Take care of yourself. I'll need a good strong man to wash walls and paint for me when you come home. I want to paint the apartment and put up a few little things to make it home.
Lots of Love,
Mother

* * *

The concept of Military Basic Training has always been to weed out the misfits and the losers. Drill sergeants worked everyone non-stop, tearing down and stripping away individual identities. As a recruit, your job was to reach down deep inside and shake it off, overcome the threats and obstacles, and over time, build yourself back up. The freedom to act independently was over. You worked as a team, an integral part of a whole, or you paid the price. Before long, the misfits and losers would be identified and sent home. Without addressing it directly, the basic human values of honesty, integrity and keeping your word were drummed into each of us. Personal pride and confidence would soon follow.

I was a young, seventeen, and barely needed or knew how to shave, but I was living, breathing and feeling the changes in me. I was getting through this. I was becoming a man—a never-give-up principled man. The quarter now bounced on my sheets, and my boots shined like glass. And I was developing confidence in myself—more confidence than I'd ever felt before. If they were going to send me back, I would accept it; I could take it, but I was not going to quit. And so it was. I made it through those six weeks, the physical and emotional demands of basic training, and graduated on time with the rest of Flight 471, Squad 3726. We had started with seventy-five guys. Fifty-four of us graduated.

* * *

Upon graduation, I was assigned to Keesler Air Force Base in Biloxi, Mississippi for further training. Several others were also assigned to Keesler. The rest were shipped out to various bases around the country to be schooled in different career fields. I was to become a radioman, a Morse Code Intercept Operator, assigned to the 3382 School Squadron.

Those of us going to Keesler boarded a chartered Greyhound bus from Lackland Air Force Base in San Antonio, Texas for the long ride to Biloxi, Mississippi. Biloxi is located near the southern tip of the state, bordering the Gulf of Mexico. We were assigned barracks and roommates and given a brief tour of the base. Schooling began shortly thereafter. This was a twenty-six-week course designed to teach us how to type, interpret Morse code, and copy coded signals with great proficiency. In addition to the schooling, there would be another thirteen weeks of physical training (PT) to keep us in good shape. We continued the daily marching-in-formation routine, up and down and back and forth along the flight line. Our marches would take us past the neatly aligned rows of T-38 jet trainers poised like spears, wing tip to wingtip, ready as arrows cocked in a crossbow. I would have given anything to attend flight school, slam the stick forward and slice through the clouds. What a thrill that would have been.

On the first day of class the instructor told us to gather around the table at the front of the room and put on the headsets that were lined up in front of us. "Now," he directed, "plug the attached wire into the circuit jacks mounted along the edge of the table and listen to sample transmissions of Morse code."

He started the tape-recorded segment of Morse code and told us, "In twenty-six weeks, you'll be able to interpret and type codes just like the ones you're listening to right now, and at twenty characters a minute with less than three errors."

I could not believe what I was hearing. How could I possibly do this? It all seemed to run together, just a lot of high pitched noises. I wasn't alone. We all looked at one another around the table as if to say, "What?" Learning how to type on the old manual Royal typewriters was one thing, but learning to hit the right keys while Morse code was streaming through your brain was another.

It was an immensely challenging experience. I figured if I could learn to do this, I could learn to do most anything.

One night a friend of mine and I jumped over the fence several yards down the line from the gated guard house. We made our way down to the flight line and huddled in the tall grass at the near end of an active runway, where the T-38s were practicing their late night "touch and goes." One by one they came in screaming just above our heads, leaving a "touchdown" puff of smoke along the runway before roaring straight up and back into the night.

I glanced behind to watch as the next jet banked left and began his final approach. He appeared to be coming in very low, and short of the runway. As he thundered just a few feet over our heads, I felt the deafening blast and scorching heat from the engines and knew we were asking for trouble. His landing lights illuminated everything including the both of us. I said to my buddy, "We'd better get the hell out of here." The pilot must have spotted us and had probably radioed the tower. He completed his touch and go without incident, then fired up the afterburners, like all the others, and darted back into formation to do it all over again.

We scrambled through the tall grass at the end of the runway, showed our IDs to the gatehouse guard, and hustled back to the barracks. Enough excitement for one night, I thought.

In July, I received a letter from Peter:

July 9, 1960
Dear Don,
*   I am sorry I have not wrote to you but I have worked all week at the Brockton Fair. I have made $10.00 dollars. I started out Sunday and worked to Wednesday. Pretty good, heh? ha ha.*
*   Since Wednesday I have done odd jobs. Please write to me. I miss you, I really have.*
*   You should have saw how fast I spent it.*
*   I got shoes, socks and I blew the rest of the money.*
Love, Peter Hussey
P.S. I passed the 7 grade. I miss you, Don

I was glad to hear from him. My mother wrote frequently, but Peter hardly ever sat down long enough to write, or sat down long enough to do anything. He was always on the go. I knew my mother and Peter were still having a tough time with money. I also knew

Peter was ambitious enough, even at his young age, to find a way to make a few bucks on his own. I was still sending most of my pay home—even though it fell far short of what they needed.

We all enjoyed much more freedom while at Keesler. We could leave the base on weekends and hang around the many hot spots in downtown Biloxi.

It was during my schooling at Keesler that I met a guy who would become one of my best friends in the service, Rene Roche. Rene (he pronounced it rainy) and I were in the same Intercept class together, a class of about twenty-five. Rene was of French-Canadian heritage, and although he wasn't fluent in French, he frequently used French phrases when he wanted to emphasize a point. Rene was from Berlin, New Hampshire.

One night, several of us ventured off Base and into downtown Biloxi. We were dressed in our "civvies," but it wasn't hard to pick us out as servicemen because of our short hair and shined shoes. We all needed a little time off to drink a few beers and listen to the jukebox in one of the many bars.

This was the first time I'd ever had a beer. In fact, the next day I developed a sore throat and blamed it on the beer. I had tasted it once when I was younger and I didn't like it, and I couldn't figure out why anyone did. After growing up with it all around me and knowing the misery it brought into my life, I figured I would never drink. My brother Peter never did. But in the service, most of the socializing centered on drinking. All my buddies were older than me and most had plenty of drinking experience. It was unusual to find someone in the service who didn't drink.

I soon found out why drinking beer was so popular; it didn't cost much and it made me feel pretty damn good. I would laugh over the silliest things, and frequently make a fool out of myself, which I would always regret the next morning. Except for some next day harassing, nobody seemed to think too much about it. At my young and inexperienced age, two bottles of beer was about all I could handle.

One night three of us, Rene, another friend of mine named Richard Creath, and I paid our tab at the bar and headed back to the base.

While walking along the sidewalk next to all the shops and bars, Rene spotted a flashing neon sign down an alleyway to our left. The sign read, "Tattoo Parlor." He stopped for a moment and then asked, "Hey, how about a tattoo? What do you think?" We decided to walk down and take a look.

The alleyway ended at the front door of the tattoo parlor. There was no other place to go. You either entered the tattoo parlor or you turned around and walked back to the main street. It was an unusually small building, like a shack, and it was painted pink except the door, which was bright red. The door was undersized and appeared to be handmade. Rene knocked lightly and it opened easily, so we decided to walk in. To enter, you had to duck your head and slip through the opening sideways. Once inside, I looked around and thought "parlor" was too fancy a word for this place. Dim red lights were strung along the perimeter of the ceiling. There were table lamps and floor lamps in each of the corners, all aglow in red. I figured this must double as a whorehouse. Although I'd never seen or been in a whorehouse, this seemed like the perfect place. Electric needles and vials of dye or paint sat on top of a red tablecloth draped over a small round table set up in the center of the room. Rene and Creath sat down in the two chairs over in the corner. Creath called out, "Anyone here?"

A short, elderly woman dressed in flowing garments of red and pink and blue appeared through the small archway over to our left. She walked slowly across the small room, held out her hand and greet-ed us warmly, and then asked if we were there for a tattoo. Without waiting for an answer, she waltzed over to the round table and sat down. Rene and Creath stood up and moved over to the table and sat down across from her. I stood off to the side taking it all in. This must be the madam, I guessed. After some idle conversation, she opened a small drawer in the table and pulled out a series of laminated cards depicting tattoos of various sizes and shapes. I paid little attention to their dealings as I continued sizing up the place.

Everything was red or pink, the drapes over the archway, the rugs, the ceiling, the hanging lights—even the small window had been painted red. I figured something sinister was about to happen, like some wild-eyed gypsy suddenly emerging from behind the arch-way with a sword or a lit candle, or maybe a snake would slither into the room from under the drapes. I was sure someone or something was in the other room. My imagination was on overtime, like that of a young boy in a strange land (which wasn't far from the truth).

Rene and Creath carefully flipped through the images and finally made their selections. They agreed on a price and the tattooist went to work. I watched her squeeze some coloring from a tube and smear it across a piece of waxed paper, then another color, then another. She hit the switch on the electric needle and began forming an image on Rene's upper arm.

I'd had enough of the madam and her colorful world and decided this wasn't for me. Nothing in that place looked clean. I watched the needle as it worked the ink under Rene's skin. I was convinced this would cause more trouble than it was worth. Besides, I'd heard that tattoos lasted forever, so I backed away. I laughed off the ribbing I got from Rene and Creath for expressing my reluctance. After paying for her services, we slipped through the same slanted door and back out into the night.

It took about three days for the tattoos to heal enough to wash. Rene's was on his right arm, on his bicep above the elbow—a heart-shaped design dedicated to his girlfriend. Creath's tattoo was much bigger, a red, white and blue eagle with the words "Air Force" writ-ten under it. They both seemed quite happy with the whole thing.

Creath was a big barrel-chested guy, not too tall but with a strong upper body, and he was proud of his very blond, but barely notice-able, moustache. I used to kid him about it. "What moustache?" I would say. "Let me get a closer look. Where is it?" I didn't tease him too much though; he was real sensitive about it.

About two weeks after the tattoos, the three of us headed back into downtown Biloxi for another Friday night on the town. We wan-dered down the main street, past the tattoo parlor, to the all-night bars that seemed to be everywhere. Creath stopped us along the side-walk and said, "Hey, let's go in here, I know one of the waitresses." The jukebox was turned up full blast to attract passersby, so we followed his lead, walked in and sat down in the second booth to the right. This is where I met the unforgettable Violet.

Violet had been standing in front of the jukebox with a fist full of quarters when we arrived. She glanced over her left shoulder and spotted us as we walked through the door, and came right over to wait on us. She was a beautiful, voluptuous blond who knew how to attract attention. Dressed in a loose-fitting, low-cut top, she would lean over and stretch her beautiful self across the table while serving up the bottles of beer. Wow, I thought, just like Marilyn Monroe!

The place was getting busy, so after serving us our beers, she turned back to the bar to make another delivery. That's when Creath called out to her, "Hey Violet, come back over here." I figured she must have been the waitress he was referring to because she was very friendly to him. She smiled over her shoulder and said, "Just give me a minute, Richard. I'll get right back to you in a minute." She called him Richard, which of course was his first name, but nobody I knew ever referred to him as Richard. It was always Creath. When she came back, she sat down in the booth next to him and across from me. Rene was to my left. "Hey Violet," says Creath, "Hussey here has never seen a tit. Show him your tits." He just blurted it out.

"Oh no!" I said out loud. I was flush-faced with embarrassment. How in hell did he know that? I didn't go around bragging about it. Without a moment's hesitation, Violet pulled down her top and there they were. I nearly choked!

She quickly covered herself up and we all burst out laughing. I figured she'd tell Creath to go to hell, but oh no, she just went ahead, and I still couldn't believe it. "How's that, Hussey?" Creath cried out, killing himself laughing. Rene was laughing so hard, tears ran down his face. Creath looked over at me and announced, "See, Hussey? See how easy that was?" He was quite proud of himself for pulling this off.

Violet laughed along with the rest of us, tears in her eyes as well. The expression on my face must have said it all. I had three beers that night and never touched the ground the whole way back to the barracks.

It seemed that no matter where we went or what we did, we were constantly tapping out Morse code—on the tables at lunch, on the bedposts in the barracks, everywhere. S.O.S. was no longer dot dot dot dash dash dash dot dot dot. It became dididit dahdahdah dididit. It was hard to pick up sometimes, but after a million tries it became as recognizable as my own name; the sounds would just roll out of my mouth. During the rhythmic cadence of the daily marching routine along the flight line, we belted out various phrases in Morse code: ditti-dah-dit, ditti-dah, dah-di-dah-dit, dah-di-dah—which spelled f.u.c.k. Rarely did anyone use that word in those days, but we got away with it because nobody knew what the hell we were saying.

We even spoke to one another in code. It was made clear to us that if we failed, if we flunked out of radio school, we would wind up in the mess hall learning how to cook and clean pots and pans. That was the Air Force's fallback position—not an appealing option.

The instructors were some of the best teachers you could hope for. They were highly ranked NCOs, (non-commissioned officers). Step by step and class by class, they methodically taught us how to type and how to interpret Morse code. Twenty-six weeks later, only two guys were dropped from the program. The rest of us had passed—including me. Twenty characters a minute for five minutes, letters and numbers in blocks of five. I must have taken the final test ten or eleven times before I met that standard. I was the last one to pass, the last one to go on leave.

My buddies waited patiently for me outside, ready to take off for home.

I had received my top secret security clearance and my orders, which read "Alaska – Isolated, 0126." That's all that was written on my orders, short and simple. I was off to Alaska. The others were sent to places around the globe: Tulle, Greenland, the Island of Crete in the Mediterranean, the Aleutians, and the Philippines.

I was given a thirty-day leave of absence to go home before heading off to St. Lawrence Island, a remote spit of land off the coast of Nome, Alaska. All my training was successfully behind me. Like everyone else in my outfit, I wanted to go home and spend some time with my family. It was early December, and I'd been away for nearly eight months. I had very little money and didn't really know how I would get home.

One of my classmates, his last name was Brown so we naturally called him "Brownie," was heading home to Greenfield, Indiana. Brownie had his own car, a '55 Chevy. My friend Rene planned to travel with him. They had been outside waiting for me. Brownie offered me a ride to Indiana if I wanted. He said, "You can ride along with Rene and me if you want. It's not Boston, but it's a start."

Rene planned to spend some time in Indiana with Brownie and then grab a bus for Berlin, New Hampshire. I told him, "Great, thanks! I'll thumb home from there."

We took off in Brownie's car. He was the pilot, I sat in the middle and served as the radio operator, and Rene, to my right, was the navigator. We pretended to be on a secret military mission. It helped pass the time. The trip north from Biloxi, Mississippi to Greenfield, Indiana took nearly twenty hours. We drove straight through, switching drivers along the way.

Traveling north through rural Mississippi gave us a wide-angle look at the vast landscape of endless cotton fields, and the people who worked them. They were young and old, but mostly young black kids, making their way through the rows of cotton bushes with gunnysacks slung over their shoulders. No one appeared to be in any rush. Old flatbed wooden wagons moved slowly through the fields, some pulled along by mules and others by tractors. Everyone wore light-colored clothing and some form of hat. There was no place to hide from the hot Mississippi sun.

There weren't many cars or trucks along the route we took. Brownie beeped the horn repeatedly as the three of us smiled and waved to the pickers. They returned the smiles and waved back, seemingly content with themselves and their work.

We were moving along pretty fast on the open road. I noticed the speedometer climbing past seventy as we topped the crest of a hill and began coming down the other side. We were somewhere in western Tennessee at this point and, unbeknownst to us, lying in wait at the bottom of the hill were the cops—a speed trap. Still flying along downhill, we rounded a corner at the foot of the hill and without warning came upon a sign that read: "Town Line—Speed Limit 25."

Nobody coming off that mountain could possibly slow down to twenty-five. The cops were hiding in their cruiser off to the right in the bushes behind the sign. We blew right past them; there was no time to slow down. They flipped on their lights and took off after us. Brownie hit the brakes and pulled over to the side of the road muttering, "Shit! Those sneaky bastards!" We figured we'd be fined more money than we had and would have to spend the night in jail and answer to some judge in the morning.

As it turned out, they weren't after us. They wanted the guy in front of us who had passed us on the way down the hill. He must have hit that town doing ninety.

We laughed out loud as the cops, with their lights and sirens on fire, went right past us. They could have bagged us, also, but didn't bother. We continued through town moving slowly around them as they cuffed their man by the side of the road.

The rest of the trip went smoothly. We made good time and eventually came upon the Greenfield, Indiana exit, somewhere around nine or ten o'clock at night.

Brownie pulled off the road and said, "Hey, you want to stay the night and get a fresh start in the morning?" I told him I was ready to get on with this, and excited about the prospects, the adventure of thumbing halfway across America. They dropped me off on some interstate highway not far from Brownie's place. We shook hands and said goodbye. I told Rene I'd see him in Alaska. Rene smiled and said, "Take care, buddy. See you in Anchorage." Brownie was headed for the Greek island of Crete.

I was dressed in my uniform, which was pretty wrinkled from sleeping in the back of Brownie's car. It began to rain as I turned and surveyed my position at the edge of the road. Directly in front of me was an eastbound expressway bridge, so I decided to cross over and get beyond the on and off ramps, to the safety of the other side. There were several streetlights along the bridge revealing the wind-driven, drizzling rain that washed across my face. Although it was a gloomy scene, it only added to my determination.

Once beyond the ramps, I turned around and began walking

backwards along the shoulder with my thumb out, looking for a ride. Within a few short minutes a semi-tractor trailer pulled to a stop in front of me. The driver had just begun running through the gears from a dead stop at the traffic lights down beyond the bridge. He reached across his seat and opened the passenger side door. "Come on in," he hollered down to me above the noise of the diesel engine. "I'm not supposed to do this, but you're obviously in the military and you're getting soaking wet."

"Thanks a lot," I hollered back as I climbed up and in. I watched him as he shifted each of the gears of the two transmissions. I'd never seen a truck with two transmissions before and found it interesting. The first gear barely got us moving, then a quick shift, then another and another. Then he switched a lever, grabbed the other stick and shifted to the higher gears. He must have changed gears twelve times or more before we were moving at the speed limit. I realized the effort he had made to stop and pick me up, and I thanked him again. He asked me where I was going and I told him I was headed to Boston. He was surprised and told me he was on a short run so he wouldn't be of much help.

He reached across his chest and into his breast pocket for a couple of small white pills. "Here," he said, "take these at our next stop. You'll be able to stay awake." I said thanks, but I threw them in the toilet when we stopped in a rest area.

I rode with him through the rest of Indiana and through most of Ohio.

"Sorry," he said," my exit is coming up. I'll pull over here and let you out." He came to a full stop on the side of the road and wished me luck as I opened the door and climbed down. I thanked him again before shutting the door and watched as he headed down the ramp to the right and out of sight.

I walked along the highway bridge beyond the next on ramp, then turned around and started walking backwards again, looking for another ride. It was early in the morning by now—another cloud-covered, gloomy day. It seemed fruitless to be walking along the highway; Boston was a lifetime away. I could have just stood there holding out my thumb, but I figured walking would give people the impression I was making an effort.

A car pulled over and stopped in the breakdown lane up ahead of me. It was an old, black, beat-up, two-door Ford. I was a little hesitant at first but quickly realized I was in no position to decline the offer. I got in and said, "Hello. Thanks for stopping."

The driver was a short, pudgy middle-aged man with thick glasses who kept moving his head back and forth from side to side as he drove. We never spoke to each other all the way through the rest of Ohio and on into Pennsylvania. He dropped me off in western Pennsylvania on Route 22, which, according to my map, would take me all the way across Pennsylvania and into New Jersey—the East Coast, a milestone.

I began walking the breakdown lane alongside Pennsylvania Highway 22. An older, retired couple in a brand new, red, four-door Buick pulled over, up ahead of me. I ran up to their car and introduced myself through the open passenger-side window. The lady said to me, "We never do this, but we saw your uniform and thought you were probably trying to get home."

I thanked them for stopping, hopped in the back seat, and said, "Yes, I'm heading home."

They asked me if I was hungry, but before I could answer, the wife turned and said, "We're going to get you something to eat. You look tired and I know you've got a long trip ahead of you. You like steak?"

We pulled off the highway and stopped at a fancy restaurant for a hearty steak dinner. After dinner she asked me if I'd like some dessert. I said, "No, that's okay." She ordered me a piece of apple pie anyway. She told me to fill up. "Boston is a long way away." I was thankful for the good meal and their kindness.

As soon as we pulled out onto the highway, I lay down in the back seat and fell dead asleep. I didn't wake up until they called back to me, "We're coming up on the New Jersey Turnpike. Sorry, young man, but this is our exit."

They pulled over before the upcoming interchange to let me out. When we stopped, I opened the rear door and stumbled to the ground.

The lady lowered her window and handed me a ten-dollar bill and wished me a safe journey. I thanked her very much and waved good-bye as they pulled back onto the highway. Then I turned around, pointed my finger north, and said out loud, "Straight ahead...the last leg!"

I climbed the concrete steps in front of me to the over-the-highway footbridge, which brought me to the northbound side of the turnpike. When I climbed down the steps I turned around and looked up at the overpass sign which read, "New England."

It was late in the afternoon by then and the traffic on the New Jersey Turnpike was heavy and moving fast, six lanes full. People heading home from work, I figured. For the first time since leaving Brownie and Rene back in Indiana, I began feeling a little uneasy. I was standing on the edge of a highway jammed with traffic. How's anybody going to stop without causing a pileup? I thought. I can't make a mistake here. I better take my time and stay well back off the road.

I decided to walk backwards along the breakdown lane next to the guardrail. I surveyed everything moving, keeping an eye out for anything unusual—ladders flying off trucks, flat tires, potential accidents that could spill over in my direction, anything and everything. I could jump over the guardrail if I needed to. The nonstop, heavy traffic created nonstop blasts of cold air, giving me the chills and unsettling my nerves. Everything was flying past, just a few feet away. I knew I had little choice. Either catch a ride or freeze. I stuck out my thumb thinking that no one would or could stop.

I was shivering, with the constant wind blasting me in the face, when some guy in a tractor-trailer gave me a long, loud blast from his twin air horns. The message was clear: "Get the hell off the road, you idiot."

I jumped away from the breakdown lane and fell down the grassy embankment. I was pretty angry with myself for being a damn coward, so I got back up and continued walking in the breakdown lane. I soon realized that no one was going to pull over; everything was moving too fast. It was getting dark by then and one by one drivers began turning on their headlights.

I figured if I didn't get a ride pretty damn soon, I'd be stuck out there huddled against a tree for the night, and it was getting mighty cold. I spotted a car way up ahead. I watched as he began moving in my direction, making his way across the four lanes of traffic. He must have seen me standing out there from a half a mile away. He cut in front of the last car in his way and thundered down the breakdown lane at top speed, kicking up rocks and gravel and sliding to a side-ways stop. I started running like mad to catch up to him before he changed his mind. Instead of taking off, he threw it in reverse and began backing up, making it easier for me.

I ran up to his car and jumped in and thanked him for stopping. He told me he had been in the service himself. "I know what it's like."

I was grateful to him. Grateful to be warm, off the highway, and heading north. I was hungry and wet and tired and dirty, but I fig-ured it wouldn't be much longer now. As it turned out, he was head-ing for Boston and could take me as far as he was going.

It was nearly three in the morning when he dropped me off. I real-ly didn't know where I was, but I knew I was somewhere in Boston, and it was beginning to drizzle again, a cold, raw, Boston rain. The early morning traffic was light. Rush hour wouldn't begin for several hours. All I needed now was a lift to the South Shore.

I walked in the rain along a roadway trying to snag one more ride. At one point a tractor-trailer thundered past me, sending a blast of wind-driven rain into my face. No one seemed to notice my wretched self, freezing to goddamned death. I began talking to my-self, saying things like, "Hey, nothing lasts forever. You'll be home soon...stop bitching!"

Finally, a Wonder Bread delivery van with a driver and his helper moved over from the center lane and pulled up next to me. The guy in the passenger seat rolled down the window and shouted for me to, "Get in!" He reached over his shoulder with his right hand and slid the panel door open. I grabbed the outside handle and helped open the door wide enough to climb in, then jumped in and quickly pulled it shut behind me. I glanced around and found an awkward place to sit among the sweet-smelling racks of bread and pastries.

"Hey, man, thanks a lot for stopping," I stuttered through chattering teeth. The driver turned around and said, "Where the hell are you going at this hour and what are you doing out here in this shit?" I told him I was on my way to Brockton.

"I hate to tell you this, Skippy," he said, "but you're heading in the wrong direction. Brockton's back the other way. Listen, it's out of my way, but I'll take you down to Avon. How's that sound? I've got a stop there later this morning, anyway."

I told him that would be great. "Every mile out of this weather is just fine with me."

He pulled off at the next ramp, crossed over the highway and headed south toward Avon. The guy in the passenger seat, who sat quietly listening to our conversation, turned around and asked if I was hungry.

"I'm always hungry," I told him. "And right about now, I'm ready to eat my thumbs."

He reached back, opened a box of pastries, and said, "Here, try of one of these. You can have the whole box if you want."

Still shivering like a frozen dog, I downed enough to satisfy myself.

About twenty minutes later, we pulled over to the curb near a train bridge in Avon, right up the street from the town line with Brockton.

"Hey man," I said, "thanks a million for the ride and for the pastries." I took a deep breath, slid the van door open and stepped back out into the cold.

Brockton Center was about two miles straight ahead. I started walking. Along the way, I stopped at an all-night donut shop and bought a bag of donuts. I couldn't come home empty-handed.

It was after four in the morning when I finally arrived. Trying not to make a sound or arouse any suspicion, I slipped into the side door of the apartment building where my mother and Peter were now living. I found the door I was looking for at the end of the first-floor hallway, and figured this must be it. I knocked softly.

My mother woke up, came to the door and asked who it was. I said, "It's your son."

She cried out, "What? Oh, my God!" She called to Peter, and after fumbling with the locks, opened the door. I grabbed the two of them, gave them a kiss and a long hug. She looked up at me and said, "Let me take a good look at you. You're a mess. What happened? How'd you get home?

"It was a long walk," I said jokingly. "I need to change out of these clothes. Can you get me a towel?" She brought me a towel from the bathroom and Peter gave me some warm clothes to put on. "Thanks," I said. "It's good to be home. I'll get some rest over there on the couch and tell you everything in the morning."

My mother was up at 6:00. She worked the 7:00 to 3:30 shift at the Brockton Hospital, so when her alarm went off, she jumped up, dressed, and hurried down the street to catch the city bus. She let me sleep. Peter stayed home from school that day, so we had some donuts for breakfast and I told him all about my trip.

Much of my leave was spent getting around to my relatives in Norwell and spending some time with my Rockland High School friend, Tom Condon. I didn't know this at the time, but Tom and seven of his friends had enlisted in the Air Force right out of high school. Since they were all from Rockland, it was a group enlistment. The Air Force referred to it as "the buddy system." Tom never made it through Basic. He had been out one day with the others in his squad drilling and exercising when he suffered an asthma attack. His lungs had tightened up from the exertion and the extreme heat, and he couldn't breathe. They rushed him over to the base hospital, and after a few days issued him a medical discharge and sent him home. It took him a long time to get his feet under him after that. It had been a lonely and disappointing experience for a young ambitious guy right out of high school.

I had been away for eight or nine months by now. My mother and Peter had really missed me. My mother had become more and more dependent on me as I grew older, and I had been Peter's anchor for much of his young life. Peter stayed in school while I was away, trying to stick it out in spite of his relentless medical problems. Now that I was home, we could spend some time together and catch up on what had happened while I was gone. I wouldn't be home very long, but that didn't matter. He was so excited to have me home, and I was glad to be there.

Peter had just learned a new dance step called the Twist. It was a song and a dance, written and popularized by Chubby Checker. It must have been released while I was away. Peter still had the simple one-record-at-a-time record player I had given him before leaving for the service. He opened the lid, placed the record on the turntable, moved the needle arm over and the song began playing. Peter smiled and began twisting around the living room to the beat of the music.

I gave my mother a hand fixing up her new place and taking the weekly laundry over to the local laundromat; she had missed not having me around to take some of the load off of her. The laundromat was in the basement of another apartment building, down a side street about two blocks away—two quarters to wash and five dimes to dry.

One night I sat down with my mother and brother, just the three of us. My mother wanted to fill me in on what happened the day I left for the service. "Don," she said, "I left Martins' and walked in the rain all the way to the Sunset Grove. I was so depressed after you left that I just had to get out." The Sunset Grove was a bar located about four miles away in the town of Whitman, just over the town line with Abington.

The Sunset Grove had been an old favorite of Bud's. My brother and I spent a lot of time in there sitting in a booth watching all the regulars drink up their hard-earned money. In fact, we spent a lot of time in and around barrooms all along the South Shore when we were young. There were many times during the hot summer months when we'd be heading for Wilkie's Pond in Hanson to go for a swim, having grabbed our bathing suits and towels and packed some sandwiches to spend the day. On the way, Bud would always stop at some gin mill to have a few drinks. He'd pull off the road, park the car and lean back to tell us, "You two wait here in the car. We'll just be a few minutes." Sometimes we'd spend the whole afternoon in that sweaty car watching the traffic go by. Peter and I made up a game to help pass the time. As the traffic passed, I would say, "Okay, the next car is mine." Every other car was Peter's and the alternating cars would be mine. Trucks didn't count. The best ones would be the cars we wanted to buy when we grew up. On more than one occasion, we played our game the entire day and never made it to Wilkie's.

My mother told me it was late in the afternoon by the time she arrived at the Sunset Grove, and she was soaking wet and didn't even care. Hard to figure sometimes, but it was on that night and in that place that she met Joe Martel. Joe was having a drink at the bar. He had just finished work and had stopped in before heading home to his apartment. He was divorced and living alone somewhere nearby. My mother was sitting alone in one of the booths along the wall, far away from the bar, next to the row of windows. She painted the scene: "I sat over there sipping a drink and having a damn good cry for myself. Joe left his spot at the bar and walked over and introduced himself as I sat in my self-absorbed, depressed state of mind. He asked if there was anything he could do. 'You seem so upset,' he said sympathetically."

She invited him to sit down and they had a long conversation. She did all the talking; he did all the listening. She told him I had left for the service earlier that morning, and she also told him where she was living and why. He drove her back to the Martins' and asked if it would all right to give her a call.

Not long after that I received a letter from her saying that things were much better. Bud was gone and wouldn't be coming back. "We're doing pretty well living in Brockton. Peter is in the eighth grade, attending West Junior High. I also want you to know that I met a wonderful man named Joe Martel. He has been so good to Peter and to me. He's a brick mason, works with his brother in his brother's business in West Quincy."

My mother and Peter moved from the one-bedroom apartment on Warren Avenue, where Peter slept on a fold-up cot in the kitchen, to a larger, two-bedroom unit on the first floor. It was just around the corner in the back of the same building, at 89 West Elm Street, an old, gray, six-story wooden building that sat on the corner of Warren Avenue and West Elm. Joe eventually gave up his apartment and moved in with them.

Peter never went to High School; it became too much for him. He was always on crutches to take the pressure off a swollen ankle or a swollen knee which was usually wrapped tightly with Ace bandages. Sometimes, when the pain subsided, he'd walk along using the crutches only intermittently for a little extra support. Most of the time he'd hobble along working both crutches with one leg elevated. The Brockton kids had no idea what was wrong with him. They were brutal. "Faker, faker," they taunted him. He'd take it just so long, then he'd swing those crutches around and drop anyone tormenting him to the floor. Why the teachers didn't intervene was always a mystery. Maybe they didn't understand his condition either. One kid beat him up so badly that he spent the whole summer recovering in the Brockton Hospital.

Between the constant humiliation and frequent absences, it became impossible for him to continue. He finally admitted to my mother that he couldn't and wouldn't take it anymore. He was quitting school. "Maybe the people at the Massachusetts Rehabilitation Center can help me get into barber school," he told her. "Maybe I'll go to barber school and become a barber, but I've had enough!"

With my mother's permission, Peter left West Junior High School and, with the help of the Massachusetts Rehabilitation Center, began taking classes at the Boston Barber School. Every day, he trekked back and forth to Boston for the duration of the program. He hopped two busses and then rode the "T." After classes, he retraced his commute back to Brockton. At sixteen, he successfully completed his barber school training and, like my mother's father, became a licensed barber.

There were several unique characters living in that old, tired-looking, wooden apartment building at 89 West Elm Street. One such character, living in the apartment across from us at the opposite end of the outside staircase, was unemployed. After a day of drinking, he would stumble up the stairs, turn right and enter his apartment, which he shared with his wife. One Saturday afternoon, I watched him amble his way though the parking lot carrying a bundle of wooden boards. He dropped the wood next to the building, then went over to his truck, which had a flat front tire, and came back with his hammer.

He began nailing the boards across the front door of his apartment.

I stood outside my door, just a few feet away, watching him as he continued hammering nails through the boards on both sides of the door frame. He turned and said something to me about his wife locking him out but I didn't respond. From the other side of the door I could hear his wife yelling, "Go away and leave me alone. And don't come back here ever again. I'm getting a divorce!" He shouted over her, "Okay, you witch, we'll see about that! If you don't unlock this goddamn door and let me in, I'll lock you in and you'll never get out!" Then I heard him again, mumbling more to himself than to anyone else. "If she won't let me in, I won't let her out! She can stay in there forever. Fuck her!"

I could see her in the window pacing back and forth. Eventually she picked up the phone and within a few minutes the cops arrived with their lights flashing. Two cops stepped out of the cruiser, approached her husband and asked him what he was doing. I heard him explain, "She's got me locked out...so I'm locking her in. What do you think of that?" Each cop grabbed an arm and they dragged him over to the cruiser and dumped him into the back seat. Then one of them opened the trunk, grabbed a tire iron, brought it back to the apartment and pried the boards off so she could get out. She opened the door and began telling them what happened. "I never want to see him again. Please just lock him up!" She agreed to come down to the station and file a complaint. "Don't worry, lady," said one of the cops. "We'll keep him until Monday morning, then he can tell it to the judge."

I walked away without saying a word to anyone, but two weeks later I was asked by the man's wife to testify as a witness. She said, "I could see you watching him as he tried to barricade my door. So would you come down to the courthouse on Monday and tell the judge what you saw?" I agreed to show up and help her out, but when I arrived, my testimony wasn't needed. He pled guilty to the charges, and the judge ordered him to pay for the damages to the building and pay the court costs. Then he sentenced him to serve thirty days in the Plymouth House of Correction so he'd have enough time to think about what he'd done.

On Saturday nights Johnnie Yeager, a short, stout, likable guy who lived alone on the first floor, would come over to my mother's place, along with Dottie from the fifth floor and Irene from the sixth, and a few others, including Clara, who ran the place for Mr. Berger. Johnnie treasured his handmade, brightly polished, wooden mandolin, and could play it like a pro. He would sit down, prop the mandolin up on his extended belly, then, resting it under his chin, play sweet, romantic songs you might hear along the canals in Venice. They'd all be drinking and singing and dancing around the kitchen, having a few laughs. Joe was in high spirits, just loving life. He flashed me the broadest grin I'd ever seen on a grown man. Of course, Peter and I were having a pretty good time as well, singing songs we'd never heard before.

My leave was nearly up. I would soon be flying out of Logan to the great northwest, on my way to Alaska. Before I left, I paid a visit to my Air Force recruiter. He was still in the recruiting office on the corner of Main and Belmont Streets in downtown Brockton. He remembered me and asked me how it was going. I told him I had made it past the hard part and was now headed for Alaska. I showed him my orders and he went though the checklist of items I needed to bring with me. We talked for a while longer and I thanked him for his help and said goodbye. He wished me luck in Alaska and told me to check in with him when I got back.

I left his office and walked back down Main Street, through the Legion Parkway to Warren Avenue, and then around the corner to West Elm Street. I laid all my gear down on the floor and started packing. I had been home now for nearly thirty days and was ready to get going, full of confidence, and looking forward to the trip. The Air Force had trained me well, not only in the complex language of Morse code but in other ways as well, such as maintaining my personal appearance, pride through accomplishment, and doing the right thing when no one was looking. Although I had not yet reached my eighteenth birthday, I was excited to see what life had in store for me.

The movie *North to Alaska* had just been released, and I was on my way. It would be the adventure of a lifetime.

FIVE

The Turning Point

On 25 January 1961, I boarded a bus for Logan Airport and then hopped a commercial standby flight to Seattle, Washington, where I changed planes to a chartered military flight bound for Elmendorf Air Force Base in Anchorage, Alaska.

Upon arrival in Seattle, we exited the aircraft doors, walked down the portable staircase, across the tarmac and through the main airport doors. From there it was a short walk down a narrow hallway to a briefing room where the others, who had arrived earlier in the day from various places in the lower forty-eight, were waiting.

The Air Force master sergeant in charge called us to attention and then read the names from his roster; everyone was present and accounted for; it was time to go. We lined up and marched through the open side doors at the far end of the briefing room and boarded a charted commercial prop-jet which was parked and fueling. The weather was beautiful and relatively warm—warmer than I had expected.

Once on board and seated, we taxied out to the runway, turned right and lined up for takeoff. The pilot released the brakes after running the engines at full throttle, then thundered down the runway past the markers, climbing into the cloudless, early-morning sky. We flew over the area known as Puget Sound and headed northwest over the North Pacific Ocean, bound for Anchorage.

As we descended below 3000 feet, I glanced out the window and marveled at the endless expanse of barren, snow-covered terrain, seemingly untouched by man. I spotted a herd of reindeer or caribou trudging through the heavy snow as we banked to the right on our final approach to Elmendorf Air Force Base.

I was in a window seat and as we were landing my eyes were taking it all in. Off to my left, and far in the distance, lay a chain of snow-covered mountains known simply as the Alaska Range. The string of mountains filled the horizon from left to right parallel to the runway. The bright blue, cloudless skies over Anchorage that day capped off a breathtaking view of Alaska's unspoiled beauty. I stopped momentarily as I exited the plane for another look—a look stored forever in my mind's eye. Then hustled, along with the others, into the building to avoid exposure to the crisp, bitterly cold air.

We walked through a series of corridors and into a small, dimly-lit room painted a drab yellow. This was the briefing room where we were given detailed instructions on severe weather survival techniques designed to prepare us for life on the frozen tundra. We were outfitted with heavy, fur-lined parkas, insulated leggings, full-length thermal underwear, and fur-lined hats, gloves and boots. I sat there taking it all in and generally resigning myself to what lay ahead: a year-long tour of duty on a frozen island in the middle of the Bering Straits.

There were only twelve of us in our group. We stayed in the temporary duty (TDY) barracks at Elmendorf for a week, and during that time, we had a chance to venture into downtown Anchorage and look around. Four of us grabbed a local bus from Elmendorf one miserably cold afternoon; heavy overcast skies accompanied by a mix of rain and snow and a biting wind. Once in town, we walked along the muddy wooden sidewalks and stopped at an old two-story building, which housed a bowling alley, a lunch counter, and a barroom. We went in, sat down at the bar and ordered hamburgers and coffee. I was surprised at the cost: seven dollars for a hamburger and a cup of coffee. 'Pretty damn expensive,' I thought.

Later in the afternoon we wandered into another bar to have a few drinks and talk with the locals. I ordered some bottles of beer from the bartender and brought them over to the round table in the center of the room, near the pool table. I took a good look around at the posters and pictures on the walls, many of which were of beautiful women in one-piece bathing suits. There were also plenty of signs from the 40s and 50s advertising Coke and Pepsi, and Schlitz beer. Most of the men at the bar had full-length beards, wore baggy overalls and heavy coats, and muddy, fur-lined boots. We drank some Budweisers, had some laughs and played a few games of pool. I couldn't imagine anyone choosing to live up there. It was damp and cold outside and not much better inside. The old wooden buildings in the center of Anchorage lined both sides of a muddy, unpaved main street. I felt like I was in a mid-1800's mining town, like in the "wild west" movies I'd seen as a kid.

One of my buddies turned to me with an idea, which at first startled me. "Listen," he reasoned, "we're going to be out on that goddamn island for a year, completely isolated, right? No women, right? So what do you think? Let's find a prostitute."

I'd never been in the company of a prostitute before and was in no rush to meet one. He explained to the rest of us that the cabbies back home in Jersey knew right where to go, and then added, "I'm sure up here it's no different." I thought about this as I finished up my beer. He stood up and walked over to the bartender and asked if he knew any cab drivers. The bartender told him who to call and gave him the four-digit number. No area codes and no prefix—just four numbers. He turned and gave us the thumbs up sign as he walked over to a pay phone hanging on the wall. He dropped in some coins and dialed the numbers on the old rotary dialer. When the cabbie answered, he asked him to come by and pick us up saying, "There's four of us and we need a ride." There was no mention of a prostitute.

When the cabbie arrived, my buddy said, "Let me handle this. I'll be right back." He went outside and explained what we were looking for, then he came back in and said, "We're all set." He bought a six pack from the bartender to take with us, and we went outside and got into the cab. The tires on the cab were dripping with mud from sloshing through the rain-soaked unpaved streets. The nervous and less-than-friendly cabbie said, in a hurried, impatient tone, "Hold on. Just give me a minute. I've got to go back inside and make a call. Don't worry, and don't go nowhere. I can put this together."

He made his call, came back to the cab and explained that "she" was waiting, and it would be "twenty bucks each."

Everyone said okay, except me. I was quiet; I was still thinking this through. I was only seventeen and had never been with a woman. I thought my first experience should be with someone special, not a prostitute. But I went along, not saying very much. I figured this would be interesting, if nothing else.

The four of us rode in the back seat as the cabbie drove for about ten minutes through the sloppy streets of downtown Anchorage to a place on the outskirts of town. He turned off the road and into the muddy driveway of an old two-story wooden house. Everything about this night was dreary.

We stepped out into the rain and walked behind the cabbie as he led us around the back to an outside wooden staircase along the right side of the building. The staircase was shaking as we walked up to the second floor. I thought it might break away from the building at any moment. When we reached the top landing, he knocked at the door. I could hear a women's voice from the other side of the door say, "Okay, it's unlocked, come in."

The cabbie turned the knob and we all walked in behind him. I was last. No one spoke as the four of us sat down on a couch in the living room. The cabbie and the prostitute walked into the kitchen to discuss the "deal." She never even looked at us. When they finished their brief discussion, the cabbie came out of the kitchen, and, as he walked past us, said, "I'll be back in an hour." Then he left. I heard him walk down the outside stairs and leave in his car. The deal had been struck; there was no bullshit here.

The lady of the night entered the living room, gave us a weak smile and said, "Okay, we all know why we're here. Who's first?" No sweet talk. This was all business.

She was a heavy-set black woman and looked to be in her early forties. I could tell she must have been a good-looking woman in her youth, and I wondered how she found herself up here in Alaska. Maybe she was born here, but from her accent I didn't think so. Her hair was pulled back on each side and held in place by small combs and some pins. She sashayed slowly past us as she turned to her left and entered the bedroom, which was directly across from where we were sitting. She changed her clothes in a flash, came out half naked, and stood in the doorway giving us a shy "come-on" look. It must have been amusing to her, seeing the four of us sitting on her couch, cramped together side by side like schoolboys on a first date.

One of my buddies jumped up and said, "Okay, I'm first." She reached for his hand and escorted him into her bedroom. A moment later she came out carrying a small pan. She walked into the kitchen and came back with the pan filled with warm water and a small washcloth draped over her wrist, then slipped into her room, swinging the door shut with her foot.

A couple of minutes later, maybe less, my buddy came out, zipping up his pants, and sat down in the chair to my right. "Any beer left?" he asked. The same routine was repeated two more times...the pan, the washcloth, etc. She knew how to move this along.

I was a little nervous about my upcoming turn. I glanced over to my left and noticed a lamp sitting on a small table next to the couch. The dim red bulb was on, and the heat from the bulb appeared to rotate the lamp shade. Round and round went the shade, revolving slowly. It was full of small holes that, as it turned, revealed the moving figure of a naked man standing sideways, urinating a steady stream. I really didn't want any part of this, and that image, that picture, said it all for me. This was no place I wanted to be.

She stood in the same doorway and looked across the room, straight at me. I drank the last few sips of my beer, trying to buy some time. With her finger motioning for me to follow her, she said, "Come on in now and get you some."

I got up and walked over to her. I said, "I'm not going in there. I don't want to hurt your feelings, but I'm not going in there."

She said it again, softer now, warm and sexy. "Now, you come on in and get you some." She put her arm on my shoulder, revealing her nakedness under her negligee. She rubbed the back of my neck and ran her hand across my ass. I told her again, "I'm not going in there." And I didn't.

I could tell she wasn't happy with me. I turned and sat back down on the couch wondering what was going to happen next. My buddies didn't say anything to me; they just sat there sipping their beer waiting for me to make a move. I wasn't moving. When the cabbie showed up to take us back to the base, they started arguing out in the kitchen. "One of 'em chickened out," she hollered in an angry voice we couldn't miss. The cabbie didn't believe her. She eventually convinced him as she pointed her finger at me from the kitchen. I looked him in the eye and gave a slight nod. They finally settled up and the cabbie walked through the living room and motioned for us to leave.

On the way back, one of my buddies broke down sobbing. He put his head down and buried his face in his hands. He had just been married the month before and was kicking himself for going through with this. Ironically, he was the one who suggested we do it in the first place.

I felt at peace with myself for not going through with it. I wanted my first time to be something special, something I wouldn't forget. And I wanted it to be different than that—a lot different than that.

* * *

St. Lawrence Island was better known to us as "The Rock." There was twenty-six feet of snow on the ground the day our C-123 left the runway at Elmendorf A.F.B. and headed out past Nome for the thirty-minute flight across the Bering Straits. It was a rough landing on the icy, cinder and gravel stretch of runway, a runway cut out from mountains of snow. This is about as remote as it gets, I figured.

I noticed a temperature gauge attached to the weather shack as we exited the plane. The weather shack was a one-room, single story wooden building that also served as the control tower. The outside temperature was 23F degrees below zero. It was late January of '61; I would turn eighteen in two weeks. Each of us was bundled up against the harsh conditions with thermals, leggings, and a heavy parka with a fur lining around the head and face, just enough opening through the fur to see through. I tried to spit into the air, wondering if the spit would freeze in mid-air. It never made it through the fur. So much for my experiment.

There were eighty-six of us stationed there, mostly support personnel. I was assigned to the 6980th Radio Squadron Mobile, Northeast Cape, Alaska. The Army Post Office (APO) was 714 out of Seattle, Washington. Alaska—Isolated. That was my mailing address.

All my training in Morse code would now be put to the test, and I was looking forward to it. As soon as I fixed the headsets over my ears and turned the dial on the receiver to the assigned frequency, live coded transmissions came streaming into my consciousness—signals coming from station operators deep inside the Soviet Union. This was for real and I quickly adapted to the cadence and the rhythm. Anyone not familiar with Morse code would have been baffled, but I was on an emotional high. I could do the job I had trained for. We scanned frequencies for signals as far north as Point Barrow, Alaska and as far south as Vietnam and the South China Sea.

I never seemed to dwell on being so far removed from civilization, especially when I was at work. I was an intercept operator. As I expected, the work was very interesting, even exciting, and it kept me pretty busy. I felt I was doing something worthwhile with my life and for my country. There were eleven positions or stations in our Operations room. I was assigned to station number two, the only station with three receivers—the busiest. My main target was an operator known to me only by his call sign. He was, for the most part, quite predictable. I'd hear the whine of his transmitter coming to life, then signing on with his familiar CQ, a call to all stations in his network. He was fast and highly proficient and I enjoyed the challenge of keeping up with him. I copied his transmissions on a daily basis for the entire time I was stationed there—so much so that I felt as if I knew him, but of course I didn't.

The U.S. Air Command had notified us of a planned mission designed to test the response time of the Soviet Air Defense System. The plan was to send an unarmed U.S. military transport out into the Bering Straits, north of our position, and fly a course north to south along the Soviet coastline. Our role was to search for any and all communications from the Soviets, and notify command headquarters immediately upon contact.

On the night of the operation, the transport took off from a classified location in Alaska. As they crossed the international dateline and approached Soviet airspace, three Soviet MiG17s were scrambled out of Vladivostok, a major Soviet city located just inland from the eastern coast. Our radar stations picked up the MiGs as they left the runway. Within seconds, our Command Center was "hot." One of the Operations officers opened the secure operations door and came right over to me. "I want you to leave your position *right now* and follow me." I unplugged my headset from my central receiver and followed him into the Command Center, which was alive with an atmosphere of high intensity.

I plugged my headset, which was still resting on my head like ear muffs, into the main terminal, and sat down at the typewriter to begin copying coded transmissions from the Soviet ground stations to the three jets. The signals were coming in so fast I could hardly keep up. I had just turned eighteen and was the youngest of the operators, but I was good and they knew it. I later found out there was a backup operator in another room also copying. But at that moment, I thought it all rested with me—my singular responsibility. I went down deep into a state of extreme concentration. Every dit and every dah ran together at nearly indistinguishable speed. There were numbers and letters mixed in side by side. I knew the operator was using a slide key transmitter—a very fast, almost automatic transmitter. A number five, for instance, was five dits and the letter H was four dits—fast with split second separation. I stayed three characters behind; otherwise I'd lose my rhythm and concentration. I kept up with him though, throughout the tense, hour-long crisis. Richard Gynin, one of the best poker players I'd ever met, was in the back room translating Russian voice transmissions, air to ground and vice versa. We had all communications covered. This could be a long night....

Up on the wall, directly in front of me, was a large, five-foot wide map of Alaska, which included Vladivostok and the eastern provinces of the Soviet Union. It was enclosed in a metal frame with a clear Plexiglas covering. With a black magic marker, the Captain of Operations began plotting the approaching intercept. I was typing and copying the signals like a man possessed. The captain would look over my shoulder at my continuous-feed typewriter paper and read out the five-number sequence codes as they appeared across the page. The MiGs were clearly in pursuit. I heard someone call out "zok vot"— or something like that—which I later understood to be "lock on." Apparently their on-board radar and weapons systems were ready and capable of taking out the transport. I had been told at the time that on board our plane were two Air Force pilots and two radiomen, each schooled in Morse code. Radio silence had been broken the moment the jets left Vladivostok. The intercept was imminent. I was not privy to the actual conversation between command headquarters and the aircraft, but could imagine what must have been said. "Abort! I say again, abort, abort! Cleared to land, Bravo One! Repeat, Bravo One!" We were informed shortly after the near encounter that our transport had banked sharply to the left and fallen from the sky, then followed a straight-in approach to a classified airfield known only as Bravo One.

The MiGs then turned sharply in tight formation to the west-northwest and returned to Vladivostok. My commanding officer tapped me on the shoulder and said, "Good job, Airman!" When we realized it was all over and that our guys had landed safely, there was a collective sigh of relief.

The next day, someone came up to me and said, "President Kennedy was awakened last night over that incident. Did you know that?" I felt the blood rush to my face. All I could say was, "How about that!"

While scanning through the frequencies another night, I picked up an S.O.S., the international signal for distress. As soon as I realized what it was, I called out to my superior, Master Sergeant Johnnie Maples. He came right over and patched into an open jack with a separate headset to listen in to the rapid ditti dit, dahdahdah, ditti dit. He wrote down the frequency, then turned and left the room. I knew he would relay this information to the men in the direction-finding shack, the DF shack. They would bring up the signal, triangulate it with antennas in our antenna field and get a fix on the location.

I never knew what came of it. Sergeant Maples told me they weren't able to get a fix on the signal. It was too weak, perhaps out of range.

Once, during a particularly ferocious snowstorm, Sergeant Maples asked for volunteers to help secure an aircraft that had just landed on the runway. It was a small single engine plane owned and operated by Wien Airways, a cargo and mail carrier out of Nome. I volunteered along with several others.

Reaching the aircraft was not easy. The five of us formed a line, one behind the other, each holding on to the man in front by grabbing his shoulder with our right hand. The lead man was holding on to the back gate of a halftrack, a truck with bulldozer-like tracks in the rear. I remember holding out my left hand, at arm's length, and not being able to see it. That was how bad it was that night. This was a blizzard, a whiteout blizzard of heavy snow coming from the west, driven by incredibly fierce winds.

The plane was vibrating and shaking like a wild horse struggling to be free. It had been tied down to the runway with several wire ropes that kept it from flipping over and being tossed into the Bering Sea. I reached up with both hands, and struggling against the heavy winds, opened the door and climbed up the step and into the cockpit. The wind slammed the door shut against my left shoulder. I sat in the pilot's seat and grabbed the wheel to get some leverage and, as the plane continued buffeting and straining against the ropes, I planted my feet firmly on the two floor pedals, stopping the rudder from snapping back and forth. As I held the rudder in place with my feet, two of my buddies grabbed a ten-foot aluminum ladder from the halftrack, and using rubber straps and ropes, attempted to secure the rudder using the ladder as a splint. In spite of the ferocious storm they succeeded in tying the ladder across the rudder and vertical stabilizer, saving the plane.

We stayed with the plane all night and into the next day, and it was bitterly cold, temperatures approaching thirty below. We found some army rations dating back to World War II in the weather shack. They'd been wrapped in several layers of plastic and kept frozen for about twenty years: canned hams, green beans, boxes of tootsie rolls and cartons of Lucky Strike cigarettes, all from the 1940s. We cooked one of the hams in the small electric oven in the back room and thawed out the tootsie rolls. There was plenty to go around.

Several months later, after the snow had melted and the unpaved roads were now awash in ankle-deep mud, we were alerted to a Soviet threat to cross the Bering Straits and occupy the island. The transmission was received through a coded intercept and indicated the shore landing was imminent. We halted operations, locked down and secured the center, and were brought into a conference area to be briefed. The commander spoke with a sense of urgency, "We don't know how credible this information is but we must assume it's their intent to come ashore. We were told to gear up with heavy clothing and assemble outside the motor pool in fifteen minutes. Weapons were issued to each of us along with hand-held radios. We were then hustled into the back of three, six-wheel trucks. It was the middle of the night and the temperatures had dropped below freezing, so the trucks bounced along the now frozen parameter road from north to south along the western edge of the island. One by one we were off-loaded at intervals of fifty yards, forming a parameter. Orders had been given to maintain radio silence unless or until, "You see anything suspicious. And, for chrissake, keep the goddamn safety locked on…no screw-ups. If this is for real, I want you to break silence and fire only if fired upon. We'll be monitoring any activity or communications from here." I followed along with the others as ordered, scared to shit. What are we supposed to do, I thought, take on the entire Russian Army? No U.S. aircraft overhead, no other activity… nothing. I stood my position for several hours with my eyes open wide and my heart pounding, expecting to be overrun at any moment.

Then the fog rolled in off the water from the west. Everything in Alaska was extreme and the fog was no different. Fog so thick I could not see a thing. Nothing in front of me or on either side. And no sounds accept the lemmings rustling beneath the underbrush or an occasional fox or two, howling. I figured if I couldn't see them, how in hell could they see me? Five hours later I heard the trucks approaching along the parameter road off to my right. The alert had been lifted and they were fishing through the night looking for each of us. I honestly figured they were lost and I would be out there until later the next day.

* * *

This sort of thing happened periodically throughout my stay in Alaska—the back and forth manifestations of the ongoing cold war between the world's two superpowers.

While stationed in Alaska, I turned eighteen. I learned how to shoot pool, play poker, shoot craps, and drink beer. The only thing I was good at was shooting pool. Not too many guys could beat me at that or at ping-pong, or table-tennis, either.

One evening, at an assembly in the movie theater, I was called up to the stage to receive my GED (General Education Development) certificate. Passing the GED exams was considered the equivalent of graduating from high school. A copy of the exams would be sent to my last high school of record and placed in my permanent folder.

I had studied and taken those exams weeks earlier and forgotten completely about them until that night at the assembly. I was pretty happy and pretty surprised. All the guys hollered out, clapped and cheered as I walked onto the stage. Now I could say I was a high school graduate.

Most of the guys accepted or resigned themselves to the dreary, day-to-day isolation of life on St. Lawrence Island. One of my closest buddies, Jack Lydon, was really struggling with being so far away from the beaches and the girls back home on Carson Beach in South Boston, or "Southie," as it was called. I was sitting with Jack one morning in the chow hall having breakfast, when he picked up a glass jar of sugar from the table and made a motion as if to throw it through the plate-glass door across from our table. He held back and instead slammed it back down on the table, popping the lid off and sending sugar flying through the air. "I hate this goddamn, fuckin' place," he yelled so everyone could hear. Jack wasn't someone you messed with. He was a tough street kid from the city. I said, "Hey Jack, what the hell, we're trapped here. Nothing you can do about it. You're one tough sonofabitch, you'll make it." Jack and I got along very well, even though I usually kicked his ass on the pool table. He called me "professor" for some reason.

My buddy Rene Roche had been assigned to one of the other bases in Alaska, somewhere out in the Aleutians. He put in for a transfer to St. Lawrence Island to serve his remaining time in Alaska with me and Creath and the others—all the guys he knew so well from Keesler. He was granted the transfer and became one of my roommates.

Our rooms were lined along a short corridor that looked like the kind you might find in a grade B motel—a narrow hallway, orange linoleum floors, light tan paneling covering the walls on both sides, and cheap hollow-wooden doors. There were four men to a room. Each room had two double bunks stacked against opposite walls. Blackout shades were installed over the only window to block out the relentless sun during the summer months...twenty-one hours of sunlight and three hours of dusk. During the winter it was the reverse: twenty-one hours of total darkness and three hours where the sun peaked at us from the edge of the horizon.

My room was five doors down the hall from the Airman's Club. The back door of the Club opened directly onto a frozen, wind-driven snow field. In the distance, about a mile away, were twin mountain peaks. They stood side-by-side and were similar in size, elevation about 800 feet. They were more or less piles of volcanic rock. A few of us hiked up one of those peaks in the late spring of '61. After reaching the summit, I tried sliding down along the deep snow-packed slope, but only managed to bruise my hip and rip my leggings wide open.

One night in the summer of '61 we all walked outside to see the Northern Lights, wispy purple and pink ribbons of magnetically charged particles swirling around in the otherwise clear night sky... positively fascinating.

Everyone in the hallway worked the same shift. We played poker together, shot craps, and drank beer, all just about twenty steps from my room. One night, a sergeant entered our hallway from the other wing of the building and started raising hell with us about the noise. He got up in the face of a buddy of mine and began humiliating him in front of everyone. We were all so close. We had to be because of the

107

isolation. Even the sergeants would drink beer, play poker, and were generally friendly. But not this guy, and not this night.

He grabbed my buddy and pushed him up against the wall, screaming at him, humiliating him to the point of tears. Then he turned and stormed back to his room at the far end of the adjacent hallway, last door on the left. He could have been related to Bud Welch, could have been his twin—a pudgy, balding, ugly guy with a pockmarked face and a rotten disposition.

I followed him back to his room and banged on his door. When he opened it, I told him what he had done wasn't necessary. "You've got the guy so upset he's crying," I said. I reminded him that we were all in this goddamn place together. Then I opened my mouth too far, far enough to change my life: "You're a complete asshole!" He slammed the door in my face.

The next morning I heard my name called out over the hallway intercom system. I was to report immediately to Major Emil Stalder, my commanding officer. I quickly made my way through the labyrinth of hallways to his office.

I walked in, approached his desk and gave him a snappy salute. Standing off to my left was the hung-over, rat-faced sergeant I'd had the run in with the night before.

The commander repeated what the sergeant had told him about what happened the night before, and asked if it was true. Without offering an explanation or a defense, I said, "Yes Sir, no excuse, Sir." My orders, which had already been cut for a promotion to Airman 1st class (three stripes), were withdrawn and my new assignment to Edinburgh, Scotland was also withdrawn. I never said another word. Just, "No excuse, Sir." Even if I had one, I was taught to admit it if you did it and then shut up.

What bothered me more than anything was the look on my commander's face. A look that told me he thought I was a misfit, a troublemaker…that I was somehow not dedicated to the job or the mission. He told me he would not make this part of my permanent record. "You're a good kid, but you cannot show disrespect to a superior." I figured he might give me a break after the Vladivostok incident and my efforts down at the flight line. But he never said anything to me about that.

So I wasn't going to Scotland and I wasn't getting promoted. I felt like an idiot. I should have kept my mouth shut. At least, I reasoned, I stood up for one of my buddies; no one else had made a move to do so that night. We were all full of beer and having a great time, and as far as I was concerned, it was the sergeant who was out of line. Still, I was really disappointed with myself and my commander. He could have given me KP duty or some other pain-in-the-ass job. Instead, my new stripe, which meant a pay raise, and my plans for Scotland—my heritage—vaporized. This was a hard lesson, one of many lessons I would learn in my life, most of which resulted from too much to drink.

I was re-assigned to Orlando Air Force Base in Florida, Detachment Three, USAFSS. United States Air Force Security Service. I would serve the remaining two years of my enlistment at this facility. It could have been worse, I thought. My buddy Richard Creath and I had been excited and looking forward to our assignment to Scotland. We were even writing to girls in Edinburgh. I was writing to a young single mother named Ruby Kerr. She'd sent me pictures of herself and her three-year-old daughter. Her letters were wonderful—nice letters to a guy stationed so far away from the rest of the world. I had been waiting with much anticipation to meet her. I'd never really had a girlfriend, and she obviously wanted a relationship with me. Everyone told me, "She probably wants a ticket to the U.S.; you better think twice." Knowing me at the time, I probably would have wound up marrying her and that would have sent me off in a completely different direction. I quickly put her out of mind, but I kept her picture.

Some time after I left Alaska and settled myself in Orlando, I received a letter from one of the guys still up there on the frozen tundra. He told me how the sergeant I had mouthed off to, found himself in quite a bit of trouble for passing bad checks at the BX. I felt somewhat vindicated. He got his, I thought.

The day I left The Rock, eight of us were waiting in the weather shack down at the flight line. My year was finally up and it was time to get the hell out of there and rejoin the human race. A storm was kicking up all across the ominous looking horizon. I looked up and spotted my ride home: a C-123 making a wide sweeping turn off to my right and descending rapidly. The pilot brought the plane in fast and hit hard. The strong winds were swirling and gusting across the flight line from every direction. He landed right-to-left directly in front of me. After braking to a stop at the far end of the runway, he quickly spun around—a full 180—and headed back to pick us up.

We were lined up on the edge of the runway, ready to leave. The twin engines were running at nearly full throttle and the brakes were straining to stop, so we grabbed our gear and prepared to jump in. One member of the flight crew slid the side door open and yelled, above the deafening engine noise, "Let's go. Hurry the fuck up. Get in. Get in. Let's go!"

As soon as we were on board and the sliding door pulled shut, the pilot released the brakes. The plane lurched forward, raced down the runway, and lifted off directly into the turbulence. We tumbled around the open cargo bay, trying to grab hold of the canvas seats strung along the wall.

The ride back to Elmendorf Air Force Base was pretty damn wild, tossing us all over the sky. It was a relatively short flight; no time to get "above it." The empty cargo bay was spread out directly in front of us. The pilot and co-pilot were sitting in their seats to my left, elevated a few steps up in the open cockpit. They were fighting the weather, trying to keep the wings aligned with the horizon. We kept climbing and diving and rocking. Snow pounded the windshield; visibility was zero. It was all instruments now. The young, wide-eyed co-pilot snapped his head around to the left and hollered, "Where are the rafts? Get 'em ready!"

I mumbled to myself, "Holy shit…the rafts! I've spent a year of my life on that frozen patch of ice, and now we're going down… and on the way home!" I knew we'd be lucky to last six minutes in those waters if we had to ditch. Still, I was young and pretty much unafraid; I figured I'd survive. We all reached under our seats and looked overhead for the rafts. Two of the guys down at the end managed to pull a couple of tightly-wrapped canvas bags out from under their seats. Inside each bag was a six-man rubber raft. We sat there waiting for the orders to inflate.

I kept thinking of what had happened a little more than a year earlier, just before I arrived up there. A similar flight, under the same weather conditions, fighting the head winds and cross-winds in a desperate attempt to get airborne. Like us, they were heading home after a yearlong tour of duty. They never made it. The plane flipped over on take-off and landed upside down on the far end of the runway, sliding out onto the ice. I never knew all the details except that several men suffered broken backs.

Across from where we were sitting, on the other side of the cargo bay, was a lieutenant colonel. I didn't know his name, but he was stretched out over three canvas seats with seat belts around his chest and legs. He was asleep, or looked as though he was trying to sleep. Maybe he was just hung over from the party the night before. We were buffeting all over the damn place and he's just riding it out. I just couldn't believe it. I thought to myself, If he's not worried, why the hell should I be?

We came in high and fast at Elmendorf and needed the full length of runway to stop. It was a "hold on to your ass" kind of ride, from start to finish.

In retrospect, we had a hell of a time in Alaska. What an experience! I enjoyed the work immensely. You could never call it routine; something could happen at any moment. I met some really great guys and we all seemed to get along remarkably well considering the circumstances. Everyone could give and take a little ribbing from time to time.

I remember thinking back to the day, the year before, when we boarded the flight out to the island. One of the older guys, realizing how young I was, put his arm around my neck, pulled me in close to him, and said, "Hey, Hussey, don't worry. I hear there's a lot of beautiful women out there. I can't wait...a woman behind every tree." Then, laughing good-naturedly at his own joke, he finished up with, "The only trouble is Hussey...there's no trees!"

Rene left The Rock a few weeks before I did. He went off to Italy and sent me a card telling me what a great time he was having. "The Italian food is great and the girls are all gorgeous!"

After attending two days of re-orientation and de-briefing at Elmendorf, I boarded a flight from Anchorage to Seattle, Washington. There I grabbed my bags and waited in line for a standby commercial flight to my father's place in Michigan. He and Jane picked me up at the airport for the half hour ride to 13212 Superior Street in Wyandotte. I had been sending money every payday to Jane to save for me until I finished my time in Alaska. I felt I could trust her to hold my money until I came back. If I sent it home to my mother, she might use it to pay bills, and I would need that money when I left the island to buy a car. Jane deposited it into a local bank, and although my father tried to get his hands on it, she refused to tell him where it was deposited. My plan was to stop in Detroit on the way home, buy a car, and drive home from there.

The day after I arrived, Jane handed me a check for $722, and my father took me out shopping for a car. It seemed like there were car dealerships on every corner. Detroit was the car capital of the world in those days. We stopped at a Chevrolet dealership and I found just what I wanted, a '55 Chevy. It was painted a two-tone, blue and white; a really nice-looking car with low-mileage and a strong, tight engine. The dealer quoted me a price. I didn't have enough. I was $150 short. He looked at both of us and said, "You can have the car if someone will co-sign for a loan to cover the one-fifty." I turned to my father and asked him to co-sign, but he said he wouldn't.

I was really disappointed. My father must have known I was good for the money. I told him I was in the service and if I defaulted on any debt obligation, I would be in big trouble with my superiors. I felt he owed me at least that much, but my argument fell on deaf ears. He really didn't know me very well; he had never taken the time to know me, or to know Peter for that matter. So what else could I expect? It was his loss and, of course, my loss as well.

I settled for a beat-up car that had been repossessed by a local bank. The banker just happened to live next door to my father. He explained the circumstances concerning the repossession and said the car was in pretty good shape, and I could have it for $350. He invited me to go take a look. "Here," he said, "take my keys and drive my car over to the bank. It's in the back." He handed me the keys to the repossessed car and I drove to the bank. The car was a convertible, a black 1956 Ford with a white canvas top.

On the way back to my father's place, I was in an accident while attempting to make a right-hand turn at an intersection. It was a four-lane roadway, two lanes going in each direction. I was in the right-hand lane next to the centerline. The light turned green and I started my turn to the right, crossing the empty lane to my right. Some guy came flying up that outside right lane and broadsided me, caving in the front passenger side door. It was obviously my fault. I crossed right in front of him, and he couldn't stop.

The cops came, and because no one was hurt and both cars were still drivable, they gave me a ticket and wrote up the report. I had a really hard time convincing the cops that I had borrowed the car from a guy at the bank. They made a call from their radio in the cruiser and let me go. I drove the banker's smashed-up car back to my father's place and explained to everyone what had happened. I was more than a little embarrassed over the whole thing, but what happened, happened. There was obviously no sense in trying to hide it. The banker took care of the ticket and he assured me his insurance company would take care of the rest. He signed the title over to me and I handed him his $350.00 in cash. Then I drove my "new car" to my father's place. I didn't know it at the time but it had been driven into the ground. The previous owner must have given it a good beating before the bank came and took it away. I spent the rest of my money on repairs. It needed a new or rebuilt transmission, and the mechanic went on to tell me, "I've also done a compression check on the engine to see why I can't keep it running. I hate to tell you this, but there's no compression coming from the left side of the engine. You're going to need a new engine head."

I stayed at my father's place long enough to have the car fixed, and then headed home to Massachusetts, driving straight through—

eight hundred and fifty miles. My mother, Peter, and Joe were still living in Brockton at 89 West Elm Street. I spent most of the next two weeks catching up with the folks in Norwell and with my mother and Peter. Beyond that, the leave was uneventful, and when it was over, I packed my car, said my goodbyes, and headed for Florida. Destination: Orlando Air Force Base.

On the drive to Florida, I picked up a hitchhiker on the Garden State Parkway in New Jersey. He was standing out on the edge of the highway with a sign that read "Miami." Having been in that position more than once in my life, I knew how much it meant to have someone pull over and offer a ride. He was wearing a full cast on one leg and had crutches tucked under each arm. He was older than me, probably twenty-eight or thirty. He opened the door, thanked me for stopping, tossed the crutches into the back seat and got in.

He never mentioned his name or introduced himself. We sat next to one another for several miles without saying much at all. He did say that I was following the right edge of the road too closely for his comfort, but I didn't respond. After a while, we began exchanging stories about our lives and families. He told me what his mother and her boyfriend did for a living. He said, as if it were no big deal, "she'd go out to the bars and pick up guys, then go with them back to their places for drinks and a little kissy-face. She'd wait for the right moment and put 'sleepy drops' in the guy's drink. After he passed out, she'd open the door, let her boyfriend in and rob the guy. I said, "I'd never heard of anything like that." He smiled at me and said, in a condescending tone, "You're a little naïve."

He also told me that his mother and her boyfriend had robbed a number of small banks down in South Georgia. I remember thinking, I'd better be careful with this guy. Maybe those crutches and that cast were just a prop. Maybe he had plans for me and my car. But by this time I was getting pretty tired and knew I couldn't drive much longer, so I pulled over for the night at some motel along the highway in South Carolina. I figured he was as tired as I was and needed sleep as much as I did. Maybe I was taking a chance, but I didn't think so. We grabbed a few hours of sleep and in the morning I was awakened by the loud chirping of robins in the grassy backyard outside the open window in our room.

When we crossed over the Georgia-Florida border, I pulled over to the side of the road and put the top down. The rich, inviting aroma of orange blossoms filled the air—fresh and clean and beautiful. So this is what it's like to be in Florida, I thought. It was as if I was entering a new world.

We continued south along Route I, and when I came upon the signs for Orlando, I pulled over and dropped the hitchhiker off. He opened the door, reached in and pulled his crutches out from the back seat and said, without shaking my hand, "Hey, thanks. I'll catch a ride to Miami from here, no problem." I was satisfied that I had helped him out, like others who had helped me earlier in my life, but I was glad to be rid of him.

I made my way into Orlando and checked through the main gate of Orlando Air Force Base. I handed the guard my papers, and he gave me directions to my assigned barracks. As I turned right at the first intersection, I marveled at the single-engine jet aircraft poised on the lawn directly in front of me. Written on the side of the fuselage in large black letters were the words "Orlando Air Force Base." The day was perfect and I could not have been happier.

On the left, about a mile from the main gate, was my new home. The small white sign in front of the building read: United States Air Force Security Service, Detachment Three. USAFSS-3. I was assigned to the Security Service voice intercept unit. It was a single-story, wood and brick building directly on the shoreline of a gorgeous, fresh-water lake. I turned into the parking area and walked down to the freshly painted wooden dock that jutted out about sixty feet onto the lake. I stopped and glanced around at my new home and thought, Wow! What a great spot. After spending a year of my young life in that frozen world up north, I figured I deserved this. A grin came over my face as I began unloading my car.

The warm Florida sun was positively inviting. I was sure I was going to love it there; the polar opposite of where I'd come from. It was everything I had expected, just beautiful. Plenty of sunshine, plenty of beaches and, thankfully, plenty of trees! I walked into the barracks, through the dayroom where the pool table and coke machines were located, then down the hall to my room, where I said hello to my new roommate, Bob Anderyt.Security Service personnel, assigned to Detachment Three, were considered the elite on Base. Each of us held a top secret security clearance. We lived in the best barracks and ate the best chow. We worked with sensitive voice transmissions between U.S. military pilots and their respective ground stations on preset military flight and ground station frequencies. Several voice-activated, reel-to-reel tape-recorders automatically recorded communications between pilots and ground stations. As soon as a pilot or ground station operator spoke, or even keyed the mike, the reels activated and began recording. These recorded conversations were then transcribed onto continuous-feed typewriter paper, which was fed directly into the manual typewriters from a cardboard box on the floor.

I transcribed voice communications from aircraft on routine missions mainly patrolling the Florida coastline. I also transcribed communications from pilots who flew in and around the region known as the "Devil's Triangle," a triangular-shaped geographic area running from Miami northeast to Bermuda and then south to Puerto Rico and back to Miami. It's an area where true north intersects or bisects magnetic north, and is long suspected of contributing to air mishaps and other strange events including the disappearance of ships at sea. After 1964, this area became known as the "Bermuda Triangle."

There were two or three mysterious occurrences in that area while I was stationed in Florida. I never felt the Triangle was particularly relevant until a U.S. Air Force tanker aircraft disappeared in 1962. The following year, two or three other incidents took place that involved aircraft collided in mid-air. I also heard about the disappearance of a ship (it just vanished) in 1963. The only explanation I could figure was that the on-board navigational instruments somehow distorted locations providing misleading information to flight crews and ships' crews. I never found a satisfactory explanation. I'm not sure there ever were satisfactory explanations.

During my two years in Orlando, I attended Rollins College as an evening student in Winter Park, a small municipality just north of Orlando. The campus grounds were immaculate and the buildings were richly constructed in ornate Spanish architectural design, featuring fluted columns and perfectly sculptured terra cotta roofs. My schedule made it difficult for me to attend on a regular basis. I had to argue my case in front of my superiors. We were on a rotating schedule, i.e., three days on "days" (7:00 a.m. to 4:00 p.m.), three days on "swings" (4:00 p.m. to midnight) and three days on "nights" (midnight to 7:00 a.m.). Then there were three days off.

I made my argument to the captain in charge of our duty schedule. "Why is it that Jabb can go to school and I can't?" I asked. Leonard Jabb was a friend of mine. His real name had been Jabblonski but his grandfather had changed it to Jabb when they came to America.

Jabb was enrolled as an evening student at Rollins. He told me it was a great opportunity to further your education. Jabb always had a book under his arm and was always studying. "You should look into it. It's practically free," he said one night.

The O.D. (Officer of the Day) reminded me that "Jabb works days, period. You're on rotation."

"So, why can't you put me on days for one semester so I can go to school, too?" I asked him directly. "I want to take advantage of this opportunity, if I can." The Air Force was picking up most of the tuition and actually had a program encouraging enlistees to further their education. I made that part of my argument and pressed him hard, but not too hard.

My duty captain finally re-arranged my schedule and granted me permission to attend one class—one evening a week—for one semester. There would be a subsequent evaluation to determine my status. I ended up enrolling in four classes over four semesters—two mathematics classes, one English class and a computer FORTRAN class. I had no trouble with the math and English. The FORTRAN was something altogether different. FORTRAN was one of the early computer languages, used to determine the means by which computers could be programmed to calculate various outcomes.

In those years, computers were enormous in size. The one we worked with was nearly six feet wide, four feet long, and four feet high. It was housed in a large cabinet that nearly filled the adjoining classroom. Each and every command was "punched out" on cardboard computer cards. This required hitting keys on a special keyboard that would make a small square hole, or a series of small square holes, at various locations along the card. Each card measured approximately 2.5 inches wide by 5.5 inches long. After punching the cards, we stacked them like playing cards and placed them along a sliding tray to be fed, left to right, into the computer. The computer would read each card and perform the calculations if, of course, you understood FORTRAN and had punched the cards correctly.

I passed the FORTRAN course, but not by much.

* * *

During the events surrounding the "Cuban Missile Crisis," no one was allowed off Base for any reason. It was October of 1962, and President Kennedy had invoked the Monroe Doctrine, signed into law in 1823, which stated that, "In the opinion of the United States, European powers should no longer colonize the Americas or interfere with the affairs of sovereign nations located in the Americas, such as the United States of America, Mexico, and others."

United States U-2 spy planes had flown over and photographed missile sites on Cuban soil, sites built and maintained by the Soviet Union, a clear violation of the stated Monroe Doctrine. It was time for a decision, a showdown—an international showdown with enormous consequences hanging in the balance. On October 24, 1962, Soviet ships reached the quarantine line of U.S. Naval ships. Spearheaded by the Essex Carrier Group, the U.S. ships encircled the island of Cuba. The blockade was in place. Soviet submarines, armed with nuclear-tipped torpedoes, ran silent, like sharks, beneath the surface.

The Soviet Commander radioed back to Moscow for instructions. Seconds ticked on. What would they do? Moscow immediately radioed back giving orders: "Hold your position. Do not engage." This was high drama on the high seas, and it nearly precipitated World War Three.

On Thursday, October 25, the U.S. Joint Chiefs of Staff instructed the Strategic Air Command to go to DEFCON 2—the highest alert level in U.S. History. A squad of U.S. fighter jets conducted a fly-over along the Cuban coastline. One jet was hit by gunfire from Fidel Castro's Revolutionary Army, but it managed to return safely. Two B-52 Stratofortress nuclear bombers were ordered in the air from Homestead Air Force Base near Miami.

The Joint Chiefs concluded that, "The Soviet missile sites in Cuba represent one-half of the total Soviet nuclear capacity at the time." The United States was on the brink of a catastrophic encounter with nuclear weapons. There could be no winners.

We gathered around the television in the barracks dayroom, watching as the Soviet ships approached the line of U.S. Naval warships strung along the Cuban coast, blockading their advance into port. Soviet President Khrushchev was known for his impulsive and sometimes erratic behavior. No one could predict what would happen. The crisis was unfolding just a few miles south of us.

I figured that if war broke out it would not be limited to the waters off Cuba, but would probably wipe the Island of Cuba off the map. The Soviet response would most likely level Miami, the southern tip of Florida, and beyond. Perhaps it would escalate, drawing a full-scale response from the Soviet homeland in Western Europe. And then what? The potential for disaster was nearly incalculable.

Dean Rusk, then U.S. Secretary of State, boldly announced to President Kennedy, his brother Robert, and the rest of their immediate staff, "They're dead in the water. We were eyeball to eyeball with them and I think the other guy just blinked."

They *had* blinked. One at a time and in deliberate slow motion, the Soviet ships began their wide arching turn and set a course for home. When the news of their departure hit the airwaves, we vaulted from our seats. The dayroom was crazy with cheering applause, and hand shaking!

We learned later that at the height of the pending crisis, the commander of the Soviet nuclear fleet had his hand on the launch controls just moments before Khrushchev issued his order to stand down. The blockade and subsequent standoff had been a success. Soviet ships were leaving our hemisphere and had, moreover, agreed to dismantle all existing missile installations in Cuba. No more missile sites and no more missiles. You could almost hear a collective sigh of relief across the world.

Shortly after these events, President Kennedy and President Khrushchev agreed to install a direct telephonic hookup between the White House and the Kremlin to immediately address any potential threats or misunderstandings in the future.

* * *

A year later, and while I was still stationed in Orlando, President John F. Kennedy was assassinated. It happened in the early afternoon of November 22, 1963 during a presidential motorcade parading through downtown Dallas. The President was riding in an open convertible with his wife Jackie, Texas Governor John Connolly and the Governor's wife. Theirs was the second car in the motorcade.

I was in the barracks when someone ran through the corridor yelling, "The President's been shot. Kennedy's been shot." I was getting ready for work, but stopped everything and ran through the corridors to the dayroom. A TV news reporter was broadcasting from the emergency entranceway outside Parkland Memorial Hospital in downtown Dallas. All we knew at the time was that the President had been shot. The news was sketchy: "The President is in surgery. No word on his condition."

Moments after I arrived in the dayroom, newscaster Walter Cronkite reported the following: "At one o'clock Central time or two o'clock Eastern time, President John Fitzgerald Kennedy died at Parkland Memorial Hospital in Dallas, Texas."

Three shots had been fired at the motorcade. Governor Connolly had also been shot. He was riding up front, and the President was sitting directly behind him. Governor Connolly was taken to Parkland Hospital also, and went immediately into surgery. He had been shot in the back along his left shoulder.

Vice President Lyndon B. Johnson was taken to a secure location and, as required by the Constitution, was sworn in as the next President of the United States.

I left for work at the usual time. My shift started at 4:00 p.m. As soon as I walked through the door at Operations, I ran into Billy

Watson, one of the guys I worked with at the time. His home state was Texas, and his hometown was Dallas. He had enlisted in the Air Force from there, and he was always mouthing off about his Dallas, how great it was.

Air Force One was about to land at Andrews AFB in Washington D.C. Most of us were pretty damn upset. It'll take a long time to get over this, I thought. I turned to Billy, who seemed somewhat detached, and said, "What do you think of your Dallas now?" He said something and pushed me, and I pushed him back. We were surrounded by expensive communications equipment. Someone grabbed me and someone else grabbed Billy, and that was the end of it. I shouldn't have been up in his face, but I was. I blasted him with, "I never want to hear another word about your damn Dallas. You hear me?"

I had followed Jack Kennedy's campaign through radio and television stations in Boston, and read about him in the *Brockton Enterprise*. I was proud to be in the military with Kennedy as Commander-in-Chief, and I wasn't too happy about Lyndon Johnson's sudden ascendancy to the presidency. The swearing-in took place on board Air Force One with the grief-stricken Jackie Kennedy standing to his left, and the body of her husband enclosed in a coffin and secured a few feet below in the cargo bay.

Later that night and throughout the following three days, I tape-recorded news broadcasts from the radio in the back room of the Operations center. I had access to the reel-to-reel tape recorders, so I came back to Operations after work and sat for hours in the back room making sure I was getting everything—Parkland Memorial Hospital, the swearing-in of Lyndon Johnston, the pending funeral arrangements: "The body will lie in the rotunda...."

While listening and recording, I was startled by yet another news flash—as it was happening. "Shots rang out in the basement of the Dallas County Jailhouse. Lee Harvey Oswald, the accused assassin, was being escorted through the basement corridor of the jailhouse on his way to his arraignment when Jack Ruby, a local nightclub owner, pulled a pistol from his pocket and shot Oswald at point blank range in the lower abdomen." I recorded all of it as it was being broadcast. I figured Dallas was in a state of lawlessness and assumed Jack Ruby would be next. I was troubled to think that everyone must carry guns down there. I sat on the edge of my chair and recorded every word.

* * *

Six months before I was discharged, I was called into the commander's office for my Retention Interview. Would I re-enlist? A $2,000 bonus waited for me if I did, along with another four years. I declined. I couldn't wait to be on my own. I had a plan, and I expected great things of myself. If I had stayed another four years, I might have resigned myself to serving twenty years and retiring with a pension at age thirty-seven, only then to start another career. It was a predictable course with plenty of security. I wanted more. I wanted to challenge myself. I wanted to see how far my ambition would take me.

I was honorably discharged from the U.S. Air Force on February 5, 1964. I had served nearly four years and was not yet twenty-one. The Air Force offered me a three-month "early-out" because my career field was being phased out; Morse code, which was my Military Occupational Specialty code (AFSC 29250), would soon become a thing of the past.

While in the service, I learned to get along and respect the differences all people bring to the table; everyone has something to offer. We were a mix of individuals with varying backgrounds, interests, attitudes, and abilities, trained to work together as a team, and for the most part we did. I could leave the service now and pursue my own interests—set my own course, find my own way. I had plenty of confidence and plenty of ambition.

I had achieved success in everything I had attempted since leaving Marshfield High School in the fall of '59. Upon my discharge, I made my way up the coast in my new car, a six-cylinder, four-door, black and white '57 Chevy. It wasn't actually new, but it was new to me. It had a floor shift, a homemade metal rod that poked through the floor and connected to the transmission. If I pulled up on it, it would disengage from the transmission and I could pull it out and hold it in my hand. Once in a while I'd yank it out to show some of the guys and they'd laugh like hell. The previous owner of the car must have thought it was pretty cool to have a floor shift, and I felt the same.

I made a stop in Washington, D.C., to look around, and had my picture taken on the steps of the Capitol Building. I thought, Maybe someday I'll make it all the way to the halls of Congress.

The possibilities that lay ahead of me seemed endless. I left D.C. and headed north for home, driving straight through to Brockton. I knew there'd be a bed or a couch for me at my mother's place…I really never gave it a thought. I arrived home with open arms, in a hurry to get started. I began looking for a job the next day.

Unemployment was high at the time. Jobs were scarce. I couldn't find work anywhere. I walked down West Elm Street to the center of Brockton and stopped at the Western Union office to see if they needed any people experienced in Morse code. They told me, "No, that went out several years ago." I walked all over Brockton knocking on doors looking for work. Someone mentioned that because of my recent discharge from the service, I was eligible to collect unemploy-ment benefits, so I headed over to the unemployment office on White Street to sign up and "collect." I was so disappointed in myself for being in those unemployment lines. I knew there must be work out there somewhere.

I spent an hour in the first line collecting my application paper-work. Then I turned and entered the second line. Both lines were roped off with the usual directional and instructional signs. The sec-ond line was for processing claims, so I began filling out the forms while moving along in line toward the final station, the interview.

There must have been one hundred and fifty people in line on that cold, rainy, dreary day. The floor was wet and dirty from melting snow and dripping clothing. I shuffled along with people who I knew would rather be anywhere else but there. I started questioning my decision to leave the Air Force. I had lots of friends in the service and an inter-esting job. I could have made it a career. There was always plenty of food, free medical and dental care, a car, a place to call home, and on top of that, they paid me. I was secure. What more was I looking for?

Still, I reasoned, I had other things to do.

Halfway through the second, final line at the unemployment office, I turned, stepped out of line and walked out the door. As I exited the building, I threw my files in a trash container to my left, just outside the front entranceway. I was not going to be unemployed; I was not going to collect. I was going to find a job. On the way home, I promised myself I would work as hard as I could at whatever I found.

The next day, I went to work at the Centre Street Car Wash across the street from the Brockton Hospital, $36 a week. It was enough to pay my way at home and register my car. The registration had expired the week before, but I had been driving it anyway.

Peter asked if I could get him a job there too. I said, "Sure, I'll talk to the guy tomorrow." Peter began working with me the next day, but after three days he got into a fight with one of the other guys and quit. I continued on, washing cars until they were spotless.

Every day I bought the *Brockton Enterprise* newspaper and searched the help wanted section trying to find a better job.

Three weeks later, I found myself standing in another line, applying for the one opening available at the local Friendly Ice Cream restaurant on the east side of town. I really wanted this job. The pay at Friendly's was double what I was making at the car wash, and it would give me some responsibility and a chance to start saving.

We didn't have a phone, so after the interview I called the manager every day from a pay phone out in the hall. "Did you make a decision yet?" I asked. I don't know how many people applied that day, but in the end I was chosen. I would now be making $65 a week.

When I returned to the car wash the day after I was hired at Friendly's, the owner smiled and said, "You'll be back; they all come back." I said to myself, I won't be back, I'm going to college.

Now I needed to save every nickel. I spent no money. Not on anything. I never went out. I was committed to this. I knew this was the only chance I would have to live a decent life, free from the depression and poverty that had surrounded and threatened me for most of my childhood. The service was a transition, my steppingstone. But now I needed a college education. A college degree would open doors; perhaps give me a chance to earn some real money. Maybe I'd go right to the top, become whatever I wanted to be. Maybe I'd run for public office and end up in Washington. The possibilities were endless, but I was going nowhere without an education, and I knew it.I stayed at Friendly's for about six months, advancing from dishwasher to assistant manager in charge of the weekday night shift. The manager liked me and wanted me to stay on, maybe become a manager someday and have my own store. I never told him of my plans to leave at the end of August. Maybe I should have, but I couldn't chance getting fired or being pushed out by my replacement. He did find out though, through a co-worker friend of mine. I told him I was sorry for not telling him, but I was going away to school and, as much as I appreciated the confidence, I did not want my own store. He reached out, touched my shoulder, shook my hand, and said, "I wish you the best of luck. I'm going to miss you."

Before I left for college, Peter asked me to go with him to see Bud. I didn't really see any point in seeing Bud again. I hated him, didn't I? Or maybe I didn't. Maybe I just felt sorry for him—but I had no reason to see him.

"Why the hell do you want to see him?" I asked.

"I'm not sure, maybe to get some things off my chest," he said.

"I'm all done with that," I told him. "I threw all that shit away years ago. Too burdensome to carry around."

Nonetheless, I agreed to go. Peter needed me to be there when he unloaded on Bud; something was really nagging him. We drove in my car to the Veteran's Hospital in Brockton where Bud was now confined. Although Bud was only in his early fifties, he apparently could no longer care for himself. I never knew the details.

We walked in the front door and approached the receptionist at the front desk. He invited us to have a seat; he would call an attendant out to speak with us. When the attendant arrived, I told him who we were and why we had come. He said it would just be a moment, then turned and asked, "By the way, does he know you're here, know you were coming?"

I looked at Peter to see if he had called ahead. "No," said Peter. "He doesn't know."

My father, "Pete" with Peter and me before divorce, 1947.

Left: Peter, age 18 months, Rockland, MA, 1947.

Below: Don, age four, and Peter, age 18 months, North Avenue, Rockland, MA, 1947.

Above: Mom with Peter and me. Christmas, 1960.

Right: Don freshman S.I.U., September 1964. (Courtesy: S.I.U. Alumni Archives)

Agnes and Alexander Black, "Grandpa Black." 21 Central Street, Norwell, MA, 1940.

"Well then," said the attendant as he looked first at Peter and then at me, "let me see if I can get him." I figured what he was really saying was, "Let me see if he wants to see you."

After fumbling with the many keys strapped to his side, the attendant unlocked a heavy metal door with a small see-through window in the middle. The door opened to a long hallway leading to the rooms. It was quite a long time before he returned. The door opened slowly from the inside as he escorted my stepfather out into the waiting area. Bud wasn't handcuffed, nor was he wearing striped clothing. But it did seem as though he was a prisoner, an inmate.

Peter and I were sitting on a long, red, plastic-covered couch in the middle of the reception area. A fresh bouquet of flowers had been placed on the table directly in front of us. There he was, Bud Welch, walking toward us with his familiar limp, looking like a broken man.

He was much shorter than I'd remembered—and older-looking than I expected. As I watched him come through the door, moving in slow motion toward us, I said to myself, This is the guy who came into my young life when I was only five and didn't leave until I was sixteen. The guy who deprived me of my childhood, smacked me around for no reason, and constantly called me every name in the book. He had never come to any of my baseball games. Never helped me with anything I ever did, and denied me time and time again the social interactions with my peers so important to a young boy, the fun of growing up.

Peter and I both stood up. Bud was quite subdued as he shuffled over and sat down on the couch between the two of us. He leaned over, rested his elbows on his knees and stared at the floor. In a soft, barely audible voice, he turned to me and said, "I was pretty rough on you, wasn't I?" I figured that was his way of apologizing to me after all the years. He had been kinder to Peter; Peter was a hemophiliac. Bud never hit him.

"Ah, don't worry about it," I said, "It probably toughened me up."

Bud's hand was shaking as he fiddled with his unlit cigarette. "You have a match?" he asked. I told him I didn't. Peter said the same. Back when I was working at the car wash, I had come home one day to find Peter sitting in the living room smoking a cigarette. I was so upset with him. "You've got enough to deal with," I had screamed. "What the hell are you doing?" I hoped the reason he didn't have a match for Bud was because he wasn't smoking anymore.

Not much else was said between the three of us. Bud's eyes were glassy and grey and had a distant look as he rested his elbows on his knees, bent over, looking at the floor.

As they say, the silence was deafening. The brief conversation had ended. Nobody knew what else to say, least of all Bud. Peter and I just got up and said goodbye.

I said goodbye to Bud for good that day. I offered no handshake and no hug, and neither did Peter. I never saw him again. On the way home from the VA, I said to Peter, "You only get one life and he pretty much wasted his."

When Bud died at age fifty-seven, my mother and Peter went to his wake and funeral. They buried him in the military section of the Hanson Town Cemetery. After the services, Peter called to tell me that nobody else had been there. "It was a depressing sight," he said. Bud had lost his way in life a long time ago. He wasted away from depression until his body finally shut down. I didn't go to pay my last respects. I didn't have any last respects.

During this time I was a little disappointed with my mother. She insisted I pay her $15 a week for my "room and board." Joe was living with her then and was working hard and trying to pay most of the bills. I figured I owed it to him, but it still bothered me. My mother knew how dedicated and determined I was to save as much as I could so I could go to college. She could have done all right without my money, but she insisted.

I managed to save $735 while working at Friendly's. It wasn't much, but time was running out; it would have to be enough. The Friday before the long Labor Day weekend, I drove over to the bank and closed out my account, withdrawing everything in cash. I returned home, packed the car, filled the tank, checked the oil and said goodbye to Peter and my mother, nobody stopping me. I was leaving that afternoon. I was going off to college, Southern Illinois University in Alton, Illinois.

SIX

I'm Not Going Home

I drove my '57 Chevy straight through from Brockton, Massachusetts, to Alton, Illinois, arriving in the early morning hours of Sunday, September 6, 1964. Shurtleff College was on the eastern banks of the Mississippi River and had just been accredited by, and transferred to, the State of Illinois. It would soon be renamed Southern Illinois University. The main campus of SIU, located in Carbondale, Illinois, was one hundred and forty miles to the south. The Carbondale Campus had been fully operational for years. Construction of a new 2660-acre campus was planned for the following year, and would be located fifteen miles to the east in Edwardsville, Illinois.

I had decided months earlier to apply to this school after talking with an Air Force buddy who was raised in the Midwest. He told me how much he loved the St. Louis area—the warm and friendly Midwestern folks, the Mississippi River, the Cardinals baseball team—and it wasn't too far from Hannibal, Missouri, the home of Tom Sawyer and Huckleberry Finn. I was convinced it would be a good fit for me, and a lot more inviting than the streets of Brockton, Massachusetts.

Upon my arrival, I checked into the Chain of Rocks Motel, which was just off the highway on the outskirts of Edwardsville. After the first couple of nights the motel owner, who lived next door in a separate house, offered me a room on a long-term basis if I would agree to work the desk and switchboard in the evenings. I needed a place, so I wound up working for him five nights a week from six to midnight.

Student registration was scheduled for Tuesday, September 8. I got up early, dressed, dashed out the door, and drove west to the campus in

Alton, a distance of about fourteen miles. Registration began at nine in the morning. I was as excited as ever to begin my college career. I stood in a line that stretched out of the Student Center building, across the lawn and out to the main road. When I finally arrived at the registration desk, the assistant registrar ran her finger down the long list of names. She told me she could not find mine. I was not listed. She turned and motioned to the building behind her and said, "You'll have to go upstairs to the Office of the Dean and find out what the problem is."

I gathered my papers, went upstairs to the dean's office and told the secretary that I needed to see him. She pushed the intercom button and asked if he could see me. She smiled and said, "Yes, he'll see you. Just go on in."

As it turned out, the Dean of Admissions was not surprised to see me. It was almost as though he was expecting me. It seemed I had not been officially accepted and therefore would not be allowed to enroll. I thought back to the day in mid-July when my letter from SIU had arrived. My mother went down the hall to our box and came back with the news: "There's a letter here for you from Southern Illinois University." I opened it right away and read it out loud. "Accepted—pending SAT results." I waved the letter in the air and said, "Can you believe it, Mom? I'm going to a university. I'm going to college. They've accepted me!" I forwarded all my SAT scores and never received any "After careful consideration…" letter, or any other correspondence, so I figured I'd been accepted.

This was the only school I applied to. I thought about Bridgewater State College in Massachusetts where I took my SATs, but decided against it. I needed to get away. I needed to get far away.

The Dean was sitting behind an impressive cherry wood desk, books and papers scattered about the room. He was quite abrupt as he peered out at me from over half-glasses balanced on the far end of his nose. His wry smile and condescending manner put me on the defensive. "We cannot accept you here at SIU because of your poor SAT scores," he announced matter-of-factly.

My mind started racing, scrambling to figure out how I was going to get around this. I thought to myself, I'm not going home and

I'm not going down without a fight. After a few awkward moments of listening to him explain, I began to lay out my case. "I've recently completed four years in the Air Force, traveled twelve hundred miles by car, have $650 in my pocket, and I want to stay." To bolster my position, I added that I had attended Rollins College as a part-time night student while stationed in Florida, and had passed all my classes, several of which I planned to transfer.

He had all my records in front of him. "Three of those classes are not transferable. They're refresher courses you should have had in high school."

Impatient with his pompous bullshit, I mustered what little charm I had left, looked him square in the eye and said, "Just give me one semester. If I don't make it, I'll leave."

Then I shut my mouth. I didn't want to overplay my hand or overstate my case. It's your move, I said to myself. I gave him plenty of time to talk himself into letting me stay. After a long pause and a few "Wells…" and "What ifs…" he granted me permission to register, but only on a provisional basis. "And," he admonished, "if you do not maintain at least a C average, you will not be allowed to continue."

I stood up, reached over his desk, flashed a broad smile, shook his hand, and thanked him. He scribbled a note on his official "from the desk of" pad and handed it to me. "Here, he muttered as if he were staying my execution, "Give this to the girls downstairs at the registration desk."

I took the note back outside to the registration tables and handed it to the assistant registrar. She smiled warmly, wrote my name at the bottom of her list, handed me my official registration papers along with an outline of courses for incoming freshmen, and I registered for a full load—four classes.

I was in: Donald A. Hussey, student number N-9728.

I walked over to the school library and picked up my books. I was so damn proud of myself. I had outwitted the dean and was now a college freshman!

The books were used "loaner" books that the university provided to students for a small fee. It was better than buying them full retail, I thought. I was told to turn them in after the quarter ended or lose the privilege next time. Southern Illinois University was on the quarter system, three quarters instead of two semesters. The fourth quarter was held in the summer for those who wanted to attend year-round. When classes began on Thursday, I drove from the motel to campus and parked my car on a narrow, tree-lined side street just around the corner from the library. I grabbed my books and headed for my very first class, English 101 with Dr. Regan. I was walking, dancing maybe, barely touching the ground, admiring the campus grounds, the brick and stone buildings, the many statues and the wooden benches sitting near a mix of oak and maple trees scattered throughout the campus. I wondered if these trees would produce a fall display as beautiful as those of my New England roots. I always loved the fall, the beauty of it all, the leaves dying off in brilliant glory.

I also wondered if I would fit in. I never had too much difficulty meeting people and making friends, so why would this be any different? Of greatest concern to me were my grades. Could I do the work? Keep up with the others? I was fully aware of the enormous gaps in my education.

I walked up three marble steps, entered the building, and stood in line with the others as we found seats in Dr. Regan's class. At twenty-one, I was older than the rest of the students. Most of them were seventeen or eighteen and had finished high school the previous June.

Dr. Regan was a young, short, good-looking man who was easy to like and easy to admire. He had been stricken with polio as a child and he made his way around the room on crutches, swinging his legs along behind him. It must have been difficult for him. But there he was, leaning on those crutches, teaching Freshman English with a doctorate in English Literature. I thought of my brother, Peter. Peter had been on crutches most of his young life, and I knew what a difficult time he had getting around.

I could not have been happier with myself. I was enrolled as a full-time student at a four-year university and my only responsibilities were to myself. I was free and far away from home. A new situation with new surroundings and new faces was something I was accustomed to. I would take my time and figure this out—a new and exciting experience, a new challenge. I was going to make the most of it.

The enormity and complexity of keeping it all together struck me rather quickly. Housing, food, clothes, my car, and of course, school. Money would be a problem, but I knew I'd find work—I always did.

Two or three weeks into the school year, I was having trouble settling into a consistent and predicable routine, and figured that maybe I was in way over my head. I thought about withdrawing as I dealt, and not very well, with the constant pressure and bouts of self-doubt.

I had never been a good reader having missed most of what was taught in high school. One day I stood on the sidewalk, staring across the lush-green front lawn in front of the Student Center, lost in my private thoughts. I realized I could walk along the red brick pathway, go downstairs to the book return window, turn in my books, and give it up. But I wasn't a quitter. I hadn't given up on or quit anything after leaving high school, and I had worked hard for the past year or more to finally be standing here. I walked over to a pay phone along the sidewalk and placed a call to my father. It was a workday. I was surprised he answered the phone. I told him where I was and that I was starting college, thinking he'd be proud, looking for some reassurance or support.

My father was living in the same house near Detroit with his second family. Without hesitating, he said, "What are you doing? That's not for you. Why don't you come live up here with us? I'll get you a good job at Ford. I have an 'in' over there."

I guess that's what I really needed to hear. Without realizing it, my father snapped me out of my hapless state. I wasn't going to live with him or settle for an entry-level job at Ford. "No thanks. I gotta do this," I fired back. He offered no reassurances or "'atta-boys." I didn't expect any...with expectations come disappointments, so I expected nothing and that's what I got.

I hung up the phone, checked the change return to see if any money came back, and went to class.

* * *

137

From the beginning, all members of the freshman class were encouraged to apply for a student activity scholarship. The only requirements to be considered for the scholarship were to be a full-time student, in good standing, and to be active on campus, which meant they wanted you to join clubs, work on campus, volunteer, and so on.

I recognized this for what it was: a great opportunity. So I went to the Student Center and signed up for the chess club. I had never played chess, but it intrigued me. Then I went over to the library and signed up for a part-time job filing books and cataloguing. I joined the Young Democrats Club, and then signed on to pledge a local fraternity. I said to myself, You want active? I'll give you active!

During this time, bulletins were posted around campus looking for students who might be interested in running for freshman class positions. I signed up for that as well by adding my name to the ballot to run for the Student Senate. Money was tight and was always of great concern to me. I really wanted that scholarship.

I was eventually awarded the Activity Scholarship and my tuition dropped to $39 per quarter. Looking back, I can hardly believe it. I was going to school for practically nothing. All I had to do was keep up this pace and do well in school.

Right from the beginning, I was quite popular. After all, I was the only student at SIU from the Boston area, where they "Paahk the caah in Haavid Yaahd." I was older, not the youngest any longer, and enjoying some welcomed respect for my age and experiences.

I met a girl in my English 101 class named Janice Gibson. She sat directly behind me, and I didn't really notice her until the third or fourth class. We were both waiting to speak with Dr. Regan after class one day. She waited for me as I finished up my conversation and we walked out together.

Janice was about five feet four inches tall, with shoulder-length strawberry-blond hair and soft, light brown eyes. I was attracted to her right away. She was shy and nervous and a little awkward around me, but had the most charming smile I'd ever seen. I even remember what she was wearing when we first met on that late September day as we walked out of Dr. Regan's class: a long purple coat with a matching beret tilted off to one side. Ahh, I said to myself, a little French girl; how nice. She wanted to know everything about me— my accent, my family, why I came way out here, and where I was living. We walked along and talked for some time. I told her about my background, and that I was of Scotch-Irish descent, and "Yankee." When she asked, I explained what Yankee meant. "According to my mother, my family has been in this country from the beginning...that is on my father's side," I said with no fanfare.

Now I wanted to know a little bit about her background, her heritage and where she lived. She thought for a moment and then said softly, "I'm from Edwardsville, about a twenty minute drive east of here. I'm mostly Irish and my full name is Janet Claudette Gibson. Claudette is after my grandmother, so I also have a little French in me, but I don't speak the language very well. Do you like my beret?" When we said good bye that day she turned and said, with a charming smile, "Bonjour, Au revoir," then laughed and hurried across the parking lot to her car. She was seventeen.

It wasn't long before I looked up her phone number and called to say hi. I never had much time for a girlfriend, but now I was looking around. Janice seemed perfect. Dr. Regan's class met twice a week, Tuesdays and Thursdays. After class, Janice and I waited for each other and I walked her to her car. One afternoon, when we arrived at her car, she turned and asked me for my phone number. She looked up at me with a warm, blushing smile and said, "You have my phone number, but I don't have yours. That's not fair." I told her I didn't have a phone.

I had moved out of the Chain of Rocks Motel and was now living in Alton, in the basement of a private home. I explained that I expected to move from there to an apartment with friends in downtown Alton, but not for a couple of weeks. Then I'd have my own phone. "So, in the meantime, I'll just call you," I said. She smiled and we said goodbye. It was never really goodbye; it was always, "See you later."

My basement apartment was located at 3404 Gillham Street in Alton. The owner, Dora Duncan, was an elderly grandmother type who rented rooms to pick up some extra income. She was a nice old lady who kept insisting I go to church with her some Saturday night.

She said she'd bake me an apple pie if I'd go. If she wanted me to go that bad, I figured what the hell, so I went.

The church service was held inside a towering white tent with rows and rows of folding chairs lined up on the grass. Additional chairs were set up outside to handle the overflow. The congregation consisted of a large gathering of Baptist folks, a couple hundred, I guessed, mostly from the local area. They were singing and hollering and stomping their feet, rolling and swaying, deep in celebration.

I really wasn't comfortable with this at all. I was, after all, a Catholic from Boston, where church services were in Latin, and were traditionally quiet and conservative, serious and solemn affairs attended by long faces. I wanted to excuse myself and wait outside, but I didn't.

As the service was coming to a close, the preacher called for silence. He extended his arms high into the air, looked up and appealed directly to the Heavens. "Let's praise the Lord for our blessings," he bellowed in a voice that could be heard across town. This must be Elmer Gantry himself, I thought.

Immediately following his speech, four young men, dressed in black suits, white shirts with black ties proceeded to the front and began working their way up the aisles with offering buckets. When one came to me, I dropped in a couple of quarters, trying to impress Granny. I didn't want to offend her by skipping out on the donation. I made sure she could hear the quarters as I dropped them in the bucket. She turned her head and gave me a little smile; she was pleased.

The cynic in me told me this overt appeal for money was so well orchestrated, so well rehearsed. I wasn't buying it. This was the last of that for me. On the way home, Granny said, "See how much fun we have? You should come every week."

"Thanks," I said. But I was all through with Elmer Gantry. She kept her promise and made me the apple pie.

I called Janice a couple of days later from a pay phone in downtown Alton. We talked for a long time. The telephone operator kept breaking in to remind me that my time was up. "To continue, please deposit an additional ten cents, thank you."

I kept feeding dimes into the change slot until Janice said, "I'd better let you go. This must be costing you a small fortune." I told her it was no big deal. Before she hung up, she said, "Oh, would you like to go on a hayride...mon ami? It's next Saturday night. Would you like to go?"

I told her I'd never been on a hayride before but added, "It sounds like fun...and yes, I'd love to go." She filled me in on what to expect and gave me directions to her house. "Okay," I said, "I'll pick you up at six. See you then." I hung up the phone and drove home. I never mentioned the "mon ami," but thought it was very charming...a nice touch to a warm conversation. A hayride, I said to myself. That's a first. Should be fun.

There was a full harvest moon that Saturday night as the horse-drawn wagon loaded with hay made its way along a dusty dirt road and out into the cornfields. The corn had been harvested days before, and the remaining stalks were beginning to wither and turn a golden brown. Twelve or more of us were hanging all over the wagon as the horse walked us slowly through the fields. Someone had a guitar, and we began singing songs and drinking beer. I sat on the back gate of the wagon with Janice, our legs hanging over the side. It was a beautiful time, our first date.

Janice was from Edwardsville, a middle-class community with a population of nearly 20,000 about fifteen miles east of the Mississippi. She'd spent her whole life there, graduating from Edwardsville High School in June of 1964. At seventeen, I thought she was a little young for me. But everyone, it seemed, was seventeen or eighteen, right out of high school. She would turn eighteen in November.

Right from the start, I was impressed with everything about her. She was brilliant, intuitive, and had a warm and inviting personality. She wrote beautifully and had a well-developed vocabulary. Even Dr. Regan was impressed. Janice wrote with her left hand, and that mystified me. I'd ever met a left-handed person in all my travels. I'd watch her write and wonder how she could write so beautifully with her hair flowing onto the paper, being held away by her right hand. Her cursive writing style slanted to the left, the opposite of anything I was familiar with. It was beautiful. And, without realizing it, she helped me fill in the many blanks of my limited vocabulary and spotty education.

In addition to knowing a little French, Janice also knew a lot of what I called "fancy" words. I would say, "There you go again with another one of your seventy-five-cent words." She laughed at all of my silly jokes and I loved to hear her laugh. Some leftover adolescent acne embarrassed her, but that didn't matter to me. I'd had more than my fair share of that when I was younger.

Janice lived with her mother, her brother Walter, affectionately known as Wally, and her sister Diane in a small six-room, one-story bungalow on Brockmeier Road. She also had another sister, Bridget, who was married and living in Georgia with her husband, Dave, and their two young sons.

Janice was the youngest member of the family. The only other member was a small, noisy little dog named Max. Max didn't like me at first; he didn't like anyone at first. He would settle down after a while and give me permission to enter his world and even allowed me to pat him.

Janice's father, Thomas, had died of cancer suddenly when she was only ten years old. He had worked for the Illinois Central Railroad and was on a business trip to Chicago when he suddenly began bleeding from the nose while walking to a meeting. He must have died a short time later. Her mother, at fifty-six, was left to raise her four children on his railroad pension.

On our second date, two weeks later, I invited Janice to the movies. *My Fair Lady* was playing in St. Louis, and I knew it would be a perfect movie for our first formal date. I was nicely dressed in my sport coat, tie and shined shoes. When I arrived, I walked up the concrete steps and knocked at the front door. When Janice opened the door, I said, "Hi there, Sunshine, ready to go?" She invited me in and introduced me to her mother, who was sitting across the living room in a light blue velvet high back chair, next to the fireplace. Mrs. Gibson remained seated as I walked over and shook her hand. I knew right away where Janice got her charming smile and sweet disposition.

From that moment on I referred to Janice as my Sunshine. She lit up my life, and I let her know it.

One day after class as we walked across the street to the student center, I told her I was beginning my campaign for the Student Senate. She was surprised and excited for me and asked if she could help. I didn't have to ask her, she asked me. "Thanks, that would be great," I said. My plan was to print some flyers and pass them out all over campus. She said she and a couple of her friends could design and print the flyers. "Would you like us to handle that? We could get started today." We agreed on what the flyers should say, and in two days she and her friends had hundreds of them ready to hand out.

I didn't know anything about running for elective office, but it seemed pretty obvious, just meet and converse with as many students as possible and perhaps give a few speeches leading up to Election Day. The main thing was to convince everyone that I wanted the job, was willing to commit to it, and would serve effectively.

One week before Election Day, I drove to the Carbondale campus where I passed out flyers at the Student Center and the cafeteria. I was stumping for votes, making speeches, shaking hands and loving it. I was on the campaign trail. While I worked the crowds in Carbondale, Janice and a couple of her friends stood all afternoon passing out flyers at the Student Center in Alton. It was an exciting time for both of us; I was on my way to winning my first political campaign.

When the election results for Student Senate were posted, I found out I had been elected. Before long I was asked to serve as Chairman of the Public Relations Committee, to act as a liaison between the university and the community.

How about that? I thought.

Janice and I found jobs together in the school book binding and cataloguing facility. The one-story wooden building had been converted from an old schoolhouse, and was located down a dirt road in the middle of nowhere. Plans for the new library were still in the hands of the architect.

Still money was always tight. The library job didn't pay much and I was running out of the savings I had brought with me from home. I stopped by the Student Aid office one day and picked up an application form for benefits under the G.I. bill. After spending four years in the military, I figured I was eligible. The G.I. bill offered veterans a monthly allowance while attending college. To qualify, veterans had to have served at least two years on active duty, be honorably discharged and be enrolled on a full-time basis at an accredited college or university. Academically, students under the G.I. bill had to maintain a 2.0 grade point, a C average.

It wasn't long before I began receiving $96 a month from the Veterans Administration. It was enough to pay my rent and other living expenses with a few bucks left over.

What a time I was having. I was passing all my classes, getting invited to parties on campus and off and had some money in my pocket and a great girlfriend. I would walk with her on campus, books under my arm, kicking up the leaves and just feeling wonderful. Janice and I met between classes, went for coffee and then headed for the library, sometimes to study and sometimes to work.

I couldn't do anything wrong. It was all falling into place for me.

Thanksgiving was coming, and the leaves were all dressed up in full color. SIU was a perfect place for me, a small campus with about two thousand students. It was a commuter college; student housing was years away. There was a quaint, small-town feeling about the area, almost like the small New England towns back home, and just a short distance from the "Mighty Mississippi." Growing up in the Boston area, I had been around or near the water most of my life, and the Mississippi gave me the sense that I was not somehow landlocked.

In the middle of October, I left Granny's place and moved into a second-floor apartment with a couple of friends. The apartment was a yellow two-story house on a small side street, halfway up a hill in downtown Alton. Judson Street, number 2305.

One Saturday afternoon in mid-November, there was a knock at the downstairs door. It was Janice. We hadn't hooked up a phone as yet, so she drove all the way from Edwardsville to see me. I was pretty surprised and excited to see her.

"Hi there, Kid, nice to see you," I said. "How'd you ever find this place?"

She smiled and replied, "It wasn't hard. I just came by to ask you if you had any plans for Thanksgiving."

Thanksgiving was the following week, and I already had an invitation from Granny to spend the day with her. Granny really liked me and we had stayed in touch. I knew what was coming, though, so I lied. "No, I don't have any plans." Janice asked if I would like to come to her house and spend Thanksgiving with her and her family. What could I do? Without hesitating, I said, "Sure, I'd love to."

I figured I'd somehow find a way to bow out on Granny. Sorry, I would say, but I really like this girl very much.

Granny wasn't happy with me when I told her. "You got a better offer, eh?" she said with a knowing look. I bought some flowers for her table and hoped she wouldn't be too upset. She smiled when I gave her the flowers and said, "You have a nice time now, and don't you worry about me. I'll be just fine. Tell your young lady friend I said hello. You're a nice boy; she's a lucky one."

I was delighted that Janice had invited me for Thanksgiving. I dressed up for the occasion in a sport coat, white shirt and tie, and my shined shoes. The table was beautifully set with a white linen tablecloth and a fall bouquet in the center with white candles on either side. White dinner plates and silverware were set out for five people with napkins and holders at each setting. Two freshly-baked pies, one apple and the other pumpkin, sat on the kitchen counter, cooling. The warm, inviting aroma of a Thanksgiving dinner reminded me of home.

When dinner was ready, Janice removed the fall bouquet from the center of the table and Wally brought the steaming hot, golden brown turkey in from the kitchen. He held it up so everyone could see, and then gently set it down in the center of the table. Janice's mother began placing bowls of piping hot white corn, mashed potatoes, and freshly cut green beans around the table. I offered to give her a hand, but Wally, Janice and Diane were all the help she needed. She said, "No, no, good heavens, we'll take care of it. You're our guest, so please have a seat right over there next to Janice."

Wally gave me a smile as he worked the cork free from a bottle of champagne. He placed a small linen napkin over the cork to contain it as it popped from the bottle, then walked around the table with a white waiter's cloth draped over his arm, filling each of our glasses and bowing his head along the way—a classy, well-dressed man who seemed to enjoy the formality and elegance of the occasion.

Janice was on my left and Wally sat to her left at the head of the table. Diane was across from me. Janice's mother sat to my right on the other end. We folded our hands as Diane said grace. Then we lift-ed our champagne glasses in a toast. Everything was delicious. The turkey was perfect, and the apple pie finished me off.

What a wonderful day. Each of them made me feel as though I was a member of the family. Admittedly, I was relieved that there was no father figure at the table, staring me down or watching my every move as I ate or attempted to enter the conversation. I had had enough of that when I was young. Through conversations at the table though, and conversations later that day, it became obvious to me that Janice's father had been a loving parent and a wonderful husband. They all missed him, especially during the holidays.

Janice's mother, Gloria, was a delight. That's the only word that comes to my mind when I think of her. She was a charming, beautiful woman who looked and acted much younger than her age. Her light blue eyes fluttered and twinkled when she laughed, then she'd glance off to the side and start all over again. She obviously loved her family, and she graciously welcomed me into her home.

Wally was much older than either Janice or Diane. He was a well-read, well-spoken and highly-educated man, a Rhodes Scholar with a quiet disposition. He taught English Literature at a high school not far away, and had become the breadwinner of the family after his fa-ther died. Wally never married, so between his salary and his father's railroad pension, they were comfortable.

Diane was a year older than Janice and had stunningly beauti-ful, dark brown hair that flowed halfway down her back. Like her mother and her sister, she was another real charmer.

Diane had been hurt in a terrible head-on collision a few years before I met Janice. She was riding in the passenger side front seat and Wally was driving. They were on a long, country road not far from home when someone came around a bend and drifted into their lane. Diane was thrown through the windshield and out onto the road. Her head and face were badly injured. The plastic surgeons, though, had performed a near miracle repairing and reconstructing her face and neck. Wally had escaped with lesser injuries. I wouldn't have known any of this if Janice hadn't told me.

At the point when dinner was finished and desserts were about to be served, Wally, without saying a word, stood and excused himself from the table, and then went to his room. Janice turned and whispered to me, "I think he's having another one of his throbbing migraines." I had never known anyone who suffered these blistering headaches. In fact, I had never heard the word "migraine" before. Apparently, Wally's headaches had worsened after the accident, becoming more frequent and more intense.

After a piece of warm apple pie, Janice and I went for a walk around the neighborhood. She pointed out each of the houses of people she knew. Directly across the street lived her best friend in the whole world, Amy Yolanda. They had been through school together right from the beginning. Janice and her family had moved from Elm Street, a block away, to Brockmeier Road following her father's death. We walked to the Lutheran Church at the top of the street, then turned around and walked back. It was a serene setting on a beautifully crisp, fall afternoon.

When we arrived back at Janice's house, she went into her bedroom and came out with a picture of Amy and herself. It was a picture of the two of them standing on Janice's front porch, all dressed up for Easter—two adorable ten-year-old little girls growing up in Middle America.

After I thanked Janice's family and said goodbye, we walked outside to my car. I gave her a kiss and said, "Thank you, I've had a really nice time. I'll see you at school." It was dark by the time I arrived back in Alton. I was happy with the way things were working out for me.

* * *

Matt Ryder was one of my roommates on Judson Street. He was majoring in Biology, and sometimes he would bring some of his "homework" home to show me. One morning I woke up and, half asleep, walked out to the kitchen to have some breakfast before getting ready for class. There, right in the middle of the kitchen table, was a fetal pig—a small, dead pig. It was just lying there on waxed paper, looking up at me, on the damn kitchen table, part of a lab experiment from one of Matt's classes. He had left it there overnight and forgot to bring it to class that morning.

Matt was the kind of guy who would forget where he left his shoes. He was always going off in several different directions at once, usually at a hundred miles an hour. He was thin and had a full head of thick, reddish hair. When he talked, he would sort of dance, shifting from one foot to the other, always with a big grin plastered across his young face. He'd talk so fast, I was always saying, "What?"

Matt was a really friendly, good-natured guy who willingly pitched in with the household chores. We got along great. He was dating a girl at school named Shyla—an unusual name, I thought.

Matt drove a red sports car, a Triumph TR-3. We rode around all over town with the top down. I bought a small ukulele and would strum away, as we drove around campus, pretending I could play the thing.

I was loving every minute. A couple of college kids, I thought. 'How great is this!'

Christmas 1964 was three weeks away. The quarter would be ending and I was planning to drive home to spend the holidays with my mother, brother and Joe. What was left of my family would be getting together at my great grandfather's house, now my great aunt's house, in Norwell.

I bought Janice and her mother something for Christmas, a "Mamas and Papas" album and a dozen yellow roses. I chose yellow roses because they were bursting with sunshine. They loved them. I felt at home there, like part of their family. I loved Janice's mother almost as much as I loved Janice. I had a nickname for her as well. I called

148

her Snowflakes. It was snowing the day I brought the gifts over, and "Snowflakes" just popped out of my mouth.

My buddy from New York, Mike Kaplan, and I, along with the guy next door who lived in Connecticut, rode in my car back to New England. We drove straight through, each taking a turn at the wheel. When I dropped Mike off in New York, he invited me in to meet his parents, Dotty and Harry.

Harry was smoking a large cigar when he answered the door. "Come in, come in," he said. Mike introduced me. I shook hands with his father and said hello to his mother, who said, "I've heard so much about you. It's nice to finally meet you."

Mike took me downstairs to show me his bachelor pad, which was set up with a leather couch, a new refrigerator, a king-sized bed, an antique Wurlitzer juke box loaded with 45s, and a fully stocked bar. Mike had been living down there before going off to school and planned to return after graduation.

I left Mike's place and maneuvered my way through Brooklyn to the highway. Driving around and through Brooklyn, New York was not easy. Everyone seemed familiar with the roads and in a mad rush—everyone except me. But I took my time, stayed out of the way and ignored the horns.

The holidays went fine; it was good to see everyone—a time to reflect on the past and think about the future. But I missed Janice, especially on New Years' Eve.

Mike and I made the return trip to Illinois together. My buddy from Connecticut didn't return with us. School wasn't for him. He decided to stay in Connecticut and raise quarter horses with his grandfather who had begun the breeding business back in the 1920s.

Mike was the only other guy attending SIU from the east coast. He once told me he decided to go to school out there because it was far away from the city, yet close enough to get home when he wanted. He became a very close friend. Mike was a Jewish kid who grew up in the Flatbush section of Brooklyn, on East 26th Street, near Marine Park. We got along very well, even though he was an opinionated pain in the ass most of the time. I over-looked much of that, figuring that's the way it is in New York City.

Mike lived in an apartment in Wood River, an industrial community halfway between Alton and Edwardsville. Wood River was largely dependent on several nearby oil and gas refineries. The air was suffocating most of the time. The choking, noxious smell from the flame-lit stacks hung heavy in the air during the warm summer months. The yellowish-brown air mass was especially noticeable at sunset. I roomed with Mike for a short time, maybe three months. We shared a three-bedroom apartment in the basement of a yellow-brick, four-story building, with our other roommate, Danny O'Brien.

Danny, Mike and I, and a couple of other guys, played cards about once a month at his place. Mike was a good poker player, and would get angry if I or anyone else "called" him when he was bluffing. He would say to me, "What the hell are you calling me for? You've got nothing."

Funny thing was, my "nothing" often beat his "nothing," and that would piss him off.

There was something about Mike that I really liked. He had a quick wit, was fast-talking and self-assured, and spoke with a strong New York, Jewish accent. He was a kid from the city, the big city, and that fascinated me. Most of my years growing up were spent in small rural towns south of Boston.

Mike was a full member of the fraternity during my pledge period. The majority of the pledges in my group feared him the most. They hung him in effigy on a branch of a tree just outside the front entrance to the Student Center. The figure was constructed out of sticks and straw, and stuffed inside a large T-shirt with *NEW YORK* written in black marker on both sides. The whole thing was taped together to look like a small man with short legs. It hung off a low tree branch, swinging in the breeze, all day long.

Everyone in the fraternity knew who it was. Most everyone at school knew who it was. The campus newspaper photographer snapped a picture of it and printed it on the front page of the school paper that week.

One day in the spring of '66, after classes were over for the day, we met up at the Stonehouse Tavern, another college hangout in Edwardsville. Mike had lost some big money in a poker game at Sammy's Restaurant the night before. The local guys at Sammy's would gamble after hours in the back room every Thursday night. Mike knew the owner and would usually join in. Sammy's was about a mile away on Main Street in Edwardsville.

"Hussey," he said, "you have any money?"

"I've got about $200 left. If you need it, you got it," I said.

He needed it, so I went to the bank and drew out the money and gave it to him. "You've saved my ass," he said. "I'll pay you back." I told him not to worry about it.

Mike helped me land a job selling stereo sound systems house-to-house. This was a cold canvas sales job working for a company known as Marquette Sound Systems. I drove around neighborhoods, knocking on doors, trying to sell sound systems to prospective buyers. I would offer to set up the system in their home and demonstrate the extraordinary stereophonic sound in the hopes of making a sale. The sound from that system, which could be adjusted to balance the music across the room was quite remarkable for its time.

After selling three units to friends in the first week, my sales dried up. I continued on for another two weeks, spending money on gas and wasting my time. I didn't make another sale after those original three, so I bought my "demo" system from the company at a discounted price and hauled it over to Janice's house where I set it up in her living room.

I was always kidding Mike about his matzo balls, gefilte fish, and lox and bagels. Words I'd never heard before. And food I'd never tasted.

He called me Husseystein. "You'd make a good Jew," he once said to me.

On another one of our trips back east, I stayed a few days with him at his parents' home in Brooklyn. I was invited to a family function and met most of his extended family, including a couple of his uncles who bore tattooed numbers on the inside of their left forearms. The numbers were stenciled there by the Nazis while his uncles were imprisoned in German concentration camps during World War II. When I saw those ink black numbers, I bristled. It shocked me. These were some of the most wonderful, welcoming people I had ever met.

I never asked any questions and they never talked about it. On the way home, Mike said, "Did you see the numbers?" I told him I did. That was all. He never mentioned it again.

How could any of that have happened? I thought. It was one thing to read about those atrocities, but entirely another to look into the eyes and touch the hands of someone who had lived through it and somehow survived. I thought about that for the rest of that day… and have thought about it ever since. It was hard for me to believe that God allowed such a thing to happen, that he hadn't intervened sooner. It's simply beyond my comprehension.

Mike received a draft notice right after graduation. Ironically, the Army had instituted a draft lottery system the week before. As it turned out, his draft lottery number was 352, one of the highest numbers. With a number that high, he would not have been drafted. But as luck would have it, he had already been drafted before the new system had been implemented, and was ordered to report to Fort Gordon, Georgia, for basic training. He once told me he could have argued the point, but decided it was fate and kept quiet about it.

After Basic, he shipped out as a member of the 5th Infantry Division to the Quang Tri Province of Vietnam. The Quang Tri Province was on the Demilitarized Zone (DMZ), an area about a mile wide on either side of the Ben Hai River, along the 17th parallel. The DMZ was established for the purpose of separating the two opposing forces—the North Vietnamese/Viet Cong, and the South Vietnamese/U.S. Forces, a no-man's land. Quang Tri was obliterated during the relentless bombing campaigns in the late 60s and early '70s. It was the scene of the heaviest and fiercest fighting of the war.

I received a letter from Mike dated 29 Sept., 1969 from Army APO S.F. 5th Inf. 96477. Inside the envelope was a brief note and a check for $200. He was paying me back the money I had loaned him in the Stonehouse two years earlier.

His letter surprised me. I had lost track of him after the fall of '68. I had been struggling through some tough times personally, and never even knew he was sent to Vietnam, and that bothered me. I had forgotten about the money long before. Somehow, he made it through that hellhole. We've kept in touch all these years.

SEVEN

Chicago Press #42865

In the spring of 1965, the harsh, blistery winds and relentless snow of the Midwestern winters were a nearly forgotten memory. Janice and I had bundled up each morning and braved the long walks in from the parking lot. The bitter winter winds were always in your face as if to say, "If you want that degree, you've got to get past me first."

By spring though, the weather was improving. Even St. Patrick's Day, usually damp and cold back home, was balmy and drenched in sunlight. I was halfway through the third quarter of my freshman year at Southern Illinois University, and it seemed as though everyone on campus was planning to take part in the upcoming annual Spring Festival. Many of the festival activities had been sponsored and supported by the membership of the fraternity I belonged to. Each of us pledged our time to help make this event a success. In addition to setting up chairs, working the refreshment stands and emptying the trash, we staged a series of comedy routines which were as much fun for us as for the audience. Tommy Carmichael was the organizer, the choreographer—the man in charge. He was short and stout, and had a full head of thick, bushy brown hair that helped round out his full face. Tommy was a full-time student at SIU and a fraternity member. He was in his late twenties, older than the rest of us. Earlier in his life, he had been a priest or was somehow involved with the Catholic Church.

Everyone who knew Tommy loved him for his warmth and humanity. His rehearsal sessions lasted for hours. We practiced songs and rehearsed a rich variety of comedy skits. Every one of his rehearsals started with his favorite song, "You'll Never Walk Alone." It was an inspirational song that must have held some personal meaning for him. "When you walk through the rain, hold your head up high…walk on through the rain, walk on through the storm…."

Tommy would be upset with us for clowning around during rehearsals, and that made it all the more hilarious. The expressions—contortions—on his face when he was angry just added to the fun. He'd eventually join in and have a good laugh himself along with the rest of us. There were twenty-five or thirty of us on stage the night of the Festival performance, belting out songs and playacting to a warmly receptive, packed house. From our perspective, we were having the most fun of any group on campus, as each of us inched our way, one class at a time, toward our respective degrees.

The most memorable act carried out on stage that night was a comedy riotously performed by my roommate, Matt Ryder, and another friend, Charlie Feeney. Dressed for a night on the town, they threw open the curtains and sashayed out onto the stage. Matt was tall and thin and handsomely dressed in his long-tailed black tuxedo with matching tie, while Charlie—huge Charlie—was dolled up in an impressive, big-breasted woman's gown with makeup all over his large round face, a grin breaking at the seams. They made a beautiful couple as they waltzed across the stage, arm in arm, singing and dancing to something perfectly ridiculous. The audience was howling.

Janice and I had signed up to compete in the first ever Spring Festival Canoe Race the next morning. The university had recently purchased eight two-seated mahogany canoes. On the day of the race, the canoes were lined up next to one another, side-by-side between the two finger piers that jutted out into the water. The piers were parallel to each other, spaced about sixty feet apart—plenty of room to line up the eight canoes.

The course was well marked. We had to paddle out and around two buoy markers located straight ahead, about fifty yards from the dock, then round the markers and sprint for home. It was a relatively short distance and a simple course. I figured there was nothing difficult here, and we should do well.

Janice and I climbed into our sleek, pre-assigned, highly polished canoe. We were in the best position, the right inside lane next to the pier. I figured we had a better than even chance of winning. All we had to do was get off to a fast start, pull out in front, block the others, and walk away with this.

We strapped on our mandatory lifejackets over our bathing suits and climbed down the wooden ladder attached to the pier. I stepped in first and steadied the craft while Janice settled herself up front. She would paddle on the port (left) side, and I would take the starboard, steering from the rear. I had it all figured out.

The eight teams were seated and itching for the start. All was at the ready. Janice glanced nervously back at me over her left shoulder and said, "I'm not too sure about this," then flashed an uncertain grin as she positioned her paddle in the water. A long rope, threaded through the eyehooks on the bow of each canoe, was stretched across the channel and attached to each of the piers. The rope kept the canoes aligned until just before the starter's gun split the air.

The race official began counting back from ten. At zero, he yanked the rope through the eyehooks and "bang"—we were off. All eight canoes lurched forward with water flying in every direction, madness followed by more madness.

We barely cleared the dock when Janice suddenly disappeared overboard, off to the left and into the dark and chilly water. I didn't know it at the time, but she couldn't swim and the lifejacket wasn't getting it done. She was thrashing about, trying to catch hold of the boat. I reached down into the dark water, grabbed her by the hair, and pulled her up next to the boat. I began shouting, "Hold on, Janice, just hold on." She was scared and blue-lipped as she wrapped her right arm around the left side gunnel. I quickly swung the boat around to the pier. "Don't tip the thing over, just hold on." I kept reassuring her that I had everything under control. When I came to the pier, I held her hand up to the ladder and called out, "Give us a hand here!" One of the officials, who was standing over us by now, reached down and helped her up and onto the dock.

I climbed the ladder to the dock and gave Janice a big squeeze to calm her down. She was shivering nonstop. I asked, "Why didn't you tell me you couldn't swim? I never would have talked you into this."

She shyly explained, "I was too embarrassed to tell you. Besides, I had my lifejacket on. That should have been enough." She was standing on the dock soaking wet, shivering, and red-faced with embarrassment. I unbuckled the wet straps of her lifejacket and helped her wiggle out of it.

"Just wait right here," I told her. "I'll grab some towels from the cart so you can dry off."

We waved goodbye to our amused friends, and made our way over to my car. Janice was wrapped up in several towels, trying to keep warm. I turned the heater on full blast and drove her home. With a nervous sigh of relief, she shivered out the words, "I need a long hot bath and some dry clothes."

Later that evening we attended the Spring Festival fraternity party, where we were the center of attention; lots of fun-loving, animated jokes that were hilarious.

When school let out for the summer, several of us drove down to a lake in the Arkansas Ozarks for an all-day and most-of-the-night picnic: swimming, drinking beer, and cooking over an open fire on the beach. When the warm afternoon sun dropped below the horizon, pastel shades of red and gold lit up the heavens, setting the evening sky ablaze. As early evening turned into nighttime, the nearly full moon peeked through the trees at the far end of the lake. Moonlight splashed over the lake, exposing the silent ripples of gently moving water. We sat together at the end of the dock admiring the wonders of nature, reflecting on the serenity of the moment.

Dick Wilcox was sitting across from me on the other side of the dock, with his feet dangling in the crystal-clear water. Suddenly, he turned around and announced to everyone that he was going skinny-dipping. "What do you think? Anyone want to join me?" We all laughed and looked at him a little puzzled. This was not like Wilcox. He was the least adventurous of any of us. It must have been the beer.

I spoke right up. "That's a great idea, Dickie. I'm game." Before anyone could catch their breath or have second thoughts, I stood up, jumped in, and thrashed around under water, removing my bathing suit. I held it up and began waving it over my head as if to challenge the others. I threw it up onto the dock and hollered out, "You mean like that, Dickie boy?"

A burst of laughter echoed across the lake as the girls bolted back up the dock to the safety of the shore. I had caught Wilcox by surprise; he was bent over laughing. I told him, "Okay, now it's your turn. Don't fink out on me now." He and Gary jumped in and we swam around in the buff, enjoying our new found freedom and taking leave of our inhibitions. The girls, giggling nonstop, ran back down the dock, grabbed our bathing suits and ran back to the car, jumping in and locking all the doors. They left the towels about halfway down the dock, just far enough from us to be a problem. Grinning like an embarrassed schoolboy, I discreetly climbed the ladder and, covering myself, walked up the dock until I reached the towels, thankful for the darkness. I spread the towels around to Gary and Dick, and we walked back to the car. The girls, still laughing uncontrollably, rolled down the window and tossed the bathing suits out. We dried off and dressed behind a couple of trees near the shoreline. That was a night to remember. We laughed about it all the way home.

I decided to stay in Illinois that summer and called my mother to tell her I'd found a good paying job in St. Louis. Mike Kaplan had asked me if I wanted to spend the summer with him in Las Vegas, because his uncle was well connected and could easily find us jobs. I told him I wanted to stay in Illinois and spend my free time with Janice. So Mike drove to Vegas and I stayed behind.

While sitting in a far corner of the library one afternoon in May, studying for a final exam or taking notes for a paper, I glanced through the long tall window in front of me onto the campus grounds below. This was my favorite place to study, up on the second floor and hidden behind rows and rows of bookshelves—the quietest place in the library. I spent the entire afternoon up there, studying and daydreaming about my past, thinking about how lucky I was to have come this far. I had established myself at school, found some peace, and was about as happy as I could imagine. I had never been a selfish guy. I always seemed to be looking out for the other guy. And now, for the first time, and without guilt, I could be the other guy.

My mind was free to enjoy school and the balance of my youth. Janice and I were growing closer and sharing both the happy times and the challenges of college life. She was becoming the love of my life and I was loving my life. One day I would beat the odds and graduate, land a great job, marry Janice, and start a family of my own. I'd ride this all the way to the last stop. Nothing, or no one, would stand in my way.

I began my summer job at the Hussman Refrigeration Plant on the other side of the Mississippi, in Missouri. It was a Thursday, June 30, 1965. They assigned me to the afternoon shift which ran from 3:30 to midnight. I had arrived early to sign some papers, meet my boss, and fill out my time card.

The plant, in the old industrial section across the river from East St. Louis, was a small steel mill with a machine shop, fork trucks, overhead cranes, racks of freshly milled steel and a workforce of hardened men—working men who went about their business not saying very much. It was a miserably dirty place. The heavy smell of raw, molten steel and black dust filled the air and clogged your senses. It was a busy place with foremen pointing fingers and bellowing commands above the endless noise.

This was a union shop: Sheet Metal Workers, Local Union No. 93. The pay was good and I figured I'd have plenty of money in the bank by the end of summer, maybe enough to carry me through for much of the next year. I'd be back working in the school library when September came along. I was in good shape, had it all planned out.

On the first day the shop steward, the union boss, approached me and said, "We'll be watching you. If you're still here after a month, we'll let you in the union." Joining the union was mandatory, but only after thirty days and only after a satisfactory performance review.

It was a production job with a quota system that involved feeding flat steel plates between the die stops of a six-ton Chicago punch press. The downward motion of the upper die would begin descending as soon as the operator stepped on the foot pedal, which was at-

160

tached to the base of the machine. The more pressure applied to the pedal, the faster the descent. When the two dies closed, or came together, they would bend, flatten or otherwise configure the inserted steel. The upper dye would then recycle back to the up position.

The machines were massive, standing about seven feet tall and about six feet wide. The manufacturer's trademark was boldly affixed on the face—*CHICAGO*—followed by a five digit number stamped in the upper right-hand corner.

I was assigned to press number 42865. There were two rows of these mammoth machines, with five or six machines in each row, all in constant motion and manned by older men who were seasoned in their trade—men who knew what they were doing.

On my first day, I was given a brief training session on the operation of the machine and told what my responsibilities were—what they expected of me. The foreman wheeled over a full rack of flat steel plates neatly stacked on a metal cart. Each plate was about three feet long and about five inches wide, and no more than a quarter-inch thick. My job was to stand in front of the press, reach over into the cart, which was parked to my right, grab one of the plates, and then slide it between the open jaws of the press until it rested lengthwise against the rear stops of the lower dye.

After setting the steel in place, I was instructed to pull my hands out from in between the dyes and step on the metal foot pedal. The foot pedal acted as a clutch which activated the downward motion of the upper die. The momentum wheel, attached to the right side of the machine, was continuously spinning, like the flywheel in a car, but nothing would happen until the clutch was activated. The wheel was just that, a large cast iron wheel about three feet in diameter. Once engaged, the upper die would begin its descent and impact the inserted steel, bending or cutting each piece to the preset specifications.

Once the dies were fully separated, I would step off the pedal, reach in between the dies, remove the newly configured piece of steel and place it in the empty rack to my left. As soon as I finished one rack, the foreman would wheel over another load—a continuous operation.

Above: S.I.U. Spring Festival Canoe Race, May 1965.

Left and below: S.I.U. Spring Festival Talent Show, May 1965. (Courtesy S.I.U. Alumni Archives).

Above: Student protest. Outhouse on campus grounds, spring 1968. Woman in photo is unknown. (Courtesy: S.I.U Alumni Archives).

Below: Downtown Edwardsville. Site of jury trial, 1971.

Jimmy Vanzo at Vanzo's Tavern.
(Courtesy: Edwardsville Intelligencer Newspaper, Edwardsville, IL.)

It was almost midnight on July 5, 1965, my third night on the job. As I fed another piece of steel into Chicago press number 42865, I turned my head to the right to check the time. The old gray, industrial shop clock was hanging from a nearby support column, held in place by a coat hanger and tilting a little to the right. The clock was covered with years of steel dust and grime, as was everything else in that place. In a few minutes I would punch out and head back across the river to join my roommates for a much anticipated party.

It was a Monday night. My shift was coming to an end, and I knew my numbers were good. I felt satisfied the boss would approve. If I kept this up, I figured the union would let me stay.

I was working too fast, trying to finish the last rack of steel and end the night on a good note. I had the routine down flat, coordinating every move for maximum speed. Grab a piece of steel from the bin to my right, slide it into the lower die, push it up against the stops, step on the pedal, watch the dyes close to impact the steel, remove it from the dye, and throw it into the bin to my left. It was a simple, one- two- three- four- five-step operation, with coordinated motions, repetitive and monotonous—over and over, faster and faster. Only a few minutes to quitting time. It would be nice to finish the whole rack before I left for the night. They would be impressed.

It happened in an instant. The upper die came down and grabbed me—grabbed my hands, both of them. My eyes shut...then opened. I looked down and up, then down again. I opened my mouth. No sound came out. I finally managed a slight, barely audible moan.

Wild, screaming thoughts raced through my brain. I felt helplessly caught. I didn't dare move or even try to move. The momentum wheel continued spinning, humming along at the usual rate, a simple, mindless machine with no conscience and no emotion. It would spin and hum forever until someone shut it down. I could hear the slipping clutch and quickly released my foot from the pedal. It was too late.

The upper die had closed on my hands. I knew my fingers had been crushed, maybe parts of my hands as well. I wasn't sure. But I knew I was badly hurt. I stood there motionless, frozen in place. "How bad is it?" I mumbled. "How bad?" I kept moaning. No screaming, just a barely audible, "Ohh, ohh, ohh." I squeezed my eyes shut as hard as I could. I was frightened and struggling mightily with the pain. I was losing consciousness, caught in the jaws of a steel trap, like an animal in the wild. I was twenty-two years old.

I stood there muttering. I heard someone say, "For chrissake, grab him! Hold him! This is going to take me a few minutes…and give me that goddamn wrench!"

I felt my legs weaken and begin to buckle from the shock and the screaming pain. Someone rushed over, came up behind me and put his arms under mine to keep me from dropping to the floor. I hung on to every word. "I've got to switch gears and cycle this up by hand." I didn't know if he was talking to me or to the others, or talking himself through the motions, thinking it through out loud. Every word was burning into my brain. The momentum of the wheel had caused the dies to close when the foot pedal was activated. It had stopped spinning by now, and the dyes were locked together. The man climbed up on a small step stool and struggled with the heavy Stillson wrench, finally locking it around a bolt or a fitting, and began turning it. Seconds later he handed the wrench off to someone standing next to him, then reached up over his head and gripped the wheel with both hands. As he began rotating the heavy wheel, the upper die slowly began to lift. He kept looking down at me over his left shoulder as he worked the wheel, sweat dripping from his forehead. I remember him talking to me in a cracking, anxious voice. "I'll get you out of this, kid. Not much longer. Just hold on!"

His name was Paul Stuckenscheider, the man in charge of our shift. He worked feverishly to free me, and gave me confidence I would make it to the hospital. Nobody else spoke to me. Nobody else said a word.

I was trying to tough it out. The heavy duty gloves I was wearing had been cleanly severed. I couldn't look down…but I did. I raised my head. I wouldn't look down again. The last piece of steel I had inserted had been impacted by the die and was twisted and embedded in both my hands. As soon as the dyes were separated enough, they lifted me away from the machine and dragged me over to a stretcher that someone had laid out on the cold concrete floor next to the foreman's office.

There was no first-aid kit, no morphine, nothing to ease my helpless, wretched state. "The ambulance is on the way," someone assured me. Then someone else said, "I'll scrape his fingers off the die, stick 'em in this envelope and send them along with him in the ambulance."

Someone walked over and laid a blanket over me and gently placed the envelope on my chest. I lay there with my eyes wide and watery, looking up at the soot covered, gray cement ceiling, waiting for the ambulance. I took only quick, short breaths now. Deep breaths caused me greater pain, and I was sick with the pain. "Where's the ambulance?" I mumbled to someone standing over me, my head snapping back and forth. No one answered. I closed my eyes, hoping I would get to the hospital before I lost consciousness.

Still, no one spoke to me. No one spoke at all. These were tough guys. Not callous, tough.

Off in the distance, I could hear the wailing of the approaching ambulance. I thought to myself, Not much longer, just count the seconds. Louder now as it approached the front of the building and wheeled around to the rear loading dock. The flashing lights streamed across the ceiling through the blackened windows to my left. Several co-workers grabbed the stretcher and walked me through the doors to the ambulance as it backed up to the dock. Once I was inside, the medics lifted me off the stretcher and onto the bed. After strapping me down, one of them started an IV while the other wrapped me in blankets, tucking them under me and up under my chin. Then I heard him holler through the open rear window to the driver, "He's secure. Let's go!"

We raced through the deserted late night streets of downtown St. Louis to Christian Hospital, lights and sirens leading the way. It must have been nearly one in the morning by then, maybe later. I asked the medic, "How bad is it? What can you tell me?" He told me not to worry, adding, "You'll be fine. I'm going to give you a shot now which should ease the pain and send you off to sleep. We'll be at the hospital in a few minutes."

EIGHT

Oh, That Morphine!

As we approached the emergency room entrance, one of the medics waved smelling salts under my nose to wake me up. He unbuckled my straps and transferred the IV to the portable hospital bed which had been brought into the ambulance. Both medics, one at my feet and the other under my shoulders, helped slide me over onto the hospital bed. One member of the hospital staff said, "How's he doing? What's his blood pressure? We'll take it from here." It was a brief conversation; they wasted no time. They locked the guard rails in place and wheeled me out through the swinging emergency room doors to a curtained-off area directly in front of me.

Mrs. Brown, the head nurse on duty that night, was waiting for me. In her soft, calming voice, she said, "We've been expecting you. Are you in any pain now?"

I told her there was no pain. "Can you tell me how bad this is?" I asked. "How much damage?"

As she took my blood pressure and temperature, she gently told me not to worry about that right now. When I asked her the readings, she changed the subject saying, "Let's get your shirt off first. I'll have to cut it off. Is that okay with you?"

I told her I had just bought that shirt and asked that she be careful.

She cut my shirt along the seams, reassuring me that I could have it stitched back up later. I thanked her and then told her that I had a girlfriend. "Do you think she'll still love me?" I asked, hoping her words would reassure me.

"If she loves you now, she'll love you, don't worry," she said. "Is there anyone you want us to notify? Do you want me to call anyone?"

169

I asked her to call my roommate, Matt Ryder, and I gave her the number. She wrote it down on a slip of paper attached to her clipboard and handed it to another nurse. It was late at night but I knew he'd be up; we had planned a party. "Tell him I don't think I'm going to make the party," I said. "And please ask him to call Janice for me, will you?" The nurse with the number left the room to make the call.

Matt told me later that when he received the call from the hospital he immediately called Janice. Janice's mother answered the phone. She woke Janice up and Matt explained to her what had happened.

Mrs. Brown picked up her clipboard again and asked me some questions. She wanted to know how old I was, my religious affiliation, next of kin. Then she said, "I'm sorry for this, but I've got to have you sign this release so we can get you up to surgery. It's a consent form."

"How am I going to do that?" I asked. "Look at me."

"Let me help you," she said with her caring voice. "I'll put this pencil in your mouth and help you sign your name, here on the bottom of the form." I could taste the eraser as I grabbed it between my teeth and tried to steady it with my tongue.

It was nearly 10:00 a.m. by the time I awoke from surgery. A nurse passed the noxious smelling salts under my nose and I shook my head back and forth before waking up. Bright sunshine was streaming across the room from every window. I glanced up at the two nurses standing next to my bed. One of them reached behind my head and helped me sit up, and I immediately threw up. They must have expected that because the other nurse was holding a pan under my chin.

They washed my face with a warm cloth and propped me up with pillows, then asked how I felt. "Do you remember what happened to you last night?" one asked.

I told her what I could remember and then looked down at my bandages. "How badly injured am I?" I asked.

She told me not to be too concerned about that just yet. "Let's get you back to normal first. You've been through a long night of surgery, and we just want you to rest."

They gave me a shot of morphine and I went back to sleep.

I drifted in and out of morphine-induced euphoria for much of the first two weeks. Sleep came easy after those shots. The effect wouldn't last very long, but I went into a deliriously beautiful rest after each shot; morphine was a miracle drug that blunted the pain and lifted my confidence. I figured I could handle this, at least for a while. I managed a weak smile whenever the nurse came through the doorway and around the corner to my bed. "Time to fly," I would whisper up to her as she wiped my right arm with the alcohol swab. She told me not to get too used to the shots.

"You can't get these forever, you know," she reminded me.

For the moment, though, I could escape, drift just a few feet above my bed. My eyes rolled back, and I could rest and be at peace with the world. I didn't have to worry about my future; my future was now, and for now, things were good. But when I was not flying high, I spent much of the time reflecting on my early childhood and wondering what was ahead of me, where I would go from here, and I frequently fell into a state of complete despair.

I thought of my father and wondered what he would say if he found out. I figured he'd just remind me of his offer to find me a good job in Detroit. It didn't matter though; I wasn't about to tell him. He had left me when I was three, left me and my little brother Peter. We were always waiting for him to return, to come back, so we could be a family again. There comes a time in a man's life when he turns aside from his youthful self-centered ways to give, rather than take. A time when priorities shift course. My father never seemed to get that, though. He walked away after the divorce, left for Michigan to start a new life. I was almost four and Peter was just a baby, a baby with a deadly blood disorder. My mother was left to find a place to live and work, and raise her two boys.

For some reason I couldn't get my father out of my mind. It must have been the drugs. When we all lived together, before the divorce, he would come home after working all day and drinking all night. He'd mumble and stumble his way up two steps and back one, up two and down one—all the way up the stairs to our second-floor apartment.

As soon as he stepped inside, he would start arguing with my mother. One night he arrived home really late, and woke me up as he shuffled past my room and out to the back hallway. I slid out of bed, walked over to my half open door, and saw him standing in front of my mother, talking loudly. Suddenly, he turned and pushed her backwards, down the back stairs. I ran out into the hallway and began hitting his legs with my hands. I turned and looked down the stairs at my mother, hoping she was all right.

She went tumbling down the stairs, bumping her head against the walls and striking each of the wooden stairs. She landed hard, crouched in a heap on the landing floor up against the rear door.

The first-floor neighbor, Mrs. Whitcomb, opened her door when she heard the crash. She bent over and helped my mother get to her feet and brought her into her place. Mrs. Whitcomb glanced up at me and my father before closing her door.

I ran and hid under the bed. My brother, a baby at the time, remained fast asleep in the room we shared.

My father never went down to see if she was hurt. He just left the house.

He was a barroom brawling tough guy. Not very tall but built like a cement truck. He worked as a welder at the shipyard in Quincy during World War II. He was a man's man, not a woman's man, not much of a husband, and not much of a father.

He wasn't afraid of anything; he lived on the edge, especially when he was drinking, and he was always drinking.

There were plenty of stories about him around town. Apparently, one night as he was making his way home from a night out on the town, he walked past a liquor store on Union Street, the main street in Rockland Center. It was late and the store was closed. He noticed, as the story goes, that the plate glass window in front of the store had been broken. There was glass scattered all over the sidewalk and out into the street. He stepped over the glass and into the store through the broken window, helped himself to a couple of bottles of scotch, then walked the rest of the way home and went to bed.

Sometime after three in the morning, the cops arrived. They came up the stairs and pounded on the door. Someone must have spotted him and turned him in. He woke up and stumbled to the door, ready to kill whoever was banging on the other side. They wanted to speak with him about a "liquor store robbery." He told them he didn't know anything about it. They asked him about the unopened bottles of scotch sitting on the kitchen table with the price stickers from the store still attached.

He said, "I was just walking home, minding my own goddamn business, when I noticed the front window of the liquor store was bashed in. That's it. That's all. I just stepped in over the glass and helped myself."

They brought him to the station, but he somehow avoided a criminal complaint. Whether he did it or not, he wound up paying the damages to the store and paying for the scotch.

Another story that floated around town concerned the time he and a couple of his friends, his hell-raising drinking buddies, pulled the fire alarm across the street from where we were living in North Abington. It was well after midnight, and they had been drinking from the time they punched out at four o'clock, the end of their shift.

After pulling the alarm, they hid in a small one-car garage across the street next to the road and waited for the fire trucks to arrive. They were laughing so damn hard that the fire chief could hear them inside the garage. They were all thrown in jail for the night to sleep it off. They all paid a hefty fine in the morning and the chief let them go.

There were more stories, many more stories. They weren't very amusing to a wife with small children, but to his drinking buddies, my father was a barrel of laughs. Rockland was his hometown. He grew up there and knew everyone, and everyone in town knew him. He owned the place.

My father and his two brothers went through high school together and played on the Rockland High School football team. When the war broke out in 1941, his brother Donald joined the U.S. Navy and somehow managed to come home three years later without injuries. He served as a WT I/c — a water tender first class on the USS Lardner DD487, an escort destroyer that saw plenty of action in the South

Pacific. Most notable was their relentless bombardment of Guadalcanal before and during the landing of the U.S. Marines. The Lardner received a remarkable ten Battle Stars for service in WWII. Donald was oversees in the Pacific when I was born in 1943. Nobody ever expected to see him again, so they named me after him.

When Donald returned home after the war, he joined the Rockland Police Department. He remained on the force for the rest of his life, before retiring.

Following my parents' divorce in 1947, my father packed up and headed west to Detroit, Michigan. There were plenty of jobs out there in the auto industry, good-paying union jobs. He eventually remarried and bought a home in Wyandotte, a small suburb just south of Detroit, where he started a new life and a new family.

They'd come home to Rockland every summer. Donald dreaded having him home. He would be the one to get the call. "Your brother's in a fight down at the Hotel Thomas!" The Hotel Thomas was downtown near the tracks and had a bar to the right just inside the entranceway. Donald would rush down there and pull him out of the place and take him home. It was either that or put him in the slammer for a few hours, which he would never do.

I thought about my mother and her yearly dance recitals. When I was only three, she taught me how to tap dance and showcased me all alone in the center of the stage doing a little dance routine called, "The Old Soft Shoe." I was all dressed up in a tuxedo with white gloves, a hat in one hand and a cane in the other.

Next to me, in the center of the stage, was a small, elevated platform with two steps on either side. I tap-danced up to the top and then tap-danced down the other side. I must have made an impression; the audience smiled and clapped for a long time. I was so young.

My mother had auditioned with the Radio City Rockettes in New York City when she was eighteen. She could dance up a storm, but it didn't work out. She wasn't tall enough. Her mother, Margaret, was pretty much the driving force behind most of this.

My mother was always writing little notes and stashing them away. She once wrote:

Mother sent me to dancing school. I grew up in a small town where maybe twenty children out of that town were sent to learn bal- let. I loved it from the beginning, and I was only five years old.

In another, she wrote:

Mother became very bitter due to the strain and worry put upon her because of my father's condition; and knowing how she felt, my father held off going to the hospital when he knew he was in need of blood and help. Financial worries were always foremost.

The word Hemophiliac was always part of my life. As a baby, I learned to say Papa and Momma and hemophiliac at the same time, it seems. I lived with it from birth.

* * *

I never knew her father, Arthur. "He would have loved you and Peter," she'd often say to me. "He was a wonderful man." He died on the operating table at the Brockton Hospital during an emergency tracheotomy. She was twenty-one at the time and it devastated her. I wouldn't be born for another eight years.

Before marrying my father, my mother had married the one true love of her life, another Rockland native, Joe Pininni. Joe was a young auto mechanic who loved working on anything mechanical. My mother reminisced with me one night, saying, "He'd come home with his greasy hands and dirty working man's clothes. I was always telling him to take off his shoes and clean up before coming into the house. I know I overdid it. I was too much of a fuss-budget for my own good."

Her mother didn't approve of Joe, but that didn't matter very much. My mother was in love with him. So, in spite of her mother's objections, she married him.

Everything changed at sunrise on the 7th of December, 1941. The Empire of Japan launched an aerial attack on our naval fleet at anchor in Pearl Harbor, on the Island of Oahu, Hawaii. President Roosevelt spoke to the American people: "Today, December 7, 1941, a date that will live in infamy…." It was all out war. The entire population mo- bilized to defend our country.

That afternoon, Joe made up his mind to join the U.S. Army Air Corps and become a fighter pilot. In those days married men were not permitted to join the service, so with great reluctance my mother granted him a divorce; he enlisted the following day. He completed flight school, became a pilot, and flew with the Army Air Corps throughout Europe for the duration of the war.

Joe survived the war and returned home without injuries. By this time though, my mother had married my father, Peter. Perhaps she should have waited for Joe, but the daily news of men killed in action—the relentless battlefield casualties—made her certain she would never see him again.

I think Joe Pininni was the only man she ever really loved.

* * *

During my six-week stay in room 200 at Christian Hospital, the nurses and orderlies did everything for me. Washed me, shaved me, and brushed my teeth. My hands were heavily bandaged in layers of white gauze, the size of boxing gloves. When I had to go to the bath-room, an orderly would come in and clean me up.

"Sorry man," I would say. "Hope you don't mind. I don't have much choice."

He was very good about it, but I'm sure he would rather have been somewhere else.

I was in a large four-man room with one bed set up in each corner. The man in the bed to my right wanted to die. He was quite elderly and refused to eat or take any of his medications. I'd talked with him all the time. His name was Mr. Eisenberg.

I tried to encourage him to take his pills, which he would hide under his pillow. He was always lying on his left side, facing me. A couple of times he pretended to take the pills as the nurse stood next to his bed scolding him. He'd look over at me after the nurse left and show me the pills stashed under his tongue. He'd then give me a wink and spit them out.

The other man in a bed over by the window, diagonally across the room from me, couldn't urinate after his back surgery, so he spent two days on and off in the bathroom running his hands under warm water. I remember the day he came back all smiles. "It worked," he said. "This is my lucky day!" He was in his late thirties or early forties and seemed to take things pretty much in stride until he was threatened with the dreaded catheter.

The fourth man, directly across from me, wasn't so fortunate; he did have a catheter and wasn't very happy about it. He must have been in his mid-seventies and was continuously moaning and swearing, "This goddamn thing…get it outta me, get it outta me!"

He would call over to me, "Ya know, every time urine comes outta me and goes in that foolish bag down there, it hurts like hell. I'm tellin' ya, they're killing me!"

It must have been painful, because when urine began to flow, he'd start roaring, "Ohhh… that hurts, goddamnit, *goddamnit!*" I hope I never have to go through that! I said to myself.

I thought about my father almost every day. The hell with him, I said to myself. He could find out from others what happened to me; a belated slap in the face from me, a little payback. Maybe it would bother him, maybe not.

* * *

Shortly after the divorce and after my father left us, my mother found a small one-room apartment behind the Brockton Hospital, where she worked as a nurses' aide. My brother and I went to live in a large house on Corey Street in Brockton, the Holmes'. Mrs. Holmes took in kids. It was more or less an orphanage, without the name. She was a large woman who always wore a red and yellow apron wrapped around her waist. It had two side-by-side pockets in the front, which were usually filled with cookies, for the kids who were good.

She usually served up peanut butter and sliced banana sandwiches for lunch. Sometimes she switched to peanut butter and marshmallow. It didn't really matter much to me; they were both pretty good. I never saw her much except at mealtime. She must have been with the babies or doing some cleaning. My mother came to visit us twice a week.

Brockton was a tough place to grow up, even in those days. I was in my first fight at the age of four. I had been invited to go with the other kids from Mrs. Holmes' place, up the street to a third-floor apartment to watch, for the first time, a television program: "The Kookla, Fran, and Ollie Show." Kookla, Fran, and Ollie were puppets who argued and fought while hitting each other over the head with sticks. I thought that was really something.

After the show, we walked down the three flights of stairs and out to the street. Some big kid came right up to me and pushed me off the sidewalk and down onto the grass. He reached down and took off one of my shoes and blasted me in the face with it. I rolled over, jumped to my feet, grabbed my shoe and hobbled home with blood running from my nose, and all over the front of me.

My mother had come to visit us that night. She was talking with Mrs. Holmes when we all trotted up the stairs and into the kitchen. I was so happy to see her, I started crying as I smeared the blood from my face with the back of my hand. Mrs. Holmes looked at me as if I was being a baby and said, "It figures. Your mother shows up and you start crying."

My mother brought me into the bathroom and washed my face with a warm cloth, and I told her my sad tale. She finished cleaning me up, then turned to Mrs. Holmes and said, "Thank God this wasn't Peter."

Peter and I stayed at Mrs. Holmes' place for over a year. I turned five in February and Peter turned two in March.

The bunch of us would play and fight and very often, it seemed, get into trouble. There was a playground with a ball field about a mile down Main Street toward Brockton Center. In the summer, we'd all head down there after breakfast to play.

I suffered the worst sunburn of my young life while living there. I was out all day playing with no shirt on, and spent two months lying in bed on plastic sheets with cotton padding and lotions all over me, my skin peeling off in sheets.

One day, after a late winter, early spring snowstorm, we made a pile of snowballs and began throwing them at trucks passing us down Corey Street. I was the one who threw the snowball through the open driver's side window of a large delivery truck, and hit the driver in the side of the head.

He jammed on the brakes and slid sideways across the road, stopping at the curb. He jumped from the truck and came running after us, shouting, "I'll kill you...you little bastards." We all turned and raced up the walkway along the left side of the house, threw open the back door, and dashed up the three flights of stairs to the bedrooms, then huddled together in one of the closets in the back room. I don't think the driver ever came in the house, but we stayed in the closet for about an hour, until Mrs. Holmes started yelling for us that lunch was ready.

I was out wandering around by myself one day and decided I'd go down Corey Street to the busy five-way intersection at the end, to see what was going on. I could see and hear trucks and equipment digging and kicking up dust on one of the side streets connected to the intersection.

I had never ventured this far from home by myself. I stopped at the lights and leaned up against a telephone pole, which gave off a strong smell of tar. It must have been installed earlier in the day because there were fresh dirt and rocks jammed into the sidewalk at the base. Suddenly loud screams broke out above the now familiar sounds of moving equipment. I watched as a woman came running up from the side street, her arms waving wildly in the air, trying to catch someone's attention. She was screaming that her boy had just fallen into an open sewer manhole drain. "My son! My son!" she cried out hysterically. I felt so helpless and afraid for her. I could only imagine her son, probably my age, falling into an open sewer drain in the street, trapped and drowning.

Her screaming scared the hell out of me. I wanted to help her, but instead, I turned and ran as fast as I could back home. I threw open the back door and bolted up the stairs to tell Mrs. Holmes. I was out of breath, choking out my words. I frightened Peter, who was sitting in the highchair staring at me wide-eyed as I tried to explain what I saw.

Mrs. Holmes comforted me and told me not to worry, it would be all right. She told me to sit down and have my lunch." I protested, "But, Mrs. Holmes, the little boy fell into a sewer. Shouldn't we do something?" She calmed me down, telling me the police would make everything all right.

"Don't worry," she said. I sat down at the kitchen table and began telling Peter more about what had just happened. He was only a baby, but I could tell he knew something was not right.

I never heard whether the boy was rescued or not, but from that day to this, I always step over or walk around manhole covers.

I was consciously aware of my surroundings and the direction I might take as I grew older and was prepared, if necessary, to take the tough route. If I had to be tough, I would be tough. It even seemed appealing to me at times, even exciting.

One afternoon I ventured out the door and up Corey Street to the Main Street intersection. When I rounded the corner of a large building, I saw that three older boys were holding another boy upside-down, shaking him so his money would fall out of his pockets. They must have pushed him around pretty good before I came on the scene. He was crying and trying to fight back.

I stayed behind a wall next to the building and watched. I wanted to tell them to stop, leave him alone, but I didn't. After his coins spilled out on the sidewalk they punched him in the head and let him go.

They scooped up the money and started laughing. They didn't pay any attention to me. I was only five years old, but that incident had an impact on me. How could they be so mean to someone? And laugh about it?

I knew then, as young as I was, that if I was going to be tough and get into fights, it would be to protect myself or to protect someone else. I wasn't interested in hurting anyone intentionally or causing any trouble. It wasn't in my nature.

I moved away from the Holmes's before the Brockton street life changed the way I looked at my world, before it owned me. If I had stayed there much longer, things might have been very different.

* * *

It would be another hour before my next shot of morphine and I kept watching the clock, which hung on the wall on the opposite side of the room. I raised my hands in the air to lesson the blood pressure, hoping to ease the pain. I pushed the red button to summon the nurse and when she arrived I told her, "I can't take this much longer. When is my next shot?" I was hoping they weren't watching the clock as closely as I was.

"I'm really sorry," she explained, "but I can't give it to you just yet. Maybe in twenty minutes, I'll check with the head nurse."

I lay there with my eyes fixed on that damn clock until the four hours were up. At exactly that moment I buzzed the nurses' station again. Someone came with the morphine a few minutes later. "How are you doing?" the nurse asked.

I looked into her eyes and said, "Thanks for coming," then extended my right arm for the shot and the relief that came with it.

* * *

A year and a half after my father left for Michigan, my mother, still working at the Brockton Hospital, married my stepfather. Bud drove a delivery van for the Norfolk County Hospital in Braintree. The Brockton Hospital was a frequent stop on his route, and that's where he met my mother. I'm sure she was anxious to find a father figure to help bring up her two boys and help establish some financial stability.

Maybe she jumped too quickly or maybe she just had bad luck with men, but in those days there were no social services to help a single mother with two small children. She needed a husband, a breadwinner.

* * *

I rolled over on to my right side and there was Mr. Eisenberg catching hell from the head nurse again for not taking his pills.

"I'm taking them…all of them," he snapped. "So get the hell out of here."

The nurse responded sternly, "Listen, Mr. Eisenberg, I'm the boss here. Your blood tests indicate you're not taking your meds, so I'm going to stand here and watch as you take these pills, and don't try to hide them under your tongue!" Mr. Eisenberg glanced over at me to see if I was watching.

"Okay," he said. "You win." And he placed the pills in his mouth and swallowed a full glass of water, then opened his mouth and lifted his tongue, convincing the nurse he was cooperating.

After she left his bedside, he looked over at me and opened his right hand to show me the pills. He had outsmarted the nurse again. I couldn't help but laugh, and I needed a good laugh, but I knew the poor guy was not leaving there alive.

I never did find out what happened to him. The day I left the hospital, I went over to his bed, said goodbye and wished him luck. He was probably granted his wish and died in his sleep.

* * *

My stepfather, like all the men I knew when I was young, was quick-tempered and a heavy drinker. He was no better than my father, maybe even worse. I don't think I ever walked past my stepfather without him whacking me on the back of the head and calling me "banana-head" or "pin-head" or "mommy's boy" or worse—remarks meant to demean and humiliate me. I stayed away from him as much as I could.

There was one man in my young life, however, who gave me a sense that not all men were abusive drunks. He was my ninety-one-year-old great grandfather, my mother's grandfather. His name was Alexander Black. Peter and I called him Grandpa Black. He was a quiet and gentle old man with one eye, and he took an interest in me and seemed to love me.

He lived, along with my great aunts—his two daughters—in a small farmhouse on Central Street in Norwell. He came to America from County Armagh, Ireland in 1882 when he was seventeen years old. Each summer I was allowed to spend two weeks of my vacation in Norwell with him, my two great aunts, and "the cats." There were six or seven cats that stayed mostly outside or in the barn chasing away the mice. I never saw any mice.

My brother was never given the opportunity to stay with them... not even overnight. Nobody would accept the responsibility. He could easily fall or get hurt in any number of ways, and they just weren't willing to take the chance.

Peter would have benefited greatly from these visits, as I did. It was a terrible mistake to deny him this closeness with family. On the other hand, I was in charge of Peter for most of my childhood years when there were no adults around. Those two weeks each summer gave me a little break from that.

Grandpa Black's house, at number 21 Central Street, was just a short distance from Main Street and the Norwell Town Common. He'd take me for walks up to the common on the Fourth of July to watch the parade. He purchased the house and the land in the summer of 1921 for $1,700.00, settlement money paid to him as compensation for losing his left eye to a thorn bush while working as a gardener.

He had a name for each of his two Nova Scotia pines, which he planted in 1925 and stood within twenty feet of each in the backyard at the end of the driveway: Mr. Cunningham and Agnes My Dear. Mr. Cunningham was a gift from a man by the same name, and Agnes was his wife. The trees were full grown with branches extending across the grass and touching each other. His wife, Agnes was from County Galway, Ireland. I never met her. She died before I was born.

Grandpa Black asked me one morning after breakfast, "Would you like to take a walk with me down back around the other side of the barn and help me with the garden?" At ninety years old, he was hunched over and walked with a cane, one slow step at a time. I said, "Yes, I would," as I held the screen door open for him. He taught me the difference between the vegetable plants and the weeds, all of which had just begun to sprout when I visited. He talked to me in his barely audible, caring voice, as he began pulling the weeds from the garden. "We want to take out the weeds, but we have to be careful not to disturb the vegetables."

After dinner, he sat in his rocking chair beside the cast iron stove in the kitchen and smoked his pipe. I loved watching him take out his pocket knife and shave off small pieces from a block of tobacco and fill his pipe, then strike a wooden match across the stovetop, bring the lit match to the pipe and draw in the fire. Once lit, he would cross his legs, sit back and enjoy his smoke.

I sat on the stool next to him and listened to his stories. At 9:00 p.m. he had his "hot toddy," a shot of whiskey, mixed together with a half teaspoon of sugar and warm water, then walk through the dining room, turn left and climb the steep stairs to his bedroom.

In the morning he'd make his way slowly down the stairs carrying his "thunder jug" with one hand and holding the rail with the other. The thunder jug was a round tin pot about ten inches in diameter with a handle attached to the side. Everyone had a thunder jug tucked under their beds in case they needed to go to the bathroom during the night.

He'd make some coffee for himself, then slow-cook the most wonderful tasting Irish oatmeal on the old oil-fired, cast-iron stove. We'd have breakfast together, just the two of us. After oatmeal, he reached into his pocket and pulled out a small jackknife, opened it up, extended the blade and cut an orange into four quarters. That was his breakfast, that and a cup of black coffee.

He never, ever raised his voice, and he would laugh at all his own stories. He'd talk about his horse, telling me, "She'd be harnessed to the wagon, but wouldn't budge 'til I cracked the whip in the air and cried out, 'On she-she,' and on she stepped. Then we'd move along quite nicely."

And there was always a tale about the cats. I developed a sense of faith in mankind from the kindness he showed me. Every little boy and girl should be lucky enough to have a Grandpa Black.

He fell to the floor one day while leaning back to sit in his rocking chair, and broke his hip. He never recovered. I was there the day before he died. He was lying on a cot, which had been brought in from the barn and set up in the living room. When I walked through the kitchen and into the living room to see him, he reached up with his right hand and held my hand, and whispered, "Take care of the well." Although the house had been connected to the town water system years before, it must have been heavy on his mind as he began slipping away. I told him not to worry. I'd take care of it.

I cried when I heard the news of his death. I hated myself for crying; crying was for sissies.

* * *

I continued drifting in and out, from past to present, and back again. The morphine would only last about an hour if I went off to sleep, so I forced myself to stay awake as long as I could. I was in quite a bit of pain now, throbbing pain with every heartbeat.

I thought of my brother, who had endured so many long hours of pain as a child, pain from swollen ankles and knees and common childhood injuries that would often turn into a nightmare for him. I could now appreciate his hell as I lay on my bed counting the minutes until the morphine would arrive and send me off flying again.

As Peter's older brother, my responsibility was to keep him from getting hurt. He was very active and hard to keep an eye on. At one of the schools we both attended in Abington, I was called to the principal's office and told to go outside on the playground and look after my brother during his recess time. I'd be called out of my social studies class every day, and to keep up, the teacher would give me assignments to take home.

It was usually my fault, at school or at home, if anything happened to Peter—and plenty happened to him. When he was seven, he almost died after a bicycle accident. At the time, I was playing baseball down at the end of the street and didn't know anything about it until I arrived home.

Peter wasn't allowed to have his own bike. My mother thought it would be too dangerous. So he borrowed a bike from one of the Mills sisters who lived two houses from us. He and his friend, Jake Delaney, began racing, side by side, up Linda Street. Jake had just been given a new bike and wanted to show it off.

When they turned left onto Green Street, Peter fell off his bike and hit his forehead on a rock. He started bleeding immediately through his nose. He climbed back up on the bike and raced for home, blood streaming out of his nose and mouth.

The bleeding would not stop. Bud was home at the time. He cleaned Peter up and told him to lie down on the couch. Then he put a bag of ice on his forehead, trying to stop the bleeding.

When my mother came home from work, she knew immediately that Peter was in serious trouble. They helped him into the car and raced off to the Brockton Hospital where he was rushed into the emergency room. The doctors tried to stop the bleeding, but he just continued losing blood. They tried one blood transfusion after another, but he kept bleeding.

X-rays revealed a hairline fracture in his forehead, just above the bridge of his nose. They wrapped huge cotton wads around two strings, then pulled the strings up into his nose from inside his mouth, and still the bleeding would not stop.

Peter's name was posted on the "danger list" in the newspaper. A priest came and offered last rites. My mother was frantic. She remembered her own father years ago and how she saw the surgeons on the elevator, covered with blood, after their attempt to save him.

My uncle Donald was called into the hospital. He had the same blood type as Peter. He lay on a cot next to Peter while the doctors set up a transfusion from my uncle's left arm directly into Peter's forehead. And after a while, it worked. He finally stopped bleeding.

Over the course of the several months he was hospitalized, Peter received twenty or thirty or more pints of whole blood, and as soon as he was released, he would be back again, bleeding from the same area for no apparent reason.

It was well over a year before he was fully recovered.

***

I opened my eyes on the third day to another shot of morphine. The nurse had just pulled the needle out when I noticed Janice and her mother standing at the foot of my bed. I muttered through my half asleep voice, "Hey…nice to see you, Kid, and nice to see you too, Mrs. Gibson." They both smiled broadly and came over and stood next to me. "I just had my shot, so you better stand back; I'll be flying around the room in about a minute," I cautioned with a grin.

Janice smiled and so did her mother. "How are you?" Janice said softly…almost afraid to ask. I told her I was fine. "A little pain, that's all. I don't know what's under these bandages, but it can't be good. We'll just have to wait and see."

She placed a card on my table and her mother set a small bouquet of flowers next to it. Janice bent down and kissed me on the forehead and touched my shoulder with her left hand. With a troubled look she said, "Please get better in a hurry; everyone is asking for you back at school." I told her I didn't plan to stay there any longer than necessary. Then the shot hit me. "Whoa…hold on. Here I go!" We all laughed together as I traveled around the room.

Janice flashed me a beautiful smile and I smiled back. She told me she couldn't stay too long but would be back in a couple of days. "I've got to get back for Wally; he needs the car."

I said, "Thanks a lot for coming in. I'll see you later. And thanks for the card and the flowers." She kissed me again, then whispered something sweet in my ear in her soft French accent, then turned to her mother, who reached over and touched my forehead before leaving.

A few days later, Dr. Weaver, the president of Shurtleff College, paid me a visit. He brought me the latest copy of *Time* magazine and the *St. Louis Post Dispatch*, the city newspaper. I was so surprised and thankful for his visit.

When I started my freshman year in September of '64, Dr. Weaver had received a letter from Dr. Ralph Carleton, an old friend of his I had met while working at Friendly's back home in Brockton. Dr. Carleton was a college professor at Curry College in Milton, Massachusetts. He came in once in a while to have lunch and I always waited on him. I had told him about my plans to attend college in Illinois. He was surprised at how small the world had become. "I'm a very good friend of the president of Shurtleff College. I'll drop him a line and tell him to be expecting you," he'd said.

I never gave it much thought until one day, during my freshman year, I received a letter inviting me to have dinner with Dr. Weaver and his wife at their home in Alton. They lived in a large house on the west end of the campus.

After dinner, Dr. Weaver brought me into his library, where he reached up and pulled a book from a shelf. The book was signed by "A. Einstein." I could hardly believe it. "I spent some time with Albert Einstein years ago while on a trip to Europe; we walked and talked for hours. I asked him to sign a copy of his book and he graciously agreed, and here it is," he said proudly.

There I was, a high school dropout, having dinner with a college president and his wife, and talking about Albert Einstein, his personal friend. I was pretty impressed with him and pretty impressed with myself.

It was a wonderful evening—though I think I may have over-stayed my visit. I was having such a nice time and really didn't want to leave. Eventually I said goodnight and thanked him and his wife, telling them how much I'd enjoyed the dinner and our conversation.

It was such a nice gesture for him to take the time to visit me in the hospital.

I had been in the hospital for about two and a half weeks when they started giving me a placebo—a shot of nothing, saline probably. No more morphine. I knew right away something had changed because the sting from the shot felt different. I asked the nurse, "What's this? It doesn't feel the same."

She didn't answer me. She left a couple of white pills to take the place of the morphine, "but only if you need them." They were obviously weaning me from the heavy narcotics. It had to happen sooner or later, and I accepted it. I had no choice, really. I had to come back to Earth, sometime.

One day the older man across from me, the one with the catheter, started early with a nonstop complaint about his bill. When the nurse came in to answer his call, he started in on her, saying, "I can't pay this, you know. I don't know how much all this costs, but I can't pay. I'm telling you right now." Throughout the day, whenever a nurse would enter our room, he'd call out the same complaint. "I can't pay this bill...I want you to know!"

The only one listening to him was me, me and my heartfelt, drug-enhanced sympathy. I felt so bad for the old guy that I arranged to have some of his bills posted to my account. I was trying to calm him down. He seemed crazy with worry. I whispered over to him, "Hey, when you get the bills, just change the patient name and bed number to mine, and then sign my name; they can bill me." I wasn't going to pay anyway; the insurance company was paying all my bills. I told him, "Don't worry, my insurance company has plenty of money."

The hospital staff caught up with that scam when he went to check out. My nurse came in and told me the billing officer wanted to speak with me; would I please come with her. I was up and walking around by then, so I followed along behind her to the billing window.

When we arrived, the doctor was standing there talking with two other nurses and the billing clerk. The doctor turned to me and said, "How did these charges get on your account?"

I just looked puzzled and bewildered but didn't say a word. "This man has plenty of money and can easily afford to take care of this himself. He owns several rental properties in St. Louis, and has plenty of resources. You should mind your own business."

The doctor was right; I should have minded my own business. So after the scolding, I turned and disappeared back to my room. That guy had all of us in the room convinced he was just some poor soul being tormented to death by his mounting hospital bills.

All this time—for three weeks now—my hands remained heavily bandaged. I looked like a prize fighter training for a twelve-rounder. I didn't know the extent of the damage, nor was I told what to expect.

The head nurse came in one morning and told me the bandages would be coming off that afternoon. I wasn't ready. Up until then I could hide behind the bandages, but now...now it was show time. I hesitated, then said to the nurse, "Okay, but I'll take them off myself, and by myself." I wanted to be alone when I did this. "Just cut through the bandages and I'll do the rest."

She came back after lunch and as promised and began cutting through the many layers of gauze, slowly but not painlessly. She was trying to be gentle, but every time she touched the gauze, I winced. Finally, I stopped her and said, "Okay, that's enough, I'll do the rest. You can leave now, and draw the curtain, please." I knew this was going to be tough, and I needed to be alone. I knew I was going to be sick.

I began removing the heavy bandages with my teeth, one hand at a time. The nurse had prepared a hot basin of saline when she first came in. It was sitting on my bedside table, ready for me to soak my hands...when I was ready. My hands, what remained of them, were a swollen mass of black and blue. Thick black stitches were threaded and sown into my skin and sticking out everywhere at odd angles.

Some areas, not yet healed, were raw red. Half of the three middle fingers on my left hand were gone, and the end of the little finger was broken at the first joint. My right hand was worse; all three middle fingers were missing. Any attempts to reattach my fingers had been futile. Everything had been crushed.

I could see where the steel plate had been twisted and embedded in both hands.

I took a peek and quickly turned away. I stared down at the bed and then up at the ceiling. I closed my eyes and began to cry, uncontrolled heaving sobs. I couldn't stop crying. I knew the others in the room heard me and wanted to help, but there was nothing anyone could do. They respected my privacy and left me alone.

I remembered a line from Shakespeare: "What's done cannot be undone." The reality of it hit me so damn hard. I glanced down and looked away again. I needed to take this in small doses. What were once my can-do-anything hands were now unable to hold a get well card. My first attempts to rationalize and accept what had happened just upset me more. I wanted to scream and swear, let it all out, but I was beyond anger.

I tried placing my hands in the warm saline, but it burned like hell. I kept trying and eventually was able to keep them under for brief periods. For the rest of the afternoon, I remained behind the drawn curtain, soaking my hands and feeling sorry for myself.

NINE

Don't Get in My Way

About a week later, a nurse appeared at my bedside and informed me, "We're out of saline, so you won't be getting your treatment today. We'll see about tomorrow." Warm saline was used every day to soak my hands before dipping them into hot wax. This helped the healing and eased the pain. I had never seen this nurse before. Maybe she was new or reassigned from another shift. She was far too abrupt with me, so being in not too good a mood myself, I snapped right back, "What do you mean, you're out of saline?" With no further discussion, she threw her head in the air, turned, and stormed out of the room.

I covered myself up the best I could, not really caring how I looked—dressed or not. I raised my hands over my head to help relieve the throbbing pain and walked down the hall to the bank of elevators. I reached up and pushed the button with my right elbow and rode the elevator up to the next floor. When the doors opened, I walked out, turned left and went down the hall to the nurses' desk. It must have been a little unsettling to the nurses, and others I passed in the hall, to see me walking down the hall, half dressed, with my arms in the air.

I explained to the nurse sitting behind the desk, "The second floor, my floor, is out of saline. Do you have any you could spare?"

"They sent you up here?" she asked, a little puzzled.

"Yes."

She didn't bother calling down to check out my story. It was a good thing she didn't, because I was ready for a goddamn fight. She must have sensed something in my voice or in my eyes.

She immediately rose from her seat and went over to a metal cabinet that was up against the opposite wall, and opened wide the white,
side-by-side doors. She reached in, selected one of the many plastic
gallon containers of saline, and cradled it in my arms. I looked into
her eyes as if to say, you did the right thing, now get out of my way,
then turned and with blood boiling, marched back down the elevator
to my floor.

"Here!" I said to my nurse, wanting to throw it in her face.

She jumped up from her desk and demanded, "Where did you
get that?"

I told her what I had done and she told me I had no business doing
that, and added, "Don't do it again!" I didn't offer any smart-ass re-
tort, but she knew I meant business—I wanted that warm saline, and
now there was no excuse. I turned and walked back to my bed with
my arms high in the air and my gown open in the rear.

I received my warm saline that day and the hot wax as well, and
never missed another a day of treatments after that.

* * *

Before the accident, I had met most of life's challenges with a
bit of charm and an attitude of, "I'm not taking 'no' for an answer."
Somehow, I always knew when to push and when to turn back. But
this…this, I thought, would be so goddamn hard. How would I ma-
neuver around this? Would I have to hide my hands the rest of my life,
keep them in my pockets?

I convinced myself that I would learn to do everything I had done
before; it would just take me a little longer, and patience was never
my long suit. I had learned to type like a whiz while in the service,
but now…now, I couldn't even blow my own nose.

Matt came by one afternoon to see if the hospital would let me out
for a while. It was the middle of summer in St. Louis, and he had the
top down on his sporty red TR-3 and wanted to take me out for a ride. I
didn't bother to ask anyone. "Why ask?" I said. "I'm going anyway."

I slipped on some clothes and we headed down the hall to the
freight elevator. We went down to the rear loading dock, and out onto
the concrete platform where he had parked his car. He made a motion

192

to open the door for me, but I told him I'd do it myself. "Thanks any-way," I said. We drove around in his shiny red sports car for a couple of hours. He pulled into a drive-in hamburger place and bought me some lunch, then filled me in on what was going on back in Edwardsville. As I listened, I realized that I needed to get the hell out of that hospi-tal. I was missing the whole summer. It was the first time I had been out in public since the accident, and I felt so damn self-conscious. His visit meant a lot to me and I let him know it.

When we arrived back at the hospital, Matt drove around back and let me out. He again offered to grab the door but I told him, "That's okay, I've got it." I thanked him again for coming by and giving me a break from my routine, then stepped up on to the platform and rode the freight elevator up to my floor. When the door opened, I turned right, made my way down the hall to Room 200, took off my clothes and climbed into bed. They never knew I had left, and I never mentioned it.

Without telling me, members of my fraternity contacted my mother and arranged for her to fly to St. Louis to see me. They told her not to be concerned; everything has been taken care of. I was so grateful to them.

They picked her up at the airport and drove her over to Christian Hospital. I was sleeping when she walked into my room with a couple of my friends at her side. She came to my bed and began stroking my hair and I woke up. I was shocked to see her. I said, "Hey Mom. How you doing? How'd you get here?"

She explained that the boys from the fraternity had taken care of everything. "They've been wonderful to me," she said. "How you coming along?" I began to talk about what had happened to me, but when I saw the troubled expression appear on her face, I told her not to worry.

"I'm doing fine," I said. "It'll take more than this to keep me down. And you know that." She was obviously relieved to find me in good spirits. She sat down in a chair that someone brought over and we talked for a few minutes. Peter had been asking for me and want-ed to make the trip with her but couldn't. He was busy working and couldn't take the time, and of course money was an issue as well.

It was time for my saline and hot wax, so she gave me a kiss and left with the others. I told her I'd be coming home in a few weeks for further rehabilitation and would see her then. "Say hi to Peter for me."

While in the hospital, I received a letter from my old friend Tom Condon, my Rockland High School buddy from long ago:

7-19-65

Dear Don,

I hope you're feeling better and that everything is all right. Right now I am on my lunch hour and it seems a good time to write.

I have told some of our friends back here about your accident. They're all very concerned and said they would drop you a card. Last Saturday I saw Lee Manion, she asked how you were and I told her what had happened. She asked me to say to you, "Get well soon."

All of us back here are on your team and were all punching for you, but remember Don, yours is the most important punch. I feel you will come through this like you always have. With your guts, buddy, you cannot miss.

Remember John F. Kennedy and all of his problems and difficulties and how much he meant to all of us. Well Don, you mean a lot to us back here so don't let things despair because we couldn't bear a change in your personality. Pres. Kennedy is a fine model for all of us and especially you and I Don, because we're from Massachusetts. Think of our heritage... think of Bunker Hill, Dorchester Heights, Lexington and Concord. The fight's in us!

Don, I know you will come through and negotiate your problems honestly and devotedly. Remember us back here; I know you have plenty of caring friends too out there, because we all want the best for you, Don. Good luck and keep punching. Let them know Massachusetts men never give up.

Get well in every way!

Tom

* * *

Tommy was on summer break from his studies at Bentley College in Massachusetts. He was one of my friends who encouraged me to go to college. "Don," he'd urged, "somehow you've got to figure it out. It's the only way you can expect to have a decent life." I had visited him in his basement apartment on Commonwealth Avenue in Boston one evening after my discharge from the Air Force. He spoke about his college experience. "Don, it's not all work. There's plenty of social life here and you make a lot of friends." When I left that evening he put his hand on my shoulder and wished me good luck.

I wanted to drop him a note and thank him for his friendship and support, but I couldn't.

I had only completed my freshman year; three more years lay ahead of me. How was I going to write, drive my car, brush my teeth? I promised myself once again, that I would do everything I had done before…I had to be patient.

A lawyer entered my room one afternoon and walked over to my bed like he knew me. I hadn't made any calls to lawyers. I hadn't made any calls to anyone. I wasn't thinking of lawyers and wouldn't have known who to call if I had. It frankly never occurred to me. I was too wracked with emotions and pain to focus on anything other than getting through this mess.

I was suspicious of him, what he wanted and why he was here. After listening for a few minutes, I figured he was there to offer some help and give me some useful advice. But still, I really wasn't interested in what he had to say. I just went along with it. He held up a clipboard with an agreement attached and asked me to sign on the bottom. "So I can proceed," he said.

"I don't know how in hell I'm going to do that," I said, holding back my anger.

Without skipping a beat, he said, "Just put an 'X' on the line and I'll witness it." He handed me the pen and I held it between the palms of both hands and made a ragged-looking X.

Thinking back on it, he had some nerve showing up at my bedside to counsel me as I tossed and turned, high on drugs and still in considerable pain. H. Horatio Harper was his name, H3 for short.

He was a tall, well-dressed, good-looking man in his forties, and he seemed genuinely sympathetic and concerned. He reached down as if to shake my hand, and instead grabbed and squeezed my right forearm. It was a tight squeeze, like a warm handshake would have been, but it increased the blood pressure to my hand, and it hurt like hell. I quickly pulled away. I didn't say anything, and he made no attempt to apologize or even acknowledge that he was aware of what had just occurred. Instead he began explaining some relevant information pertaining to the Worker's Compensation laws in Missouri.

Although I was living in Illinois at the time, I was injured in Missouri and therefore the Missouri laws would apply. H3's law practice was in downtown Alton, Illinois, but he was familiar with the laws of Missouri and how they pertained to personal injury cases. He told me he would handle the legal matters related to my Worker's Compensation case and, with my permission, would file a lawsuit against the manufacturer of the Chicago Brake Press, Dreis and Krump Manufacturing Company, asking for damages in the amount of $250,000.

At the time, that seemed like all the money in the world, more than I could ever imagine. H3 explained that there would be court depositions and legal briefs, and eventually a jury trial, which would likely be held in Edwardsville, Illinois, the county seat of Madison County, Illinois. He also explained that if we couldn't settle out of court, it would be at least two years before the case would go to trial. In the meantime H3 would arrange a settlement agreement, a lump sum figure, with the Workman's Compensation Board of Missouri.

I interrupted him before he finished and said, "I want to get paid for the three days I worked there. They're not going to skip out on that." I was angry and very broken over the whole thing, and wasn't easy to deal with.

(I didn't receive any weekly compensation checks for job related injuries, as is the norm in most states today. Mrs. Kennedy at the State of Illinois Vocational Rehabilitation Division, 307 Henry St. in Alton, changed all that. Once I was discharged from the hospital, I visited her office looking for another job; I was running out of money. After our lengthy conversation, she explained that she might be able to help me with some form of compensation to pay my living expenses while I completed my rehabilitation and until I could get back to work. I told her that I didn't want to lose my chance to come back after rehabilitation and complete my education. Mrs. Kennedy asked me some questions and filled in the blanks on the state application. I still couldn't hold a pencil. "Now, just wait right here, I'll hand-carry this through the 'bureaucratic process,'" she said with a warm, knowing smile. She walked through an inner office door, and in less than ten minutes, came back and said, "You'll be notified in a couple of days. It looks good. I'll keep an eye on it for you, don't you worry." I knew she had presented my case to someone in the back room, someone who had the authority to act almost immediately. A very short time later, I began receiving a weekly check from the State of Illinois. I never forgot Mrs. Kennedy's name and I never forgot her kindness to me.)

I was discharged from the hospital in late August of '65. Liberty Mutual Insurance Company, the Worker's Compensation carrier for Hussman Refrigeration, sent me home to Boston for rehabilitation. I stayed for a time at the Lenox Hotel on Boylston Street to be close to the center.

The medical staff continued with my hot wax treatments and physical therapy, trying to work my hands to get some motion back. Several other tests were also conducted. Among them was a lengthy I.Q. test. When the results came back, I was told that I had an I.Q. in the top ten percent of the population for my age group. I was pleased to hear that, at least I figured I had the mental capacity to succeed in school. I just had to get beyond the physical and emotional crap.

During my stay at the Lenox Hotel, I spent much of my time with the other guys who were in there with me. One afternoon, four of us left the Lenox and walked down the sidewalk and down the stairs to the Boston subway. We jumped on the Blue Line, which took us under Boston Harbor and over to the Wonderland Greyhound Dog Track in Revere. Earlier in the day, we'd picked up racing forms from the local street vendors in Boston, sat down at a lunch counter for some lunch and coffee, and began studying the forms hoping to pick up some winners.

I'd never been much of a gambler. I worked too hard for my money to put it at risk, but I found this pretty interesting—studying each dog, its weight, its running history against other dogs in the race, the pole position, the condition of the track. Was it raining? It all seemed to make some sense. I thought it was just gambler's luck if you won, but there was logic to it.

All the guys I went with had also been injured on the job and were undergoing some form of rehabilitation. They were mostly older men who taught me how to read the racing forms and how to place a bet.

I was very cautious, so I would play the favorite to "show." The favorite, and the others, were posted on the electronic board out in the field, the open space in the center of the track. They told me that the most money would be bet on the favorite, that's why he was the favorite, pretty obvious. I won most of the time, because a "show" bet became a winner if the favorite won the race or came in second or even came in third. How could I lose?

Of course it didn't pay much. A two dollar bet usually gave me back my two dollars and two dimes. I'd make twenty cents. I lost one race and it took the rest of the day to recover my two dollars.

One of the guys in the rehabilitation program with me had lost his right leg while standing on a loading dock. He just shook his head when I asked him to go with us. He was not very steady on his prosthetic leg and hadn't felt comfortable using his crutches. But mainly, he was much too upset over the loss of his leg to go anywhere. He had worked as a truck driver, hauling supplies to industrial warehouses in and around Boston. During one delivery, he backed the truck up to the dock and then walked the steps to the platform. Suddenly, a young inexperienced fork truck driver came whirling around the corner from inside the warehouse and ran one of the blades through his right leg.

* * *

After several weeks of rehabilitation, the head nurse told me I was making good progress and could begin the outpatient phase of my treatment. "We're now going to scale down your visits to three days a week until we finish up," she said. I could go home and spend some time with my family. My treatments were coming to an end. They could do no more; the rest was up to me.

I was pretty damn unsure about this. The thought of rejoining society and weaning away from the support and comradeship of reha-bilitation was beginning to unnerve me. The swelling had diminished considerably, but I still needed physical therapy to improve motion and establish some limited dexterity.

I left the Lenox Hotel and walked to the nearest subway station to catch a train and then a bus from Boston to my mother's place in Brockton. I clumsily reached into my pockets for change to pay the subway fare, and dropped several coins onto the floor. I wasn't going to just leave them there, so I began fumbling around trying to pick them up. The guy in line behind me, realizing I was not having much success, reached down and gave me a hand. I thanked him but was embarrassed as hell.

My mother and Peter were still living at 89 West Elm Street, a couple of blocks from Brockton center. The apartment was small but my mother made it seem like home. It needed some minor repairs. Several chunks of plaster had fallen from the walls in the small bed-room I shared with my brother.

The living room walls weren't much better, but much of the miss-ing plaster was hidden behind the couch or covered over with a pic-ture. The bathroom sink faucet never stopped dripping and the heat was controlled in the basement by the landlord, Mr. Berger. It was late summer by now, so that wasn't a problem, but my mother did tell me how cold it had been the previous winter.

Each week, Mr. Berger came down the back stairs to the hallway outside our back door, and with the same familiar knock announced, "This is Mr. Berger. I want my rent." It was more like, "I vont my rr-hent." I would mimic Mr. Berger after he left. My mother thought I was so funny. But the rent had to be paid. I told her about the pend-ing lawsuit for $250,000. "Hey, Mom, don't worry too much about money," I said. "I'm gonna be rich and take care of everything."

Janice wrote to me a least once a week. I smiled when I saw the French in her come out. I wrote back as often as I could, fumbling with the pen trying to figure the best way to hold it, but I managed.

As I recall, the salutation of her letter, which must have arrived sometime in mid-September of 1965, was in French ("Mon Cheri"), which I thought was very charming. She was very concerned that she hadn't heard from me and wanted to know how things were progressing. She told me not to worry about my activity scholarship. It had been approved. The only problem was she couldn't find the approval letter. My roommate, Matt, had the paperwork and he had gone home to be with his parents who were going through a divorce.

She had been trying to register me for classes for the fall semester but was running into some difficulty with Central Registration because she didn't have the scholarship approval letter. She and Mike Kaplan went through everything in my apartment to try and find the scholarship paperwork.

I also remember that my car, my '57 Chevy, was parked in her driveway and had apparently raised some eyebrows for those who didn't know I had returned to Boston for rehabilitation. She had a big laugh over that.

I remember that she signed off with, "Mon amour, Janice," then added, along the bottom, "Poopy, ha ha."

* * *

The nickname "Poopy" came from a hilarious moment that happened while riding in my car one day on the way to school. The radio began playing "Hang on Sloopy," by the McCoy's and just goofing around, I started singing, "Hang on Poopy." I was being silly, laughing my way through the entire song, pretending I knew all the words. Whenever that song came on the radio after that we'd start laughing. "There's your song again," I'd say. We loved each other and loved singing songs together, especially that one.

The fall quarter of 1965 had begun shortly after Labor Day and Janice was still trying to register me for classes; it would probably be a late registration, that is, if my classes were not full. I knew if I completed my rehabilitation soon enough, I could return to school and would only miss the first or second class. I could explain my way around that to my professors and catch up quickly.

A week later, I received another letter from Janice which, as I remember, caused me great concern. I had to get back to school.

I remember she was very upset with the school administration for not allowing her to register for me. They had explained to her that because I was not a new student, I'd have to wait until later in September and then register "late." She explained my situation but they would not make an exception, and she was furious.

While in the registration office she checked to see if the classes I wanted were still open and they were, so she explained in her letter that it should not be a problem to register late. I remember her telling me that we were both going to be in the same Physics class together and admitted that was going to be her worst subject, and I'd have to help her. I didn't tell her that Physics was not going to be a walk in the park for me either.

She mentioned something about reading a book on the "Science of the Stars," which described in great detail the characteristics of an individual based solely upon the month in which they were born. I remember it fascinated her because as she said, it spelled me out to a "T."

She felt bad that she could not register me and acknowledged she had missed me and couldn't wait for me to return. Then signed off again with her "Mon cheri, Janice." And added the "Poopy" thing again as a P.S.

* * *

After hearing this, I told the staff at Liberty Mutual that I wanted to leave and get back to school. If I needed to continue treatments, I would have to take care of that on an out-patient basis in St. Louis. The head nurse explained her position: "We just can't drop your case until we're satisfied with your progress, both physically and emotionally. We understand your concerns and will try speeding things up for you." I told her I would stick around for another two weeks, but no longer.

I kept busy the next two weeks trekking back and forth to Boston, and learning how to take care of myself, especially my personal needs. I walked over to a typewriter that was on a desk in the corner at the rehabilitation center. I looked at my hands and then at the typewriter. "Goddamn it," I mumbled under my breath. The realization affected me profoundly. A cruel, empty feeling shot right through me.

I had been able to handle a typewriter with ease, thirty-five, maybe forty words a minute, without looking at the keys. Letters, numbers, punctuation marks, slashes and dashes, everything. I had memorized all the keys and could use all ten fingers to hit whatever key I wanted. Three and a half years of training in the service had perfected that, and now it seemed impossible. I needed time and patience.

The rehabilitation in Boston was finally coming to an end and I began preparing to return to school. The prospect, however, of leaving rehabilitation and having to face up to reality continued to unnerve me. Many questions, with few answers, continued to haunt me. I constantly worried about how others perceived me. I knew my thoughts were often a manifestation of my own insecurity, and I had to adjust to that. I needed to keep these feelings buried deep within me.

I felt trapped in a corner with no way out. This is the hand I was dealt and I had to play it—win or lose.

I planned to carry my books in my right hand, my worse hand, so no one would notice it. My little finger was healed and strong enough to balance my books while the palm of my hand held them against my body. I carried around thoughts that no one could have realized. What would I do if, or when…?

And what about holding hands with Janice? We always held hands while walking back and forth to school. Would she back away now?

I said my goodbyes to my mother and Peter and boarded a flight from Boston back to St. Louis. Liberty Mutual had booked my flight and gave me a voucher, which paid for everything.

During my absence, Matt Ryder had invited Robert Reeder, another student from SIU, to live with him. I'm not sure if I ever sent Matt any money for my share of the rent, but with Robert living there, he was able to pay the bills and keep the apartment.

All my personal belongings remained in the apartment through the summer. Then Matt, with the help of Janice and others, moved his and my clothing, beds, paintings and posters, and everything else to an apartment on Main Street in Edwardsville. When I returned to school in late September of '65, that was my new home. It was a two-bedroom first-floor unit just down the street from the Wildey Theatre in the center of town.

The Edwardsville campus was now open and fall classes were underway. When I returned, I found my scholarship paperwork and registered "late" for my fall classes, which were still open. The Pratt Academic Building was the first classroom building to be completed on campus, and the Lovejoy Library and Student Center, across from the quadrangle, was also open. The rest of the campus was still under construction.

Most of my insecurities vanished from my mind the moment I stepped off that plane and walked down the staircase. There, standing at the bottom of the stairs, was Janice. There must have been others there, but I only saw her. I dropped my bag and wrapped my arms around her, and she did the same.

I smiled broadly and told her, "I'm so glad to see you."

"I'm so glad to see you, too," she said. I kissed her on the cheek and we embraced once again.

Janice's warm embrace made me feel at home right away. I had really missed her and I missed the life I had carved out for myself in Illinois. But I also felt uneasy. I wanted everything to be the same as before, but I knew it would be an uncertain road.

* * *

Janice and I walked from the airport terminal to her car. I held her so close to me while we walked that I almost tripped myself. She drove from Lambert Field in St. Louis to her house on Brockmeier Road in Edwardsville. My '57 Chevy was still parked where I'd left it, off to the side in her driveway. We pulled into the driveway and went inside to say hello to Janice's mother. Gloria was happy to have me back. She smiled her charming smile and said, "It's so nice to have you home. How are you?" I told her I was happy to be back.

"It's nice to see you too," I said, "and thanks very much for taking care of my car."

Janice handed me my keys and we walked outside. I opened the car door with both hands and sat in the driver's seat. The stick shift was on the floor to my right. I looked at it and said to myself, I can do this; I've got to do this.

I turned the key and, surprising to me, it started without hesitation. Janice smiled and said, "I've been starting it up every other day since you left, and letting it run for a while." I kissed her and said, "You're the best."

I didn't want her riding with me and watching as I fumbled through the gears with the floor shift, so I asked her to follow along behind me in Wally's car.

When I arrived at my new place, I saw the cars but didn't think anything of it. Janice and Matt had arranged a welcome home party for me. I made a left off Main Street onto "E" Street, the side street next to my new apartment, and parked. Janice pulled in behind me. "What's going on? Who's here?" I asked. She smiled and said softly, "It's just some friends who want to welcome you home." I stopped for a moment, looked at the ground, and made up my mind to shut out the intervening ten weeks and pretend nothing had changed...but I was nervous as holy hell.

We walked in and everyone began singing, "For he's a jolly good fellow...that nobody can deny." I was excited to see so many of my friends. Everyone began slapping me on the back and offering me a beer. Nobody mentioned my ordeal. Nobody wanted to see....

They didn't stay long, just long enough to let me know how much they cared, and after a short time they all went home. They knew Janice and I needed some time alone. We sat and talked for a long time after that. She probably never knew how much I loved her and needed her. She had been there for me throughout this wretched ordeal, and I would never forget that.

I settled in at my new place, which was just a couple miles from Janice's house. I realized it would make life easier for her and her family if I picked her up in the mornings on my way to school. Wally could then have full use of his car and I would love her company. When I asked her what she thought of the idea she said, "Yes, I'd like that very much."

From that day on, and for the next three years, I drove to her house and picked her up each morning. I'd pull into her driveway, step out of my car and walk around to open her door. I was a gentleman and she was impressed. At the end of each day, we'd meet and go for a bite to eat, and then I'd take her home.

Every day began and ended with her.

I had registered late for school, and only for three classes. That was enough for now, I thought. I'd catch up later. I needed to adjust and ease my way into a gradual academic routine. I still couldn't write very well. I tried holding a pen every which way, but it always slipped out of my hand.

I held on to my innermost thoughts. Janice probably wasn't aware of the difficulty I was having adjusting. I never brought it up or complained about it, but I was an emotional mess.

The new campus was overwhelmed with contractors and their heavy trucks and earth-moving equipment. Too much was happening, too many changes. I missed the quiet academic life of the Alton campus, and the close-knit social circle I traveled in. Life had seemed simpler then.

I had not declared a major as yet and would not be compelled to do so until the beginning of my junior year, but I decided, after the accident, that I'd major in Elementary Education and minor in Math. I knew I'd make a good teacher and I felt I'd live a somewhat sheltered life, away from the harsh realities of the real world until I fully adjusted.

I bought a tape recorder and began recording class lectures. It would be awhile before I could figure out how to hold a pen and write. Simple things like combing my hair, brushing my teeth, and taking care of my most personal needs became a challenge. I would have to learn to do these things all over again, and I was determined not to let it upset me, or interfere with my desire to finish school.

Liberty Mutual paid a manufacturing company, skilled in developing prosthetic devises, to produce a flesh colored "glove" with fingers for me to wear. When I met with them at their plant in St. Louis, I dipped my right hand in a vat of plaster-of-Paris, thereby creating a hardened mold. From the mold came the plastic glove which would help me hold a pen. I thanked them when I picked it up a few weeks later, but when I tried it on I decided it looked completely absurd, and I refused to wear it.

I realized that there was no alternative. I'd have to learn how to write with what I had left.

I lay that glove down in the street and ran over it with my car, shattering it into hundreds of pieces.

The fall quarter of '65 was successfully behind me and I signed up for the spring quarter, which would begin shortly after the Christmas break. I decided I was ready to assume a full load, four classes. Janice did the same. One cold Saturday evening in early January of '66, I invited Janice over to my place to spend some quiet time together listening to music: Johnnie Mathis, Tony Bennett, the Monkees and the Mamas and Papas. Matt Ryder and my new roommate, Gary Hitchcock, had not returned from Christmas break yet, so we had the place to ourselves. There was a fireplace in the living room and I thought it would add to the evening if I had a roaring fire going while we danced to the music and sipped on a few beers.

The only problem was we didn't have any firewood, so I threw my coat on and went out back to gather up some twigs and sticks. It was a bitterly cold January night. I walked around gathering up some firewood, and when I turned around to go back inside, there it was, off to my left, an old wooden ironing board propped up against the back of the house. It didn't look like anything special to me, just an old wooden ironing board. I leaned it against the rear steps and stomped on it, smashing it into small pieces. With my arms now loaded with wood, I called to Janice to open the back door and let me in. When she did, I said, "Look at this. There's enough wood here for a roaring fire!"

A few days later, Matt returned from break and noticed the ironing board was missing. He brought it right up. "What happened to my ironing board?" he asked. "That's an antique, you know!"

I was embarrassed as hell. "Oops. Oh shit," I said. "You're not going to like this. I used it the other night when Janice came over...to build a fire. Sorry, man."

He wasn't happy with me, but he got over it. To make up for it, I told him I'd wash and wax his car for him as soon as the weather warmed up. That settled him down for the moment. He loved that car of his.

It was early spring when I received a call from someone in H3's office; they had my Workers Compensation check. The Missouri Compensation Board had issued a check for $12,000. It seems that every part of the human body has a dollar value. At the time, the family of anyone who was killed on the job would receive a lot less than the "sum of the parts."

Pretty crude, I thought, but that's the way it was. I netted $9,000. H3's fee was $3,000.

As soon as I received the check I drove over to the Pontiac dealership in Edwardsville center and traded my '57 Chevy for a brand new 1966 Pontiac GTO. I ordered the car through the dealership. They told me it would take a few weeks because it was a special order. I chose a beautiful, soft canary, yellow color with a black convertible top and a reverberating speaker sound system. The 3.8 cubic inch engine was ordered with three carburetors, "tri-power," as it was called. I decided on an automatic transmission because I didn't think I could shift a four-speed.

Three weeks later, I received a call from the dealership informing me, "Your new car has just arrived from Detroit, and wait until you see it!" I rushed over, gave them the title to my '57 Chevy, along with a check for the difference, then fired up the engine. What a power house! I flipped open the two latches releasing the top from the windshield, pushed the button to lower the top, then drove over to Janice's house. What a feeling! What a car! When I pulled off Brockmeier Road and up into her driveway, she came running out. "Wow, what a beautiful car!" she said nearly giggling. I opened the door for her and we both sat there listening to the radio and admiring the many gauges and the rich cherry wood dashboard. She was so excited.

She turned and asked, "Can I take it for a little ride up town and do a little showing off?" I said, "Sure, go ahead, I'll wait here."

I waited in her backyard for what seemed like a very long time. When she returned, her cheeks were blushing red and her smile lit up her face. She turned off the engine and sat there with both hands clutching the steering wheel, admiring every detail of the car, then glanced up at me and said, "How do I look?"

I said, "You look terrific!"

I loved riding with Janice back and forth to school and listening to the radio. The sound system speakers were engineered to alternately delay the music by a split second, creating a reverberating, echo effect—just a beautiful car in every respect.

Before leaving the Alton campus, I had completed the pledge period and was brought in as a full member of the local fraternity. Now that we were settling in at the Edwardsville campus, a new group of pledges had been enlisted and were following right behind us. They had endured the several weeks of hazing and were soon to become full members. They were busy putting the final touches together for "turnabout." Turnabout was the twenty-four hour period when pledges would "get back" at the regulars for the frequent humiliation they endured while pledging.

We all knew it was coming but didn't know when.

Turnabout was well underway when I left my house to pick up Janice one night. Matt and Gary and I, and another friend, Fran Bowles, had planned to get together at my place for a brief party before heading down the street to the Wildey Theater. Fran and his girlfriend had already arrived and were waiting for us inside.

Gary was a pledge at the time and must have tipped the others off about the party, because when Janice and I arrived, I spotted four guys carrying Fran out through the front door, holding him up over their heads like they were taking him to his wake.

Janice started laughing and screaming at the same time. "Roustabout! Roustabout!" she cried.

I said, "Oh no, it's turnabout! Quick, roll up the window. Don't let Wilcox in."

Dick Wilcox and several of the others surrounded my car; they really wanted me. I must have given them a hard time while they were pledging. I leaned over and looked out the passenger side window and starting taunting him, laughing and sticking out my tongue. Wilcox wasn't getting me unless he was willing to break the window of my

208

new car. I wasn't completely sure he wouldn't.

Wilcox kept pleading with Janice to open the door. I told her again, "Don't let him in!"

Janice was enjoying this and I wasn't sure if she'd open the door or not. She was having fun teasing him and teasing me, and laughing over calling it "roustabout." I inched my way through the frenzied mob and made it to the end of the street without running anyone over, then turned left and drove around the block, watching from a distance as they dumped Bowles into the back seat and headed out of town.

Janice was laughing so hard tears were running down her cheeks. I don't think I'd ever seen her so excited. They never captured me, though. I hid out for the night in my car behind the library on campus.

* * *

Gary Hitchcock and I became really close friends. He was a very gentle, caring guy who grew up in Caseyville, a small rural town in the backwoods south of Edwardsville. It seemed like all the towns in and around Southern Illinois ended with "ville." Maryville, Caseyville, Collinsville, Belleville.

Gary was thin, about five foot-six, and had plenty of wavy dark blond hair. He had bounced around from one parent to another while growing up and eventually moved in with his uncle before graduating from high school. He came from nothing, much like me. I don't remember how we met, but I liked him right away. He was looking for a place to stay, so I invited him to move in with us.

Gary was the only one in his family to attend college; his mother and father didn't make it beyond junior high. His brother spent much of his life in jail out in California. "College was not even in our family vocabulary," he once told me.

Gary was going to take a different road; he was determined to break free from the shackles of endless poverty and insecurity that defined his youth. It was after his parents finally split up that he moved in with Uncle Ted. A smile lit up his face as he began to reminisce with me about his uncle. "Don, you've got to meet him. He's a care-free, smooth operator—a charmer from the old Mississippi Delta days. He loves to gamble and tell stories, and he loves to drink. He doesn't have much and he lives alone now. I'm sure he'd like to meet you. He loves company."

Gary and I took a ride down there one Saturday afternoon. His uncle lived in a small three-room house, more like a shack, down a dirt road deep in the rural backcountry of Southern Illinois. We pulled off the dirt road and parked in Ted's front yard. There was no driveway. It was all just bare ground. No grass, no flowers, and no walkway.

Gary said, "Here we are, this is it. Just pull over there and park next to the porch." The front porch had an overhang roof that was held up by a series of two-by-fours braced against stakes in the front yard. No one answered when Gary knocked on the screen door, which was hanging off to the right. The screws holding the upper hinge were missing and the door was ready to fall off.

Gary said, "Let's go around back and see if he's in the backyard." Around back, attached to the house, was a newly built screened-in porch. Uncle Ted was standing next to a table on the porch attending to something in a large pot. We startled him at first, but then he realized it was Gary.

"*GARY!*" he shouted. He was positively delighted to see him, and seemed genuinely happy to meet me. Right away he said, "Come on in and have a glass of homemade dandelion wine. We got to celebrate."

"Thanks," I said, trying to be polite but a little unsure about dandelion wine. He ladled a small amount into two paper cups, one for Gary and one for me. Gary thanked him and swallowed hard, then opened his mouth for a gulp of fresh air. "Man," he said, shaking his head. "That's all right." I took a taste and nearly spit it out.

"Ohhh…phew…wow…is this stuff bitter!" I cried, trying not to offend him too much. Uncle Ted burst out laughing.

"You gotta get used to it; it's good for you. Made it myself," he said with pride and a warm smile.

"I hope you don't mind, but I think I'll just have a beer instead," I said apologetically.

"Okay, then let me grab you one," he offered.

"No, that's all right," I said. "We brought some along with us.

Some for you and some for us." Ted wasn't listening as he went to the kitchen to get me a beer.

Uncle Ted was about sixty-five and looked every bit of it. Lots of white hair, unshaven—a naturally friendly guy with a warm inviting smile. I felt at ease with him immediately. There was nothing complicated about Uncle Ted.

He obviously loved Gary and was very excited to see him, and delighted to have the unexpected company. We hadn't been there very long before he waved his index finger in Gary's direction, as if he suddenly remembered something. "Hold on a minute," he exclaimed.

He turned around and reached up to the top shelf of an old cabinet that was leaning against the wall on the porch. After knocking over a small lamp, he brought down three yellow cups without handles. "Don't worry about that," he said, referring to the lamp.

He was excited now and in a bit of a hurry as he pulled a little table from over in the corner out into the middle of the room. He stood over the table and placed the three cups down in a row on it, then turned each upside down. I watched him and wondered what in hell he was doing. With a broad grin, he held up his hands and rubbed them together as if to get them warm, then said, "Oh shit. Hold on a minute—"

He stopped himself in mid-sentence, then stepped outside to the backyard and picked up a small rock. He brought it in and held it up between his thumb and first finger so we could get a good look. Gary turned to me with a knowing smile and said, "Watch out. Here he goes."

Ted, now sly as a fox, closed one of his eyes, tilted his head to one side, turned to me and whispered, "You got any loose change?"

"What's he up to?" I asked Gary.

Gary was sipping his wine and grinning at the same time. "Hold on to your wallet," he said.

Uncle Ted grabbed the cups and the rock and knelt down on the floor to show me how the sleight-of-hand tricksters—the street peddlers, he called them—made their living. "Watch this very carefully," he said. I could tell he was a seasoned trickster himself. He placed the stone—which he referred to as a pea—under one of the three cups and began singing a little song while shifting the cups around in circles, back and forth and around again.

"There," he said. "Where's the pea?"

I had been watching him closely and knew exactly where that "pea" was. I was right. "Can't fool me," I bragged.

Uncle Ted burst out laughing. Gary just stood back quietly, shaking his head and sipping his wine. I knew I was being taken for a ride. I wanted to play this out and watch how he operated, but I knew I was being set up. I figured if I'm going to lose any money, I'll gain some experience and have a few laughs along the way.

I played along, feeding him coins and keeping my eye on him until I was out of loose change. "I'll be goddamned if I can figure this out," I said.

Gary warned me again. "I told you to watch out. He's been charming the loose change from pockets most of his life." We all had a good laugh, especially Ted.

Uncle Ted was now ready to play some poker. Now I've got a fighting chance, I said to myself. I knew how to play poker, but I didn't know a thing about the damn little pea and the three cups.

Ted was tickled with himself for out-foxing me and I was equally amused. Ted stood up and without any music began dancing around on his tiptoes. With his head down, looking at his dancing feet, he started singing a song from long ago. "I hate myself for loving you, 'cause I know you love somebody else." He explained that it was an old song from the '30s that really tickled him. This is Bojangles himself, I thought. I figured Ted must have been an entertainer of some years ago. I could just imagine him performing for the gamblers and the dance hall crowd on board one of the Mississippi River boats during the warm summer months in Southern Illinois.

We talked and drank and laughed some more before walking through the house and out to the front porch for a game of poker. We played poker throughout the night and into the early morning hours. Ted was a fun guy to be around and a shrewd operator. And as confident as I was, he taught me a few lessons about poker as well. Half asleep and out of money, Gary and I finally said goodbye to Uncle Ted. We somehow made it home just as the sun was coming up.

I think about that night with Uncle Ted every time I hear Arlo Guthrie's song, "The City of New Orleans"—a Monday morning Chicago train, by the same name, that passes south along fields of old black men and rusted automobiles, through the back country of Southern Illinois, down to the sea. But I didn't have time to let any of it dominate my life. I needed to focus on school and, of course, Janice.

I introduced Gary to Janice's best friend, Amy Yolanda, during a party we were having one night. Gary and Amy hit it off from the start and were soon dating regularly.

The four of us became very goods friends; we did everything together. "Gary and Amy" became one word to me. They were married in May of 1966 in a small ceremony held in a chapel a few miles east of Edwardsville in the town of Belleview. It was just the preacher and his witness-secretary, and Janice and me.

They were going to have a baby. It had to be a little overwhelming for them at the time, I thought, but they were so young and so much in love. They were perfect together.

Not long after they were married, Gary called and wanted to meet me at Vanzo's for a beer; he needed to talk. Vanzo's was one of the places where we hung out after school, a restaurant/bar kind of place, but mostly a bar. It was an old established saloon that had been around since before prohibition, and it was always packed with lawyers, politicians, courthouse personnel and the local folks and those of us attending SIU

Vanzo's had a narrow entranceway with a floor-to-ceiling rack of empty beer cans stacked to the left along the wall as you entered. Many of the empty cans were from breweries long since shut down. To the right, beyond the entranceway, a long bar ran about thirty feet, almost to the rear door. The "conference room" was in the back, through a small door, just beyond the end of the bar, and the juke box was at the far end across from the bar and next to the restrooms.

The entrance to the restaurant and pool room was along the wall to the left. There were antiques hanging from the ceiling and political placards and posters everywhere. Someone had glued a quarter to the floor, about halfway down the bar. It caught my eye almost every time I walked in there. I tried picking it up more than once to the amusement of those sitting at the bar.

The owner and frequent bartender, Jimmy Vanzo, was a thin, soft-spoken man who everyone knew and liked. Hanging from the ceiling, and directly over the bar, was an old schoolhouse bell with a long rope. Jimmy would scoop up the change left as a tip on the bar, grab the rope, ring the bell, and toss the change up over his head, above the mirrored wall, and into a two-foot opening between the wall and the ceiling. You could hear the change trickle down behind the wall and settle in somewhere on the other side, lost forever. At least until someone opened up that wall. (Which did happen, I'm told, in late 1988. Workmen shoveled coins for days after tearing down that wall during major renovations to the entire block).

It was a hot summer's afternoon when Gary walked through the front door. He had left Amy moments before. She was angry at him for something. I didn't ask. They had just moved into a small second-floor apartment in Edwardsville, and he was having a tough time working and going to school. He said, "I just needed to get out for a while, let her calm down."

He had one beer and I asked him if he'd like another. He said, "No, I don't want to drink too much, say the wrong thing and regret it later." He was always the voice of reason. For his young age, he had more than his share of common sense.

Still, he had his hands full—newly married with a baby on the way and trying to get through school with only a part-time job to keep it together. We sat for a while talking about school and work and what a strain everything was financially.

A couple of days later, I drove over to their place to pay a visit. It was so hot that day in their upstairs apartment. With only a small fan to keep her cool, Amy, now several months pregnant, was standing over an ironing board ironing Gary's shirts. Gary was now working two part-time jobs and going to school full time. Money was tight and the future seemed uncertain at best.

TEN

Thirty-eight Points

One bitterly cold and dark night, after a party at my place, I drove Janice home, gave her a kiss and said goodnight. When I returned, a girl was standing next to the refrigerator in the kitchen and having a beer. The party was over and her date, if she had one, had left or was too drunk to drive, so she asked me if I would drive her home. I said, "Sure, where do you live?"

The roads were icy that night, black ice everywhere. As it turned out, she lived out in the country. We drove for half an hour along country roads that weren't well marked. Miles and miles of open farmland on either side. I finally reached her house and dropped her off. She thanked me for the ride and I turned around in her driveway and headed back home. On the way back I slid through a "T" intersection and slammed into an earthen embankment directly in front of me. My face smashed against the steering wheel and my left hand and knee hit the dashboard. I reached up with my right hand and adjusted the mirror to see if my eye had popped out. It hadn't.

The back half of my car was still out in the road. The front was buried in the embankment. Not only was it cold and dark, but it was also drizzly, and there were no street lights anywhere. I looked to my right and saw a semi-tractor trailer coming around a corner and heading right through the intersection. I figured if I didn't get the car out of the way, he probably wouldn't see me until it was too late.

My engine had died upon impact, so I reached down and turned the key and, although it sounded like I was grinding up parts of the radiator, it started. I quickly put the car in reverse and was able

215

to inch it out of the way just as the truck came roaring through the intersection.

I breathed a sign of relief as I drove the mangled car over to the side of the road and on to the frost-covered grass. I forced the door open, climbed out and stood at the edge of the road with my bruised and bloody face, looking to hail down the first car that came along. An older couple, on their way home, stopped and gave me a lift to the nearest hospital. They offered to call a tow truck and have the car delivered back to my place in Edwardsville. I said, "Thanks a lot, that would be great."

There were no rooms available in the hospital, so they set up a portable bed in the hallway, next to the nurses' station. Two Edwardsville cops arrived and took a statement from me. I wasn't cited, and they gave me a copy of their brief report for my insurance company. I spent a couple of days in the hospital. No big deal; I'd recover.

I hired a tow truck to haul my car back to the same auto dealership where I bought it originally, traded in what was left of it, signed over the insurance papers—and ordered another 1966 yellow Pontiac GTO convertible.

It was another special order, so it took several weeks before it arrived from the factory. It was identical to the first GTO except for one thing: I ordered it with a four-speed, a floor-mounted stick transmission. When it arrived, I wrote a check for the balance and drove off the lot and back to my place.

I now had about $3,000 left in the bank.

I had a little difficulty driving the four-speed at first, but I quickly figured it out. When Janice saw it, she thought it was the same car, but she quickly realized she could not handle the floor clutch and the four-speed transmission. I tried on several occasions to show her, but the car would jerk forward and stall or screech rubber. She gave up trying; it just made her too nervous. It was a great car, though, a complete blast to drive.

I began making plans for spring break, 1966. Many of the college kids were leaving town and heading for Florida, so I thought it would be fun to invite some friends along to join with me on a road

trip to Daytona Beach. But before making such a trip, the manufacturer's warrantee suggested I "break-in" the engine gradually. It rec-
ommended that I run the engine at speeds under fifty miles per hour
for the first five hundred miles, then change the oil and the oil filter.
After that I could drive the car without concern for speed or long
distance travel.

So I decided I'd drive around town and out into the country, keeping the speeds under fifty, until I passed the five-hundred mile requirement. I didn't want to push my luck, so I took my time and reached
the five-hundred mile mark three days later, then changed the oil and
filter and called Gary to see if he wanted to go with me. He said,
"Sure!" Then I called John Goodwin, a "laugh-a-minute" guy we all
called "Bird," to see if he was interested. Then I asked Mike Eaton,
another friend. On Saturday morning, the first day of spring break, I
picked everyone up and headed southeast for the Florida sunshine.

I had asked Janice to come with us, but her mother thought it
wasn't a good idea, so she stayed home.

We had a lot of laughs in Daytona driving along the beach and
soaking up the night life. I remembered my days in the Air Force,
when I was stationed in Orlando. Back then, I'd often drive to Daytona, park on the beach, swim in the ocean to clear up my acne, and
leave with my usual "fair-skinned" sunburn.

Ten days later, we arrived safely back from the nonstop, fun-filled
chaos of spring break and settled in for the final quarter at school.
After this quarter, I would have my sophomore year behind me. I was
still short two classes, so I planned to take them over the summer to
catch up and graduate on time with the class 1968.

Janice and I had been dating for over two years by then and became engaged on Christmas Day, 1966. We were sitting together on
her living room couch exchanging gifts, when I stood up and said,
"I'll be back in a minute, I've got something else for you. It's in the
car." I went out to my car, opened the glove box and put the small
case in my pocket. She was still sitting on the couch when I returned.
I walked over to her, reached for her hand, and dropped down on
one knee. I slowly reached into my jacket pocket and presented her

217

with the ring and asked her to marry me. She accepted right away. I slipped the ring over her finger, gave her a kiss, and held her tightly for a long, warm embrace.

The engagement ring had a solitary diamond of thirty-eight points—not very big, but big enough. Her mother walked in from the kitchen and said with a broad smile, "I wish I'd known about this. I could have bought some champagne!" We were so happy together. Her mother was obviously delighted as well, and that meant a lot to me.

Shortly after the holidays I received a call from Peter. He was in Chicago. We had exchanged Christmas cards and a phone call on Christmas Day. When I spoke with my mother and Peter and told them I had just become engaged to Janice and how excited I was, there was no mention of a trip to Chicago.

Except for brief stays on leave from the service and a few trips home for the holidays, I had been away for nearly six years. Peter really missed me during this time. He had quit school after the eighth grade and was trying desperately to get started in life—trying to find a niche and become a success.

He called collect; the operator asked if I would accept the charges. I said yes, I would, and she said, "Go ahead, your party is on the line."

His call from Chicago really puzzled me. "What are you doing in Chicago?" I asked. He said it was a long story. "Just tell me…. I'm listening." I said.

"Before I tell you that," he said, "let me start off by telling you I graduated from barber school in Boston. I used to take the bus every day from Brockton to Dorchester and then pick up the subway, which brought me to the corner of Washington and Dover Street. That's where the barber school was located."

"Who paid for all that?" I asked him. He explained that he had applied for assistance through the Massachusetts Rehabilitation Commission, and they agreed to provide funding for him to attend the school.

Then he went on to explain how he had met a girl in Brockton named Alice. She was sixteen and so was he. One night Alice's mother stopped by to tell my mother that Alice was pregnant, and insisted that Alice and Peter get married. He said, "She was a real manipulator with plenty of street smarts."

Peter went on to tell me that because of his age, he needed my mother's written consent before he could get married. So Peter and my mother walked down to the Brockton District Courthouse and filled out the necessary forms giving Peter her consent.

Although Peter never mentioned it, I think my mother went along with it partly to get Peter out of the house. She had told me that he was coming and going at all hours of the night, and he and Joe weren't getting along at all. Peter was becoming impossible to deal with. As young as he was, he was pretty much on his own, a fired-up, impulsive young man with fire in his belly and bottled-up ambition.

Peter and Alice were married by a Justice of the Peace in Raynham, Massachusetts, a small town fifteen miles southeast of Boston. It was just Peter, Alice, her mother and her mother's boyfriend. No formality and no reception. My mother and Joe didn't attend. Although there was plenty of tension between Peter and Joe, I was surprised that my mother wasn't there. I asked Peter about it and he said, "Don, it was just a shotgun wedding, that's all."

Following the marriage, they moved into a small, unfurnished apartment about six miles away, in Abington. Now that he was a licensed barber he was working every day at the barber shop inside the main foyer of the West Elm Hotel in Brockton. He didn't have a car, so he'd grab the city bus from Abington to Brockton and back again.

Somehow they managed to furnish the place and by now it was becoming obvious to Peter that Alice had been lying about the pregnancy. They were together for about five months when Peter stepped off the bus from work one night and opened the door to his apartment to discover that Alice had left him. She had taken all of her personal belongings and anything else of value.

Peter walked across the street and waited for the next bus back to Brockton. He stopped at my mother's place to tell her what had happened and ask her if she knew what was going on. They decided to walk over to Alice's mother's place for an explanation.

Alice was there, but it was her mother who did the talking. She told Peter that Alice wasn't pregnant, and that they, Alice, her mother and her mother's boyfriend, were leaving for Chicago. Her boyfriend had just been offered a job out there with United Airlines.

Alice turned and said to Peter, "We should stay in touch, though. Maybe you can come and visit me out there."

Peter simply replied, "No…and don't bother contacting me."

The following day, Peter and my mother walked down to the Brockton District Courthouse and filed divorce papers. Peter wasn't going back to live with my mother and Joe again. He knew they didn't want him there, and preferred to be independent anyway.

Peter finished up by telling me, "I went back to Abington and gathered up what was left after Alice cleaned me out. Then the manager of the West Elm Hotel, knowing my situation, offered me a small room for next to nothing. So I took him up on his offer and moved in. It was down in the basement, but that was okay with me. That's it, until Alice called me."

"Hey, so what are you doing in Chicago?" I asked again. He was in rough, tough South Chicago and needed to get the hell out of there. Apparently, Alice had missed him; at least that's what she led him to believe. She wanted him to come out to Chicago and see her; she had made a mistake. My brother, with his softhearted underbelly admittedly exposed, said he had also missed her and confessed he'd love to see her again. He didn't have any money for airfare, or even enough for a bus trip. So, he asked, "How'm I going to get there?"

Alice reassured him, "Oh, that's not a problem; my mother will pay for you to fly out here."

Peter stopped himself in mid-sentence. "Hey, enough with the questions. It's a long story. I'll tell you everything on the way back. Just come and get me. Get me outta here!"

"Okay," I said, "I'm on the way."

I gassed up my car and left that afternoon with a friend of mine who knew Chicago inside and out. He'd grown up there. He told me all I needed to know about South Chicago. "We don't want to be there too long," he said.

It was well after midnight when we left the highway and slipped into the neighborhood where Peter was staying. He had been waiting on the sidewalk for more than an hour or two, sitting under a dimly lit lamp post, just outside Alice's place, his small, faded yellow suitcase sitting next to him.

I rounded the corner and saw him up ahead to my left on the sidewalk. He waved when he saw me coming, grabbed his suitcase and when I pulled over, climbed in the back seat, saying, "Boy am I glad to see you, and glad to get out of this damn place. I almost got into a fight. They're a mean bunch of bastards, all of 'em."

We turned down a couple of side streets and were soon on the highway heading south, back to Edwardsville. We drove for the rest of the night, and sometime late in the afternoon on the next day, we arrived back at my place.

During the trip back, Peter told me the details of his relationship with Alice.

"So," he began, "I received the flight tickets in the mail, packed some clothes and took the bus to Logan and flew out here to Chicago. Alice and her mother picked me up at O'Hare Airport. I wasn't sure what this was all about. I wasn't sure if she missed me or not. It all seemed a little fishy to me.

"Anyway," he continued, "I figured I'd be out of Brockton for a while and on an adventure—my first flight and all. When I got there, they insisted I move in with them and stay awhile. And guess what! This time, Alice was pregnant, pregnant by someone else. It was some guy in the Navy stationed at the Great Lakes Naval Training Center. He had completed his training and was shipping out, and that's the last she was going to see of him. So Alice and her slick mother hatched a plan. They wanted me to come to Chicago and stay with them. I would sleep with her, and they could blame her pregnancy on me. Then I'd be on the hook for paying child support. It didn't take me long to figure the whole thing out. That's when I called you.

"I can return to my old job once I get back to Brockton, no problem. So, all I need now is my driver's license and a car, and then I'll be all set."

Peter stayed with me at my apartment on North Main Street in Edwardsville for a couple of weeks. I introduced him to my friends and he met Janice. I helped him get his Illinois driver's license while he was there. He had been having a difficult time passing the Massachusetts driver's test, so I said, "Let's try and get it out here and then you can transfer it when you get back home."

When his Illinois license arrived in my mailbox, I bought Peter a Greyhound Bus ticket back to Boston. It was good to see him and I was glad I could get him out of that mess in Chicago—and happy that he finally had his driver's license.

* * *

Things weren't coming along fast enough for me. I couldn't run from or hide from the fact that my disfigured hands were a constant torment. My patience, or rather lack of patience, contributed to my often unpredictable and impulsive behavior.

I needed Janice more than ever. She was becoming more of a social extrovert while I was shaking off some poor grades in an advanced Physics class. And I was running out of money. We were having periodic arguments triggered by the stress of school and my increasingly obsessive behavior. Our once warm and loving affection for each other was wearing thin. We needed a break from each other.

I began having severe stomach cramps, so I went to a doctor for some tests to find out why this was happening and what could be done about it. When the tests came back the doctor told me I was on the verge of developing stomach ulcers. He put me on valium to help settle me down. The valium didn't seem to do very much, so I threw them in the trash.

Sometimes, after eating, I would develop outrageous pains in my stomach which radiated into my back. I'd arch my back and force myself to throw up, but the pain still wouldn't settle down. I took Maalox and Rolaids and drank milk—anything to get some relief.

I had never been dependent on anyone after leaving high school, but I was now dependent upon Janice and our relationship, and although I was frequently "the life of the party," I began drinking too much and too often, and putting on weight.

I sold my yellow '66 Pontiac GTO convertible in March of 1968—my junior year–to raise money. I loved that car; there were so many memories. But it had to go. Kenny Tibbetts, the salesman who had sold the car to me originally, said he would be willing to sell it for me. "No problem. I should have it sold in a week or so," he assured me.

So now I needed another car, just something to get me to school and back. I answered an ad in the local newspaper for a used car salesman's job at a place called "Cars for Less" on Main Street. They hired me on the spot. I told them I didn't have a car, so they gave me one to use. I could have the car for as long as I continued working there. If I quit, I'd have to turn it back in. It wasn't much, but it was transportation.

While working there, I met the other used car salesman who looked and acted the part—a sleazy, "fast Eddy" type. He was tall and dark, with greasy hair and long, thick sideburns. He wore an open shirt, gold necklace, and pointed leather cowboy boots. He'd jump up out of his seat when a potential customer pulled into the lot. It was often my turn, but I really didn't care. He always used the same slick routine. He'd reach out, shake the customer's hand and say, "Ring Dang Do, I'm with you."

His approach was in a class by itself. I thought to myself, How in the hell is he going to sell anything looking like that and using that absurd, slapstick introduction?'

I never sold one car, figuring there was nothing there worth owning; my heart just wasn't in it. I wanted to turn in the loaner car and quit, but I needed to stick it out until Kenny sold my car. Kenny finally called me and gave me the news I'd been waiting for. He said, "Meet me at the diner up the street at noon. I have your money." I met him there, and while we were sitting at a small round lunch table in the middle of the dining area, he slipped me sixteen one hundred dollar bills under the table.

I took the money and slowly counted it out. I looked at him awkwardly, wondering where the rest of the money was. I knew the car would fetch more than this. "Is this all?" I asked. He said there'd be more...later.

Kenny called me a week or so later; he had more money for me. We met at the same diner and sat at the same small round table and he handed me another three hundred under the table. "That's it," he told me. He added, "By the way, the engine blew up shortly after I sold it."

I never believed the story about the engine blowing up. Kenny had used the same line with me when I'd traded in my '57 Chevy way back when I bought my first GTO. I figured I probably lost about five hundred on the deal, but I just wrote it off as his hefty commission— the price of doing business with Kenny Tibbetts.

A few days later, I ran into one of Kenny's salesman friends who asked, "How's it going with Kenny? Did he sell your car okay?" I told him what had happened and he just rolled his eyes. Kenny was a smooth operator with a reputation that somehow slipped past me.

I had some money now and could look around for something else, something used. Nothing on that lot interested me. I came upon a small, red convertible sports car in the "autos for sale" section of the school paper. It was a used Austin-Healey Sprite. The owner wanted $800. I called him up, and after taking it out for a short ride, I decided to go ahead a buy it.

Later the same day, I returned my loaner car and said goodbye to the used car business. The little Sprite ran forever on a gallon of gas, and although it was not very roomy, it was fun to drive. I figured I had done pretty well, and I didn't dwell on the other car, or what had happened with Kenny.

Sometime in the spring of the following year, my Aunt Betty apparently contacted my Aunt Pat and told her what had happened to me. My Uncle Donald must have then contacted my father out in Michigan, because one Saturday morning I received a call from Jane asking me how I was and what happened. I had never told my father. I figured he'd find out sooner or later. "Why didn't you tell us?" she asked. "Wait, hold on…your father wants to talk with you."

I'm pretty sure he wouldn't have made the call without Jane's insistence, not because he didn't care about me, but because he wouldn't know how to deal with it, or wouldn't know what to say. He asked me how I was. I told him I was fine, no problem, still in school. We didn't talk long. He handed the phone back to Jane and I told her what was going on in my life, about Janice and our engagement, and that we hadn't set a date as of yet, but probably would after graduation. She told me everyone in Michigan wanted to see me again. "We'd love to meet Janice, and Jimmy and Paul are always asking for you. Can you drive up for a long weekend and bring Janice with you?"

I told her I'd have to plan it out and talk with Janice. "I'll get back to you," I said. I reassured her that I had recovered from the accident and was back in school and doing fine, nothing to worry about. I thanked her for the invitation and we said goodbye.

Not long after, Janice and I drove to Michigan in my little red sports car to meet my father, Jane and the boys. Jane had written to Janice's mother, inviting us to come and spend a weekend with them. All the proper arrangements were assured. Janice would have her own bedroom and I would sleep in the attic.

We left on a Thursday, a beautiful summer day in 1967. We packed a bunch of sandwiches and drinks and took off north to Wyandotte. I drove straight through. The little red car ran fine. I put the top down and we rode along with the radio blasting and the wind in our hair. We had a nice trip.

While we were in Detroit, though, Janice got a glimpse of what my father was like. On Saturday afternoon, he said, "Come with me, let's go down to Chauncy's for a drink." Chauncy's was a local bar and grill located at the end of his street, his favorite haunt.

I said "Okay, I'll drive. You can see what it's like to ride in a sports car." He was a heavy guy and had trouble getting in, and when he did, the car nearly sank to the street.

While we were at Chauncy's enjoying a game of pool and a couple of drinks, Jane told Janice about her sorrowful life with him. He was a hardworking man, but a rough man to live with and a brutish father. She said he was especially hard to live with after drinking, and he drank every Thursday, Friday and Saturday night. Jane told Janice that she planned to divorce him after her boys reached eighteen and were out of school. Before we left for home, Jane quietly confessed to me what she had said to Janice.

I think that conversation had an impact on Janice. I didn't know what she was thinking and she never spoke to me about it, but she seemed unusually quiet during our trip home. I sensed she was concerned, wondering if I would be like my father. She must have known that I wasn't like him at all, but whatever she was thinking stayed with her.

A week after Janice and I returned from Michigan, I stopped by the Stonehouse Tavern to see who was there and what was going on, and I ran into Bird. By now, Bird was becoming a really good friend. He was the closest thing to a free spirit I'd ever met. Nothing, and I mean nothing, ever seemed to bother him. He was a tall, good-looking guy, thin as a stick with long blond curly hair—the girls loved him. He was sitting at the bar having a beer and talking with the bartender, Danny O'Brien. When the owner wasn't around, Danny, my old roommate from the previous year, would slip me my drinks for free.

I sat down with Bird and we reminisced about our trip to Daytona Beach during spring break earlier in the year. Bird had just received his student loan money to help pay for tuition and books for the upcoming fall quarter. He was flush with money, and the more we drank the more we began talking about going to Las Vegas. He started challenging me: "I'll go but you won't," he said, and I came right back with the same. So that night we decided to go to Las Vegas.

It was a completely impulsive, spur-of-the-moment thing. I wasn't sure I wanted to do this, but I figured it would be good for me to get away. I had the time and a little money. The fall quarter wouldn't be starting for another two weeks, and I wanted to live a little on the edge. I thought I could return to my happy-go-lucky, youthful, adventurous self and finally shake off these bouts of melancholy, and I figured Janice could use a little break from me as well. I knew she wouldn't be upset with me for too long. Maybe I was taking her for granted, assuming she would be there for me no matter what.

I told Bird I'd pick him up in half an hour. "You go home and pack, and I'll do the same," I said. I'd had way too much to drink, and so had Bird. Not the best idea for a guy who was engaged to be married. I figured I'd better get some of this out of my system before settling down, or I might never have the chance again.

I packed some shirts and socks, nothing else. I jammed everything into an old suitcase and drove over to Bird's house, a place everyone called "Palmer House." He threw his loose clothes in the trunk and climbed into my small Austin-Healey Sprite. That was Bird; he never seemed to be bothered by formalities. So there we were, heading west to Las Vegas. Bird drove the first leg. I curled up and went to sleep— too much drink and too much youth.

It was nearly dawn when Bird pulled off the road into a rest area. He needed some coffee and a chance to stretch his legs. We had made it all the way to Abilene, Texas. He told me that he had picked up a hitchhiker earlier that night. "How in hell? Where did you put him? There's hardly enough room for you and me."

He said, "Well, he slouched down behind the seats, kinda sideways like, and draped his legs over you." I told him that I didn't remember any of that and he said, "I know, you were sound asleep. I thought you were dead."

From there we headed northwest to Denver, Colorado. It was my turn to drive. An empty feeling began creeping up on me, like I had done something wrong. Janice would be disappointed, I was sure, so I called her from the road to tell her where I was and where we were off to. "Be back in a few days," I said. "Hope you don't mind." I could feel her disappointment through the phone.

Before we reached Denver, Bird started complaining about a toothache. He told me it was coming on when we set out, but he didn't think much of it. Now it was throbbing, killing him. I turned off the highway and stopped at a liquor store. He wanted to pick up a pint of whiskey, hoping that would settle it down a little. He was good-natured about his toothache and I knew he was really hurting. Riding along in the passenger side of my cramped little car, he'd take a long draw from the whiskey bottle, then look over at me with a smile and say, "Ah, now that's better."

We eventually pulled into downtown Denver and found a dentist somewhere along Colfax Avenue. We both went into the office.

Bird, with his broad smile and wily charm, told the young secretary, "You've got to pull this out." He pointed into his open mouth to show her which tooth. Almost in an instant, she fell victim to his boyish charm. He could turn it on, even with a pounding toothache. Someone once said of Bird that "he never met a stranger." He could charm anyone.

The secretary's eyes widened and a cute grin broke out across her face as he explained, with much animation, how bad it hurt and how he was drinking to relieve the pain—all the details of his sad tale. She paused for a moment and then said, "I'll be right back." She turned away from the counter and walked around the glass divider to speak with the dentist. Bird turned and gave me a wink as if to say, "She likes me."

In a minute or two, she came back and gave him the good news. "He'll see you later today. How about four o'clock?" She was obviously enjoying Bird and amused by his antics. He was tilting his curly blond head to one side, crossing his big blue eyes, and crinkling up his face—exaggerating the pain.

He assured her, "It's got to go; it's got to come out, so don't worry, we'll be back at four. Don't go anywhere."

She smiled broadly through a slight giggle and said, "We'll be expecting you."

We left the office and went for a drink. Both of us wanted to try some of that world famous Coors beer. Coors had a reputation for being one of the best beers in the country—maybe the world—and at the time it was only available in the Denver area. We spotted a place not far from the dentist's office, right on Colfax Avenue. We walked in, found a couple of seats at the bar and enjoyed the cold, Rocky Mountain taste of Coors beer.

A few minutes before four o'clock, we arrived back at the dentist's office and sat down in the waiting area. The secretary came out, recognizing Bird right away. She quickly motioned with her index finger for him to follow her back to where the dentist would promptly yank his tooth free. He looked at me with a smile as if to say, "I'd follow her anywhere!"

Just a few minutes later, Bird came out from the inner office with a weak, shy smile and a large wad of cotton sticking out of his mouth. "Let's go have another beer," he mumbled. I laughed and said thanks to the secretary. Bird mumbled something with a forced smile and paid the $65 fee. We left the office, hopped back in the car, and left Denver in the rearview mirror.

* * *

We came over the ridge and down off a mountain and could see Las Vegas in the distance. The wispy clouds were aglow, as if it were sunrise or sunset. The whole valley was on fire—high noon at one in the morning. I shaded my weary eyes from the glare, found a parking spot on a side street, and wandered with Bird over to the Four Queens Casino. We walked in as if we'd been there before and sat down at one of the blackjack tables. Seated to my left was a beautiful woman who, after losing a hand with a nineteen, reached up under her sweater and began pulling one hundred dollar bills from her bra. I whispered to myself, "Holy shit! What have we got here?" Bird had settled in at another table and missed all the fun.

In a matter of minutes I went through all of my remaining money, about $75. Except for a few coins, I was flat broke. Bird wasn't doing any better. Between the two of us, we had three dollars and some change. So here we were, in Las Vegas, with no money and no way to get home. There were no credit cards or ATMs in those days, so we both had to call for help.

I placed a collect call to Janice from the Western Union office next to the Four Queens Casino, telling her where we were and that we were out of money. "Could you go to my apartment and see if I have any money in my room? Look in my top drawer. I think there's twenty or thirty dollars in there. Send it out here through the Western Union clerk downtown at Schwartz's Drug Store, so we can get back, okay?"

I gave her the Western Union number, and about two hours later, I received the money. As it turned out, I didn't have any money in my top drawer, so Janice borrowed it from her mother. (I paid her back when I returned.)

About an hour after I received the money from Janice, Bird's father came through with $25. While waiting for the money, we both
had fallen dead asleep over in the corner on the floor of the Western
Union office. With some new-found money in our hands, Bird announced, "Come on Don, let's go…let's do some more gambling." Bird
couldn't wait to get back to the tables, taking risks and plotting out
his next move.

"Ah…hold on, Bird," I said a little exasperated, "we better get
the hell outta here now that we can. If we lose this, we're screwed."

"Let's give it one more try," he said.

I told him I'd watch, but added, "I'm all through gambling, Bird.
I have enough to get us home, I think. But that's it."

We went back into the Four Queens and walked over to the craps
table. After losing the first bet, Bird placed most of his remaining
money on "eight-the-hard-way." "Bird," I said, "Are you nuts, you'll
never roll two fours! If you lose this, we're outta here."

He picked up the dice in one hand, brought them up to his mouth,
blew into them, shook them good and let them fly down the table.
The dealer announced, "Eight the hard way." A four and a four. I
could not believe it!

Bird screamed out, "Holy shit, Hussey, look at this, man!" The
dealer slid over a stack of chips that must have measured six inches.
Bird picked them up and flashed them around to show me and started
laughing like he'd just won a million. My eyes were as wide as his.
"See that," he chuckled. "I told you our luck would change." Maybe
our luck was changing, but I figured we'd better get on the road home
while we still could.

"Hey, Bird," I said, "we've got some money now, and we're both
tired and hungry, and we need to get back to school. So let's get the
hell outta here while we can, okay? If we don't leave now, we'll be
both in deep shit."

We had a brief conversation about going to California to buy
some Southern California University T-shirts. We figured we could
sell them back on campus and make a fortune. But we decided that
was a long shot and we might *never* get back. So we split a chicken

salad sandwich, the cheapest thing on the menu, then hopped in the car and headed home.

We drove southeast along a route which took us past the massive Hoover Dam. It was nighttime by then and the dam, which was off to our left and down in a valley, was a spectacular sight. We both thought it looked like an alien space station tucked into the side of a mountain—an eerie, forbidden place.

We continued east through the dry, hot states of Arizona, New Mexico, and west Texas, then northeast through Oklahoma and Missouri, and finally across the Mississippi and into Illinois.

When we finally made it back, I said goodbye to Bird and dropped him off at Palmer House, then headed across town to my apartment. Later I drew some money out of the bank to pay back Janice's mother, and I also bought Janice a present—a beautiful white cashmere sweater. The store clerk carefully wrapped it in bright colored paper and handed it to me.

Janice really liked the sweater, but I could tell she was not happy with me for taking off in the middle of the night for Vegas and not telling her.

* * *

The breakup had been brewing on and off for some time. We started arguing over little things. Janice wouldn't call for a couple of days and I wouldn't either. We were two stubborn lovers in a game of one-upmanship. Her mother tried to reason with both of us. She knew how much I loved her daughter, and I assume she knew Janice's feelings as well.

Janice was always much too reserved—or perhaps too shy—to engage in any what she would call, "public display of affection." I felt otherwise. I'm sure that at the time it was my self-conscious, somewhat damaged ego needing a little propping up. But I would have appreciated a little overt "loving me in public" sort of thing. Nothing ridiculous…maybe a hug, or a simple kiss.

We had been together ever since Thanksgiving Day back in '64, and had been engaged since Christmas of '66. In all that time we'd had many romantic moments together locked in each other's arms, but no wild and wonderful love making. Janice had a deeply-held belief that she would go down the aisle and into her wedding bed a virgin. I honestly respected that, even though it was difficult every time we were alone and close. It seemed I always needed more than she was willing to give.

We were out one night, at a friend's house in St. Louis, and we both had too much to drink. On the way home, a car came screaming over the hill on the expressway, right in front of me. The driver was on the wrong side of the highway, my side of the highway. His lights nearly blinded me when he cleared the rise; there was no time to react. It was a head-on collision that never happened. When he flew past me, going like hell, our mirrors touched. None of us would have walked away from that. I still don't know how we missed each other.

When we finally arrived back at Janice's place, I pulled into her driveway and leaned over to give her a kiss goodnight. She wasn't interested; she just wanted to go inside and go to bed. We were both upset about the near accident, but it was more than that. She was becoming distant, perhaps losing her love for me. And I was beginning to take her for granted; maybe I'd had too much of a good thing for too long. We both needed some time off.

Though I can't say exactly why, I asked her to give me back my ring. She looked over at me, still sitting in the car, took off the ring and handed it to me. She never uttered a word, just opened the door and went inside. I drove down to the end of her driveway, turned right and headed back to my place.

When I woke up the next morning, I saw the ring sitting on my bureau where I had placed it the night before. It was just sitting there looking down at me as I lay on my pillow. The sunlight was streaming through the window and reflecting off the diamond and into my eyes—a not-of-this-world, surreal moment that I'll never forget. What had I done? It was an impulsive, reactionary, knee-jerk move on my part, and I had to straighten it out.

I showered and dressed, put the ring back in my pocket and headed over to Janice's house. On the way I stopped to pick up some flowers. I had a brief, hurry-up conversation with the florist, and when

I reached into my pockets to pay the bill, I was a nickel short. She smiled at me as she handed me the nicely wrapped flowers. "Don't worry about it. I'm sure she'll like these; they're beautiful."

I drove over to Janice's house and handed her the flowers and told her how sorry I was and asked her to put the ring back on. She refused. I can only imagine how she must have felt—and the conversation she must have had with her mother before I arrived that morning. I had made the mistake of my life. She never wore the ring again.

* * *

Janice and I had spent almost four years together, important years, years not to be wasted. In many ways, we had grown up together. I remember the day she turned twenty-one. The both of us, along with Gary and Amy, went into a club in the newly renovated nightclub area in St. Louis, Gaslight Village. We sat at a table in the front next to the dance floor and ordered some drinks. As soon as the drinks arrived I turned to Janice and handed her a birthday present wrapped in light-blue and soft pink paper with a card attached which read, "Happy twenty-first birthday, Sunshine!" I had bought her a pair of long, black, lacy nylons, which in those days was considered quite risqué. When she opened the present and pulled out the nylons, everyone around us began oohing and aahing. She was laughing so much— a little shy, and a little embarrassed, but loving it.

I'd had a steady girlfriend while stationed in the Air Force in Orlando, Florida, but I knew that relationship would break off when I left for home after my discharge. This was different. This was something special. This was a truly loving relationship, and they don't come along very often, sometimes not at all.

We went out occasionally after Janice gave me the ring back, but it was never the same. She began dating other guys.

This was the '60s, a time of revolutionary change, a time for breaking loose from established norms. Free love, "rock 'n roll," hippies, drugs, long hair, sandals, and the sexual revolution had arrived to our traditional thinking mid-western university. There were campus riots and student protests over the war in Vietnam. The Beatles, The Monkeys, The Mamas and the Papas, Johnnie Mathis, Sonny &

Cher, and "Laugh In" were all part of the new world around us. The whole fabric of society seemed to be evolving, and we were a part of it. It was an exciting time full of rapidly changing ideas and priorities—a time of turmoil.

Late one night in the fall of 1968, several of us staged a campus protest, a protest over the lack of on-campus student housing. In the middle of the night five of us climbed into a pickup truck and headed out to an old farmhouse on the outskirts of Edwardsville along Route 157. Out back in the woods at the edge of a swamp was an old abandoned outhouse. We backed up to it, jumped out, gathered around it, picked it up and slid it onto the bed of the truck. It was as heavy as hell. It took all five of us to lift it. And the smell....

We roped it down, securing it to the truck so it wouldn't fall out or over, and drove to the campus. It was well after midnight when we turned right off Route 157 and passed through the entrance and down the main road to the campus center. I was a little surprised that campus security never spotted us. It was a bold move.

We slid the outhouse off the back of the truck and placed it on a mound of grass, right in front of the student center. When the sun came up in the morning, it stuck out like a black eye. One of my buddies, with great haste, painted the words "SIU Student Housing" on the side of it. It made the school newspaper and landed in the 1968 yearbook. On-campus student housing wouldn't happen for several years, but the point was made, and we had fun making it.

Throughout the fall and winter of '68 I was finishing up the remaining courses and credits needed for graduation. Janice was always on my mind. I stayed focused on my coursework as best as I could, but admittedly spent much of my time looking for her. I even dreamed about her trying to find me or trying to avoid me. It was a constant heartbreak.

Late one night, I went into the Stonehouse Tavern. My friends and I were always hanging out there or at Vanzo's when we weren't in school or doing something with the fraternity. The Stonehouse was not far from my apartment. I could, and sometimes did, make my way down there while on my afternoon run.

Janice was there, sitting by herself at the near end of the bar. I thought it was so uncharacteristic of her to be sitting at the bar. In today's world I'd think nothing of it, but although this was the '60s, it was still the Midwest, the conservative moral conscience of the country—family, church, grandma, and apple pie. Girls sitting at the bar sent a message.

This was my girl, "My Fair Lady." I'm sure there was some "proper-Boston" thing going on in my heartsick head, and I tried to shake it off. She was wearing her new pullover dress printed with a glorious sun, bursting with rays of sunshine splashed on the front. I had always been a gentleman with her and she was my lady, and now she was sitting at the bar and I was ready for the rubber room.

The bar was to the left as you entered, and I ignored her when I first went in. I walked past her and down to the other end of the bar, and turned right into the dining room. Off to the left and sitting by herself in a booth was a friend of mine from school. I walked over and asked her if she wanted company and she said, "Hey, how are you? Please sit down."

I began telling her about Janice and our breakup. She knew all about what was going on between us, or not going on between us. Everybody seemed to know a little about our broken relationship. I asked her to walk out to the bar with me while I ordered some beer to go. I said, "You pretend you're my date, my new girlfriend." She knew what I was up to and agreed to play along.

When she finished her salad, we walked out to the bar, and she really put it on. Janice was pretending not to notice, but I glanced down to the end of the bar and she quickly looked away. With her right arm warmly holding on to me, my new girlfriend leaned up and kissed my left cheek. I couldn't have scripted it any better. This should get her attention, I thought to myself. I paid for the beer and we walked right past Janice on the way out. Although my friend lived just three blocks away, I gave her a ride home. I held the door for her as she got out and said, "Thanks a lot. You were great!"

"I hope Janice got a good look," she said as she leaned over and kissed me good night. I waited for a moment as she walked around the front of my car and crossed the street to her apartment. She turned and waved before closing the door. I waved back and then headed up the street to Vanzo's, and there was Janice. Apparently she'd had enough of the Stonehouse. Whatever impression I worked so hard to create, vanished the instant she saw me. I walked over to the jukebox where she was playing a familiar song, and said, "Hi."

She turned to me and asked, "Where's your date?"

"I was just trying to make you jealous. She's just a friend," I said.

That was a stupid thing to say, and I knew it even before I said it—that had been the whole idea; make her jealous and maybe wake her up. But it seemed as if everything I did and said was wrong; it all somehow turned against me. I couldn't find the handle, the key…the trees in the forest.

* * *

One afternoon I spotted Janice in a line of traffic that had backed up waiting for one of those endless Illinois Central trains to pass up ahead. I had been out walking and running, getting some exercise. I was determined to lose the weight and take better care of myself.

When I saw that old familiar light blue, four-door Nash Rambler make the turn at the Hillsborough Street intersection and fall in behind the others, I started running as fast I could to catch up to her before the train passed and traffic started moving again. I reached her car, opened the passenger side door and hopped in. I was completely out of breath, my heart pounding. I managed a "Hi, how about a ride home? Where are you going all dressed up?"

She told me she was going to a bridal shower or a baby shower; I really wasn't listening. She looked remarkably self-assured in her beautiful kelly-green suit. The shy little girl I once knew had matured. I had given her so much love and attention during the time we were together; I had lovingly escorted her down the road into adulthood. She was a woman now.

She drove me home and agreed to come in for a minute. She sat on one end of my living room couch and we exchanged a few pleasantries, but I could tell she was in a rush. "I really have to go, I'll be late," she said as she stood, adjusted the strap of her purse over her shoulder and headed for the door. She was quick and cool, and matter-of-fact. I sat there on the couch after she left, thinking about where she might be going and who she was dating now. I wasn't dating anyone.

I saw her from a distance at school one afternoon as she was coming out of class. I hurried to catch up with her and when I did, I asked if she'd like a ride home. I said, "We could stop at Vanzo's for lunch or a beer, if you like." Surprising me, she said okay.

I opened the door for her and we drove off campus to the center of town, and pulled into a parking spot in front of Vanzo's. The place was nearly empty. It was early afternoon and the lunchtime courthouse crowd had finished up their daily routine and returned to work. Sitting by himself at one of the round tables to the left was Roger McBride. I had known Roger from freshman year when we both tried out for parts in the '65 Spring Festival Play. During that time, my buddy Mike told me a little bit about him. Mike had been dating Roger's ex-girlfriend, Stephanie, and Stephanie had broken off her relationship with Roger because he was too difficult to get along with.

I said, "Hi Roger, mind if we join you?"

Unknown to me, Roger had just moved into a small cottage on a side street directly behind Janice's house. She had noticed him a few days earlier mowing his lawn and had become interested in him. We sat down and I ordered a pitcher of beer. Janice started talking with Roger, talking very fast—nervous talk. She was ignoring me. The look on her face was obvious.

I knew her so well. I knew then and there that she would wind up dating him. I got up to go to the bathroom, leaving them alone. I could only imagine the conversation. We finished the beer and I drove her home.

Fate, that mystical and seemingly random phenomenon, provided the only reasonable explanation for the events that followed. What happened during that brief luncheon date at Vanzo's brought an end to what was left of our fragile relationship. The next day, I called Janice to see if she wanted a ride to school. She said, "No, Roger is picking me up, I'm riding with him." Roger had now taken my place. She rode to and from school with Roger from that day on, and that really broke my heart.

About a week later, I was racing off to class as usual. It was early afternoon and my car was acting up—not firing on all cylinders. It needed a tune-up, but I kept putting it off. I left my apartment and drove the familiar route to school, past the Stonehouse, then up the hill, under the train bridge, to the main campus road. I was alone now, with no one to share the ride or the term paper deadlines or the walk in from the parking lot, or anything else.

As I slowly turned right on the main campus road, I looked to my left, and there, directly in front of me, was Janice. She was stopped at the intersection, sitting in the passenger side of Roger's car. They were leaving campus together. I don't think he saw me, but Janice and I exchanged glances for what seemed like forever. I can still see her sad, reflective eyes looking up at me. It was—and is—a snapshot burned into my brain. Maybe she was wondering how I was doing… maybe not.

* * *

I eventually went to see an allergist in St. Louis. I told him I was having trouble with asthma and eczema, and on top of that, I was having a rough time trying to get through school. I trusted him and explained the many details of my personal life—stuff I usually kept to myself. He gave me a heavy shot of cortisone in my left hip. Then he wrote a prescription for some pills to calm me down. He told me to take one in the morning and that I should feel a difference in how I dealt with all that was going on in my life.

It was a prescription for amphetamines, or "speed" as it was called by those who knew more about those things than I did. Those pills made an enormous difference. I could focus on my schoolwork, get my papers in on time, and help me deal with everything else in my life. As the medication wore off though, toward the end of each day, I would fall into a wretched state of despair.

I frequently called Amy or Gary to see if they had seen or spoken to Janice. Amy did tell me during one such conversation that Janice had been to a doctor and was now taking Valium or Librium or something like that to calm her down. I asked her, "What's that all about?"

"It beats me," she said. "I can't figure her out. You know, Don, Janice has never opened up to me. I don't think she's ever opened up to anyone, and I've known her all my life. That's just her, I guess."

I took those pills for four or five months, throughout the summer and fall of '68. I'd take one in the morning, and then in the afternoon after my classes, I went for a run. I'd come back soaking wet with sweat, then take a shower, get something to eat and have a few beers. The beer helped keep the depression from overtaking me. I had a more self-directed routine now. I was losing weight, getting into shape and doing better in school, and it was becoming easier to block Janice from my mind.

* * *

Every five to six weeks, I'd visit my doctor and he'd give me another shot of cortisone and ask me how I was getting along. He was a wonderful man who really cared about me.

Every day I continued inching closer and closer to finally completing my requirements for graduation. I had to keep going no matter what. I kept reminding myself, over and over and over again, that I was out there to get an education, to get that degree—that brass ring.

It was early December 1968 and the final quarter was coming to a close. Janice's twenty-second birthday came and went; Thanksgiving had been the same, and now Christmas—nothing but haunting memories. I shook it off, convincing myself that none of it mattered. My objectives were clear and my priorities consistent. I would soon have all the credits I needed to graduate, and that remained my singular focus.

During that last quarter, I tried so damn hard to make the dean's list. It was never really that important to me until now. But I wanted to prove to myself and perhaps to the world that I was ready to move beyond the present and achieve the level of success I knew I was capable of. I was in a senior-level Anthropology class and had written a lengthy extra-credit paper, contrasting the peaceful mid-nineteenth century Zuni Indians of the desert southwest to the warlike Kwakiutl tribes of Vancouver, British Columbia. This was the only class holding me back. I submitted my term paper, a class requirement, and received a B+. Many of the answers on the final exam were narrative in nature and therefore somewhat subjective, requiring sufficient time to be clearly and honestly evaluated. Instead, the professor flipped through the exams, grading each of them as they were brought up to his desk during that final class. We busied ourselves with a reading assignment until class was over. When he finished grading the papers, he called each of us up to his desk and handed back the graded exams. At the top of the exam, he wrote two grades. One was for the final exam and the other, circled with a red pen, the course grade. I received a course grade of B+. Not good enough. I deserved more.

As the professor was leaving, I caught up with him on the walkway outside the building. I asked if I could drop by and see him for a moment. He invited me to come by his office after lunch. I figured if I could get to him before the grades were posted, he might agree to make a change. I had never done this before but I felt justified and wanted my name posted on the Dean's List. I knocked at his door at one o'clock and after a brief moment of light conversation, I launched into my request for a grade change. I detailed the amount of time and effort I had devoted to his class and reminded him of my extra credit paper. I asked him to bump my grade to an A-. He told me that a B+ was nothing to laugh about. "That's a good grade. I don't give out A's very often." Then he asked, "Do you need this for a student deferment? Are you being drafted?" I told him no, I'd already served my time in the military. He refused to make the change. I never explained to him why it was so important to me. Maybe I should have, but that was my business. I missed the dean's list by .125 of a point.

* * *

Nineteen sixty-eight was a troublesome year for me, as well as for the country: the raging war in Vietnam, the assassination of Martin Luther King, Jr. in April, the assassination of Presidential Candidate, Robert F. Kennedy in June, the Democratic National Convention in Chicago, student protests on campuses across America. What would the rest of the world think of us? It all seemed like a long, endless, and personal nightmare.

ELEVEN

A Rainy Wednesday

My plan now was to travel home, work for six months and come back to attend the commencement exercises in June—full cap and gown, a member of the Class of '69.

Before leaving for home, I placed a call to my doctor in St. Louis to thank him for his genuine concern for me over the past six months, and tell him that I had finally and successfully completed my course work and would graduate in June. I ended the conversation with my warmest regards. "You saved me from myself, and I will never forget you."

I had completed the mission and it was now time to throw away the crutch and wean myself off of those pills, which had been holding me hostage. I knew it wouldn't be easy, but nothing I ever did seemed easy. It would be another challenge, another obstacle. And it would take me several months of hit and miss before I escaped from that prison.

I left Edwardsville, Illinois, on a bitterly cold mid-December morning in my green, four-door, '55 Pontiac sedan. The odometer reading had just passed 126,000 miles, and I wasn't sure if the beast would make it across town, never mind to Boston.

I had sold the Austin-Healy Sprite three months earlier to raise some money for the final stretch. Jim Fishman, another fraternity brother of mine, sold me his '55 Pontiac for $25 and a glass of beer at Vanzo's, and I drove it back and forth to school for most of my last quarter. By the 18th of December I had finished all my class work, submitted my term papers, taken my finals, and begun packing the car for my trip home to Massachusetts.

I stopped at the gas station to check the oil and fill the gas tank, and then I drove over to Janice's house to say goodbye. Her new boyfriend was sitting at the dining room table having a cup of coffee when I arrived. We exchanged hellos. I gave her mother a hug and then went outside with Janice for a final, private moment. She handed me an envelope with $100 inside, explaining that it was payment for the Marquette stereo system I had set up in her living room the previous year. It was the demo set I had paid for and used in my door-to-door sales job.

At first I said, "No, that's all right, you keep it. You don't have to pay me for it."

She insisted, telling me, "It's from my mother and me. Please take it." I reminded myself of the long uncertain journey ahead of me—twelve hundred miles to Boston. I accepted the money and put the envelope in my pocket. This was one of the last ties between us. I knew from then on she would be sitting in the living room with someone else, listening to music we'd listened to so many times. It was just another kick in the head. I don't know what I expected when I went over there that December day, but the cool way she handed me the money was unexpected, and, it deepened the anguish about leaving.

It was very cold outside, so we only talked for a few minutes. I hugged and held her for a long time. We paused and looked into each other's eyes. I whispered something about her eyes and told her she would always be "my browned-eyed girl, my Sunshine." Neither one of us said goodbye. She turned and walked inside, and I just turned and left.

I was leaving Janice behind. It wasn't supposed to end like this. We'd made so many plans and been together for such a long time, shared so many experiences—practically grown up together. I had made this trip back and forth from Illinois to Massachusetts many times, but now I wouldn't be back again for six months. That seemed a lifetime away. With unspoken words stuck in my throat and a rigid sense of purpose, I stepped into my car, drove down her driveway, and took the familiar right hand turn onto Brockmeier Road.

I rode around downtown Edwardsville for fifteen minutes or so, taking pictures in my mind—my old apartment, the Wildey movie theater, Vanzo's, The Stonehouse Tavern, Schwartz's, and the restaurant where we used to go for pizza. I wanted and needed to get on the road and put some time and distance between me and Janice. I took a deep breath, grabbed the wheel with elbows locked, and headed for the highway.

I was ready now. If there was any chance of ever getting back together, any chance at all, I needed to be gone. I figured it was up to her to find out for herself what I already knew about her new boyfriend. Maybe she would tire of him, and maybe my absence would give her reason to pause. I'd just have to wait until June when I returned for graduation.

But for now, I had to focus on getting home. This last trip would be the toughest. I carried a lonely heart down that ramp and out onto that highway. I was leaving so much of me behind; I knew that all too well. I couldn't and wouldn't let myself turn back. I had put myself through enough. I was given the opportunity and completed the mission, and was damn proud of myself. Right or wrong, I was leaving.

The heavy car rode down the ramp and out onto the highway like an Army tank, slowly reaching the speed limit. The heater was working and so was the radio. I made my way through Illinois and Indiana and then into Ohio. There was an approaching snowstorm moving east out of the Great Lakes that I never knew about. Even so, everything seemed to go as expected until I was about halfway across Ohio. I started making my way up a long, steep hill. At the crest of the hill the road leveled off and then went down a steep decline. Light snow was falling and it was very cold. This was a two-lane highway, with one lane going downhill and the other coming up. I came upon the row of cars in front of me too quickly; they all had slowed down for some reason. I hit the brakes and started skidding. There was ice, black ice, and I knew I would not be able to stop in time, so I quickly swerved into the approaching lane. It was either that or smash into the car in front of me. There was nowhere left to go, no room to my right, just a long deep drainage ditch.

Cars were coming up the hill now, heading directly toward me. How in hell am I going to get out of this? I asked myself. As I continued down the hill, straight at the opposing traffic, I spotted a quick break in the line of cars to my right. I cut the wheel right, skidded some more and maneuvered the car sideways through the opening in the line of traffic, then bounced in and out of the ditch before slamming into the side of a hill. I'm not sure how, but I managed to miss hitting anyone. The right front fender and headlight of my car were bashed in pretty good. This was a heavy car, solidly built and strong. It could take a beating. When it was safe, I managed to back off the hill, through the ditch, and out onto the road again. I quickly pulled the lever down into drive and headed—once again—down the hill.

I said out loud, "Holy shit! What a ride. How in hell did I get away with that?" I didn't get out to check the damage. I really didn't give a damn. I was still moving.

By the time I reached the Pennsylvania Turnpike, the snowstorm had developed into a blinding blizzard. The snow was so deep; I don't know how or why the car kept going. Without warning, my windshield wipers froze. At first I could see very little, then I could see absolutely nothing.

I reached out with my left hand, trying to sweep the snow from the windshield. No luck. I leaned out the window to try and see where the hell I was going. The snow blasted my eyes and face.

I must have been all over that road. A tractor trailer came up on my left and nearly sideswiped me, giving me a long blast from his twin horns. I turned the wheel to the right to get out of his way and struck the guardrail. 'I know where I am now,' I said to myself. I couldn't see a thing. I just kept going. I bumped into the guardrail again. Sticking my head out the window did no good. I knew if I stopped, someone would plow into me or I would freeze to death packed under a mound of snow. As long as that car was willing to go, I was willing to go with it.

Suddenly—directly in front of me—there was as toll plaza. "Thank God," I said out loud.

I didn't know it at the time, but my right front tire was soft and going flat. When I pulled into the covered toll plaza, the man said, "How you doin', man? It's pretty rough out there." I told him how glad I was to see him, and that I was happy to pay the toll. "Hey," he said, "do you know you've got a flat tire?"

The flat tire hadn't successfully competed for my attention. The last three miles of driving blind and bumping along the guardrail was all I could handle. Like King Lear, I was "feeling my way." I said to myself, Hell, I can fix a flat tire. I figured it must have been damaged back in Ohio when I bounced in and out of that ditch.

"There's a gas station just up ahead. You can see it from here," he said.

I stepped out of the car, shielded my eyes from the driving snow, and took a look. He was right; I could see the neon sign just up ahead. I cleared some of the heavily packed snow and ice off the windshield, forced the door open against the wind and slid back into the car. Then I took aim and made a mad dash for that gas station.

Notwithstanding the smashed headlight and front bumper, and the scrapes and twisted chrome along the right side, I was in pretty good shape. The mechanic guided me into the service bay and began pulling off the tire. He said, "Open the trunk and get me the spare." I opened the trunk, but there was no spare.

"You don't have a spare?"

"I guess not." I answered.

He told me I could purchase a new tire and inner tube. "I'll have you back on the road in about twenty minutes, if you're crazy enough to continue in this storm."

I asked him if he could patch the old tire. He said he could, but it might not get me where I was going. "Where are you going, by the way?" he asked. I told him and he just smiled and said, "Good luck."

I figured the heavy snow had somehow protected the tire from too much damage. He patched the inner tube, stuck it back in the tire, mounted it and filled it with air. He said, "Well, it looks pretty good. Maybe it'll hold. No guarantees though." He poured warm water on the windshield and the wipers, removed the ice and managed to get the wipers working again. Things were looking up, I figured.

"What happened to the headlight?" he asked.

"Oh, don't bother about that. It's a long story. I'll get by. Just leave it hanging there," I said. I checked the oil, loaded up with gas and paid my bill. I thanked him very much and shook his hand with both of mine.

I was back on the road again; damn the snow. I never stopped again unless it was for coffee and maybe a sandwich. I drank the coffee and slapped myself in the face when I needed to stay awake. Pennsylvania was now behind me and I was making my way up the east coast. All was going pretty well, I thought. At some point it had stopped snowing, or I just outran it—maybe both. I sailed through New Jersey and crossed the border into New York.

Then it happened again. The same right front tire went flat. I bumped along down the road to the next service station, driving slowly, hoping to save the tire. This time the man told me I needed a new valve stem and new inner tube. He explained the situation: "The tire itself looks okay, but the inner tube is split wide open at the stem. If you put in a new inner tube and a new stem, you might be all right. "

I asked him how much. He said, "Not much."

I told him that's how much I had, not much.

He laughed and told me not to worry. "Besides," he said, "what choice do you have?"

I told him to go ahead, at least the tire was holding up. I was nearly out of money. I thought about Janice and her mother, and the $100. She'd never know how much I needed it.

When the tire was fixed, I maneuvered past the parked cars and out on the road; this was the last leg. I cruised through New York and into Connecticut. I was somewhere north of Providence, Rhode Island, when it happened the third time.

"Sonofabitch," I said out loud. I followed that up with another line I'd heard many times from a buddy of mine in the Air Force: "Goddamnit shit." He never, ever, said "goddamnit" or "shit" without putting the two together, and it was funny as hell most of the time.

By now I was so damn tired. I slammed my right hand on the steering wheel and said it again. "Goddamnit shit." This was no longer a challenge; this was a test of will. I began talking to the car as it bumped along on its flat tire. "Go ahead," I threatened. "Keep it up. I'll drive you into the ground." I thought about leaving it there, on the side of the road, and thumbing the rest of the way home, but as long as it kept running....

I must have damaged the frame or the wheel housing for this to happen three times, but by now, I was too exhausted to care. I calmed down and started figuring out how to get around this. "Screw it," I said out loud. The tire was round and the rim was round, so what the hell, I'll just keep going. And the faster I went, the less it annoyed me, bang, bang, bang, bang, bang, bang, bang....

I hadn't slept in nearly three days and I was just a little crazy. I pulled off the road several times to rest my eyes and get some sleep, but it was so cold outside that the heat in the car would be lost in a matter of minutes. It was a waste of time and a waste of gas, and I was running out of both.

I was ripping the tire to shreds, and it finally disintegrated. What was left of it flew from the rim as I crossed into Massachusetts. I didn't care and I didn't stop. The road was frozen solid, so I figured there'd be no damage to the roadway. I kept over to the right in the breakdown lane as much as I could. It was late at night, and I could see sparks from the steel rim reflecting off the snow packed against the guardrail. People were passing by, looking at me and pointing their finger as if I didn't know what was going on. I paid no attention. I just gripped the wheel with both hands, hell bent on "maintaining course and speed."

I continued slam-banging my way up the coast in the breakdown lane until I saw road-signs for Brockton and Avon and Randolph. "By God, I made it," I said, somewhat astonished. This madness would soon be over. I turned off the highway and drove along the back roads through Brockton and Whitman where I circled the rotary onto Plymouth Street, then passed over the line into Abington. Straight ahead, about a mile up on the left was my mother's place. I slowed down to a crawl and turned into her driveway, pulling over to the frozen, grassy area off to the left.

I hit the brakes, jammed the gearshift up into park, then reached down and turned off the key. The car sputtered and shook and shuttered, then backfired and quit. It was as tired and confused as I was. I sat there for a long time, resting my head in my arms, wrapped around the steering wheel.

I would sleep now...maybe forever.

My mother was living with Joe in a rented farmhouse at number 931 Plymouth Street in Abington. I slowly opened the car door, stepped out and walked up to the front door. I was greeted like a soldier returning from war. I must have looked the part.

"I've been worried sick," she said. "I'll make you some hot soup and you can get some sleep." Joe helped me open the couch and make up the bed. I never touched the soup. I just went off to sleep.

* * *

The next day, Joe and I picked through the old barn next to the house in search of a tire for my car. The barn was home to an assortment of auto parts, garden tools, old furniture, and cardboard boxes full of other stuff. I noticed a fully inflated, mounted tire in the corner leaning up against a side door. I asked Joe if this was okay to use.

"Sure, but I don't think it'll fit. The holes probably won't line up. I think it's from an old Ford or maybe a Chevy," he said.

Joe helped me jack up the car and remove what was left of the rim. I told him what I had done, how I got home, and he laughed out loud and I laughed along with him. I pulled off the rim, which was beaten up pretty good, and then wheeled over the tire. I lifted it up and slipped it over the bolts. I couldn't believe it and neither could Joe. It went right on—a perfect fit.

"Can you believe it?" I said. I took the tire iron and tightened down the bolts. Joe lowered the jack and said, "Well, what do you know? You're back in business." I shook his hand and got in. When I turned the key it cranked right over...ready for another adventure.

"Hey, Joe," I said, "where can I get this thing looked at? I'm sure it needs some work. I know there's something wrong with the front end."

"Let's go up to Balboni's garage," he said. "He's up on the right on

Route 123, on the way to Rockland. He's a good guy and will take an honest look at it for you. Just follow me."

I put the beast in reverse, backed out onto Plymouth Street and followed Joe down to the intersection with Route 123. When the lights turned, we made a right and headed down about two miles to Balboni's Garage.

Mr. Balboni had an open bay when we arrived, so he told me to drive right in. He raised the car up on the lift, locked it into position, and went under to take a look. "Hey, holy— Take a look at this," he cried. He was calling out for me and the other guys in the shop, too. "Hey, come take a look at this! I've never seen this before."

Joe and I walked over as the others gathered around assessing the damage. The right front wheel housing had nearly broken free from the car. Two of the four bolts that secure it to the frame were missing and the third was just hanging there. "What happened?" he asked with a puzzled look. "How did this get so bad? And how did you drive it here?"

I told him what had happened, and he just shook his head and smiled. He turned to Joe and said, "He's a pretty damn lucky guy." I asked him if he could fix it, and he told me he'd have to take the wheel housing off and straighten something out. Then he paused and said, "I think I can fix it, but I won't know until I replace the bolts, do a front end alignment and take it out for a ride. It'll take me a couple of days. Call me Friday."

"Thanks a lot," I said. I rode back to the house with Joe and had some hot soup and a sandwich my mother had ready when we returned. During lunch I gave them a more detailed account of my exciting adventure, how I made it home. "It's no big deal," I said. "I made it, that's all that counts."

Friday came and I called Balboni's to check on my car. They told me it was all set and how much I owed them. Joe had left for work early that morning and I didn't want to wait for him to get back, so I borrowed some money from my mother and walked down to Balboni's. When I arrived, Mr. Balboni told me it was all fixed and ready to go. Then he smiled and said, "That was quite a story. How did you ever keep it on the road? You must have had a wild ride. I'm surprised you made it and I'm also surprised you didn't get pulled over."

I agreed and told him I didn't have any answers. "I must have been lucky, but there's no sense worrying about something that didn't happen," I said offhandedly, as if I didn't want to talk about it.

I paid him what I owed and thanked him for the fine job of putting it back together in such short time. When I came home, I told my mother I'd pay her back as soon as I found a job.

I wasted no time. On Monday I called eleven different school systems, from Brockton south to Plymouth. Although I wouldn't officially graduate until June, my major was in Elementary Education with a minor in Math. I explained my situation and asked each of them for applications for teaching positions, and also mentioned that I'd be willing to substitute if they needed me. When the applications arrived in the mail, I filled them out, enclosed the requisite paperwork, and mailed them back, all in the same day. Two days later, I began following up with phone calls.

My first opportunity was a fifth grade substitute position at an elementary school in Brockton. This was going to be a long-term opportunity lasting several weeks.

What an eye-opener that was for me. These ten and eleven-year olds were wild. I had no control over them at all. Nothing I did or said made a difference. I was a sub, and they were going to "sink the sub."

I worked for one day, and after school the principal asked me to come in and sit down. "Tell me a little about your teaching philosophy," he asked. I explained what I thought: If you're kind and helpful, eventually they will come around. He told me that wouldn't work here, and then he said, "Don't bother coming back." That was a very good lesson for me. I made up my mind at that very moment that no kid would keep me from finding a job.

I began substituting in several other towns, including Norwell. I was broke and knew that my future was riding on this. Teaching was what I wanted to do, and I was not going to be denied.

While substituting in Norwell, I quickly earned the reputation of someone who was tough and could control a class. I was fair, but

I wouldn't let the kids get away with anything. Norwell called me back repeatedly to sub, and soon I was working every day. Not much money, but enough for now.

Sometime in early February of 1969, I received a letter from Janice. I was home alone at my mother's place in Abington when the mail arrived. I was so happy and excited to hear from her, but hesitant to open the letter. I sat down on the couch and began reading her letter.

As I remember, she asked me how I was doing and wondered if I had found a teaching job as yet, realizing I was probably broke or living on the financial edge. I hadn't written to her. I was too busy trying to put my life in order. She wished me the best and told me the guys from the fraternity were asking for me and wanted my address. She also mentioned the winter storm that I must have encountered on my way home, and what affect that must have had on me, but said she knew I'd get through it—she knew me that well.

She recalled the student teaching assignment I had at the old Lincoln School on Main Street and how the kids really loved me, especially this one boy whose mother worked as a waitress at the Stonehouse. Apparently, she had a long talk with Janice about me and the wonderful experience her little boy had with me as his teacher.

Janice mentioned that she was in her next to last quarter at school and only had her Social Services Practicum to finish before graduation. She thought she might work in the prison system helping to rehabilitate prisoners. It would be a demanding job and maybe a little scary too.

She told me about the night at Vanzo's when Jimmy Vanzo walked out from behind the bar and over to her while she was playing a song on the jukebox. Apparently he had asked about me and wondered where I was. She told him I'd finished up my classes and left to go home to Massachusetts. Jimmy wanted her to say "Hi" from him if she spoke with me again. She told me the place isn't the same without you, and everyone misses you, including me.

She ended rather coolly though, as I recall, asking me to write to her once in awhile and let me know how things are going. She signed off with something like, Bon jour…Mon amour. Janice.

* * *

I remember the tone of her letter left me wanting more. I had expected, or perhaps anticipated, a stronger attempt at renewing our relationship. The line about writing to me once in awhile was as if we were, or had been, simply casual friends. And I knew she was with someone else now. I read and re-read the letter several times. "You've got to try harder than this!" I announced to an empty room. I never wrote back.

I refused to be emotionally sidetracked for very long. I kept telling myself, stay focused…stay busy. I continued substitute teaching and making every effort to land a permanent job. I had completed all my requirements for graduation. My degree would be conferred in June. Now I needed some financial independence.

I moved out of my mother's place in Abington to a small cottage across the street from a lake in Pembroke. I had to move out. I was out every night drinking and going to hell. I had gone into a fit of rage one night, wandering around Rockland, hitting all the bars that my father must have torn apart when I was a baby. On that one miserable dog-eating night, I called my mother from a sidewalk pay phone in the center of town. I was full of fire, ranting and raving, telling her off, and venting so loudly that people started watching me from inside the bar. I had hit bottom.

Things wouldn't be much better for me while in Pembroke, but at least I could try and get some control over myself…straighten myself out. I was so goddamn miserably lonely.

Rent for the one-room cottage was $50 a month. The cottage had a gas stove, a small metal shower, a fold-up cot, a small, round table with one chair, and no refrigerator. I set up a phone so I could receive calls to substitute. I was substituting every day, mostly in the Town of Norwell. I was making $50 a day and still clunking along in my never-say-die '55 Pontiac.

In March of 1969, the Norwell School Department called to ask if I was interested in a long-term substitute position in grade four at the Grace Farrar Cole Elementary School. The current teacher was leaving in April to have her first baby. I gladly accepted.

In early May, the school principal, Walter Kaetzer, called me into his office after school and asked if I'd like a permanent full-time teaching position. He said, "I want you to know that everyone likes you here and you're doing a really nice job with those fourth graders, but the main reason I called you in here was to tell you we have a grade six teaching position available in the fall and we'd like to offer it to you. Do you think you'd be interested?"

Without hesitating, I said, "Yes, I would, and thank you for thinking of me!"

I was ready to begin my new life and eager to do the best job I knew how. The responsibility of teaching mathematics to one hundred and twenty students in four classes was handed over to me. My job was to prepare them for junior high. I couldn't wait.

When the Town of Norwell hired me, they gave me a chance to take back my life. I had a purpose now, a reason to think positively and focus on my future. I was going to be the best teacher in that town.

I picked up the phone and called Janice. I was still living in that one-room shack in Pembroke and finishing up the school year with my fourth graders. I wanted to know how she was doing and to tell her about my good fortune. During our all too brief conversation, she asked me if we ever had sex. "Did we ever…go all the way?" She just blurted it out.

How could she be so insensitive? No other issue in our long relationship had created so much turmoil. I never let on how much that miserable question hurt me. I gently but coolly responded, "No, we came close but you wanted to wait.

"No, Janice, it never happened," I repeated sincerely. "You'll know when it does."

"Well," she said, almost apologetically, "Roger wanted to know."

Without thinking, I asked her, "Have you been to bed with him?"

"That's none of your business!" she fired back. She was brutally frank and it jolted me.

We didn't talk long after that. I waited for the right moment to hang up in her face. I pictured her holding the phone to her ear and then…click. I never said a word about my new job or anything else. I ended the call abruptly with, "Well, have a good life. Bye."

I slammed the phone down before she could say another word and then turned on the radio to drown out the numbing sadness that consumed me.

Like water on a drowning man, the radio began playing a song that turned me inside out: "Those Were the Days My Friend," by Mary Hopkins. . . .

Once upon a time there was a tavern
Where we used to raise a glass or two
Remember how we laughed away the hours,
Think of all the great things we would do

Through the door, there came familiar laughter
I saw your face and heard you call my name
Oh, my friend, we're older but no wiser
For in our hearts, the dreams are still the same

Those were the days my friend
We thought they'd never end
We'd sing and dance forever and a day
We'd live the life we'd choose
We'd fight and never lose
For we were young and sure to have our way

I reached for the knob on the radio to turn it off but decided I needed to hear the whole song. I needed it to cut into me…and it did. Maybe then, I could get rid of it. I turned away, flopped down on my cot and buried my face in my pillow. When the song had finished, I turned over and stared up at the ceiling. After a few miserable minutes, caught between anger and tears, I stood up, washed the mess from my face and stumbled down the road beside the lake, to a late night sandwich shop. That was the loneliest night I can ever remember.

Three days after my phone call to Janice, my mother called to say a letter from Janice had just arrived in the mail. I couldn't get over there fast enough. I walked in, said hello, snatched the letter, which was postmarked in May of 1969, and drove down to the harbor in Scituate. Her letters always seemed to reveal much of what was going on inside of her. She could say in a letter what she couldn't say in person or on the phone. I parked my car down at the far end of the pier, just beyond the Scituate Yacht Club. Whatever was in this letter would be important to me and I wasn't going to rush it. I wanted to be alone when I opened it. I stepped out of my car, sat on the seawall and began reading.

What follows is from my memory, as with all other correspondence from Janice. I was a little surprised to receive a letter from her so soon after our last telephone conversation, which of course did not go well.

It was addressed to Don, Mon Cheri. I remember it was an emotional letter filled with sorrow, pain and regret, but acknowledging at the same time that it would be better for both of us to hold the love and regard we have for one another in our hearts…tucked away for no one else to see. Our time together and the love we once shared will be stored away forever in her heart.

She mentioned something about me closing the final door and thought it best, considering all aspects, that we not expose ourselves to this any more. I could say more, but it is probably best that it not be said at all.

I remember she simply ended the letter with, "all my love and goodwill, I say goodbye." There was no signature.

* * *

I read her letter again and again, then lifted my eyes out over the harbor searching for some peace—a beautiful setting on a warm day in May. I stared out, scanning the vista, taking in the sailboats, the sounds of the wire halyards snapping against their masts, the names neatly stenciled for all to see (*Lady B' Good*, and *Time Out*, and many more), and watched as the bright mid-day sun skipped across the slow moving waters directly in front of me.

"Close the final door?" What was this all about? I never closed the final door. That's what she heard, but it was never my intent. I

255

wanted her to work at getting me back—work as hard as I had during those final months at school before leaving.

The tide was rolling in, so I slipped off my shoes and dangled my feet in the frigid salt water. I read her letter again, consumed with memories of her and our time together. My love for her and her love for me would now be "stored away in her heart forever." I thought to myself, How in hell did this get away from me…away from us? So this was the end, the "Dear John" letter.

* * *

With little or no warning, fate, that life-changing, capricious trickster, slipped into my life once again. This time perhaps, to make amends. The Norwell Junior High School Assistant Principal introduced himself to me one day during one of my substitute assignments at his school. He opened the door, walked into my classroom, came right over to me and said, "Hi, I'm Joe Noble, the assistant principal here. I heard you were here this morning and wanted to meet you." I had been substituting throughout the Norwell School system before taking on the fourth grade assignment and had spent many days at the junior high, but up until now I hadn't met Joe. From that day on, each time I was called to sub at the junior high, he would visit my room to see how I was doing. Joe was the school disciplinarian. The kids all respected Joe.

Joe had never married, so he and I spent quite a bit of time together, especially on the weekends. Joe lived in Scituate with his father in the house where he'd grown up—number 72 Turner Road. Scituate is a small coastal town about twelve miles to the east of Pembroke. Joe's mother had passed away recently and Joe, knowing I was living alone, asked if I'd like to move in with him and his father. "Hey, we've got some extra rooms upstairs. You pay for your own food and how's $60 a month sound? Is that too much? Think about it, let me know." I smiled and said, "There's nothing to think about. Count me in."

A week later, I packed my sheets and pillow and clothes and moved in with Joe and his father. As soon as I settled in, Joe took me around town and introduced me to all his friends, and believe me, Joe knew everyone.

On a Saturday morning in late May, I rode with him to the boat-yard on the other side of the harbor, where his boating friends were scraping and sanding and bottom painting their boats for the upcoming season. There must have been a hundred boats dry-docked and up on blocks scattered all over the yard—some sailboats but mostly inboards and outboards. Everyone, from owners and their friends to mechanics and painters, was climbing ladders, tuning up and making repairs to engines, cleaning bilge pumps, airing out cabins and installing props.

Joe was half owner of a 36' wooden cabin cruiser, *The Y-Knot.* It was an older boat, maybe twenty years old, and needed plenty of maintenance, including a fresh coat of bottom paint. I asked Joe to give me something to do. He handed me some sandpaper and I went to work sanding down the forward deck.

Each of the next three weekends was spent with Joe and his friends getting the boat ready for a mid-June launch. There was always plenty of music, sandwiches and ice-cold beer to go around as Joe and I and everyone else worked in the yard. My social life, which did not exist until I met Joe, was now coming along nicely. I was turning the corner, bouncing off the bottom, and putting the past behind me.

One Sunday afternoon, Joe brought me across town and introduced me to the family who owned the Cliff Hotel. "The Cliff," as it was known, was a five-story, turn-of-the-century hotel located on Glades Road, overlooking the broad expanse of the Atlantic Ocean. What a view! The hotel was situated on an ideal coastal track of land, where the tide washed over rock outcroppings, small islands and white sandy beaches. The locals, mostly of Irish descent, called that part of town the "Irish Riviera." The hotel owners called it the "Gateway to Cape Cod."

Joe was close friends with the owners, and worked there during the summer months as a bartender. On his recommendation, they hired me on the spot to do the same. I was a little surprised they would hire me because of my obvious disability. It must have occurred to them that I might not be able to handle mixing drinks and working a manual cash register, but no one mentioned it. After showing me around and explaining the workings of the bar, Joe slapped me on the back and said to the owners, "At least you know he won't have his fingers in the till." Well, everyone broke out laughing over that, including me. I became instant friends with the owners.

I wasn't going to disappoint them or Joe. I started working weekends to familiarize myself with the drinks and the prices, and to figure out how to operate the cash register. From Memorial Day to Labor Day, the Cliff Hotel was the hot spot around town. I was looking forward to the nonstop night-clubbing atmosphere that lasted all summer long.

I explained that I would be away for a few days in June but would be back around the 15th. "I'm heading out to Illinois to attend my graduation. I have no other plans after that, and when school lets out for the summer, I'll be available to work full time, right through Labor Day."

The owner told me not to worry. "Your job here is safe," he said. "Have a nice trip, and we'll see you when you return."

TWELVE

The Class of '69

With great anticipation, I made plans to travel by car back to Edwardsville, Illinois. Graduation day would be the 10th of June, 1969. My mother agreed to make the trip with me. It was important to me to have her witness my graduation. College had been a long and sometimes difficult period in my life, and I wasn't sure if Janice or anyone else I knew would be there. Some people asked, "Why would you drive all the way to Illinois just to attend a two-hour ceremony? They would mail you your degree if you made the request."

I would answer them simply, "I just want to be there." If I had revealed my innermost thoughts, I would have said, "Believe me when I tell you, I worked for it. I want the honor and soak up the satisfaction. I'm going to walk across that stage, receive my degree, then reach up and touch the sky."

The '55 Pontiac had long since been traded in for a light blue '64 Pontiac with a white convertible top. I figured I owed it to Pontiac to remain loyal. After all, my GTO was a Pontiac and the '55 beast survived that dead-of-winter, rebellious trip home last December.

I had mapped out the route: south through New York to New Jersey, then across Pennsylvania and out through Ohio, Indiana and finally Illinois. It was the same route I had taken so many times before.

My mother didn't complain very much, but after nearly fifteen hours of driving, stopping only occasionally for coffee and a quick bite to eat, I knew she needed some rest and admittedly, so did I. We finally pulled off the road stopping for the night at a motel somewhere in Ohio. The twelve-hundred-mile trip took two days. I kept awake pushing all day and throughout the night. I was driving the car, and getting there was driving me.

It was late in the afternoon of the third day when we left the highway for the final leg of the journey which let us north along the familiar Route 157. We made the right-hand turn off 157 and up the long curved driveway arriving at the front door of the Comfort Inn. The Comfort Inn was a few miles east of Edwardsville Center and just around the bend from the main entrance to S.I.U. We checked in and brought our bags in from the car, and I flopped down on one of the beds and went to sleep. The next day I took my mother around to all the familiar spots in town, including the apartments where I had lived, and then drove out to the campus. It was summer recess and the campus was pretty quiet—no students milling around between classes, nothing except activities in preparation for graduation.

On the day I graduated we went out for a late breakfast and then drove to the SIU campus. Commencement would begin at two o'clock; we were early.

I hadn't seen Janice since I left Edwardsville six months earlier. The graduation was open to the public and I wondered if she would attend. I escorted my mother to a seat near the front and then walked over to the tented pavilion, where I put on my cap and gown. All of us were given instructions as to where to stand and how to proceed according to the prearranged schedule.

While standing in line, I turned around and said hello to Sarah, who was moving along behind me. Sarah and her boyfriend, Jim, had double-dated with Janice and me on several occasions. She asked me how I was and I told her I was fine and that I had just arrived by car from Massachusetts, and that I was excited to officially, and finally, graduate.

I asked Sarah if she was still in touch with Janice, and without waiting for a response, I mentioned that I would be stopping by to see Janice after graduation. I was looking forward to seeing her, looking for some sign that Janice had missed me and would love to see me. "In any event," I continued, "it would be nice to see her again after all this time."

Sarah, never known for her diplomacy, said, "Don, there's not a chance of getting back with her, if that's what you're thinking. She's getting married to Roger McBride." The words just spilled out of her impulsive mouth—no filter between her brain and her mouth.

Sarah's cold, insensitive tone shot right through me, but I just blew it off pretending it didn't bother me. I had come all the way out here to finally, officially graduate and to see Janice once again...and what was this pending marriage thing? And to Roger McBride? I still wasn't buying it. Hundreds of folding chairs were neatly arranged on the freshly mowed lawn in front of an expansive portable stage. The first three rows were reserved for dignitaries and those receiving advanced and honorary degrees.

I began looking around for Janice and her mother. I was sure they knew I'd be here and were aware of the date and time. It would be nice, I thought, if they would show up and share this moment with me. Janice was the only person in the world who knew how difficult it was for me to finally be standing here.

My name was called. It was now my turn. I climbed the three short steps and slowly walked across the open-air, wooden stage to receive my Bachelor's Degree. I shook hands with the president of the university as he presented me with my leather-bound document. That was it. So quick. Too quick.

After the congratulatory greeting and the handshake, I began my slow exit from the stage, walking past the podium and the two rows of deans and other officials seated on stage. I stopped for a moment, glanced over my left shoulder, and began scanning the audience—left and right, and front and back. It was one last chance to capture this moment in my mind—and look skyward to thank God for his hand in this.

One of the officials seated behind the podium to the far left stood and motioned for me to move along; I was holding up the line. I gave him a nod and a gentle knowing smile and walked the rest of the way across the stage and down the steps. I entered the row and sat next to my mother as the others—the rest of the Class of 1969—paraded right to left, across the crowded stage. It was a festive event on such a warm cloudless day, everyone hugging and throwing their caps in the air. I looked around for people I knew or had known. Most of my friends had graduated on time, a year earlier.

Janice and her mother never showed up.

My mother and I sat in the hot sun and suffered through the tiring speeches, and when it was over, we walked over to my car. I turned and faced my mother as she snapped a picture of me with my degree tucked under my left arm...and that was it.

I had been anticipating this moment for such a long time. I had it pictured in my mind, frame by frame. I would be caught up in the emotion, enjoying the sense of accomplishment—the end and the beginning. The wondrously enchanting images, born in my mind's eye, evaporated like trailing smoke from a snuffed-out candle. I don't know what I expected. Janice running up to congratulate me? Bands playing? Balloons popping? Cannons going off? Music in the air? Old friends shaking hands and talking about the great times we all had together...?

I glanced around again, one last time, then turned to my mother and said, "I now have what I came out here for, Mom. What do you think...let's do a little celebrating ourselves...just you and me. You game?" She congratulated me, then smiled and agreed to join me for a few drinks at the Stonehouse Tavern.

We drove out of the parking area to the main campus road, turned left beyond the entrance, and headed down the highway, passing under the train bridge and turning right into the parking lot next to the Stonehouse. We walked in and sat down at the bar. The place was completely empty. I ordered a couple of drinks and when they arrived, we raised our glasses in a toast to success! My mother, always good company, sat there patiently listening as I shared some of my memories of the Stonehouse with her. "I remember sitting right here, in this seat, at this bar," I began with a smile, "on the night Bird and I decided to head out to Vegas." And I told her about the night I walked right past Janice as she sat at the bar sipping her drink. "She was sitting right down there at the end of the bar next to the door."

I continued on, "Mike Kaplan and I used to play cards in here.

262

We'd sit around one of those tables over there along the wall and play gin; penny a point, nickel a box and quarter a game. He'd usually clean me out, but not always. My bartender friend, Danny O'Brien, used to hand me drinks for free over there through the service bar opening next to the cash register." I kept blabbing on non-stop, one memory after another.

It had been a day filled with anticipation and memories—an emotional day. "Hey bartender," I said, "When you have a moment, give us another round here, would you please?" I was deep in celebration and reminiscing to the extreme. I finally said to my mother, "I think we should leave before I have too much to drink." She agreed without hesitation. I paid the tab, left a generous tip, and managed to drive back to the hotel, and went straight to bed. I woke up late the next morning, put myself back together and said, "Mother, I'm going over to Janice's house to say hello and show her my Bachelor's Degree and then say goodbye. I'll be back in an hour or so. Is that okay with you?" I picked up some flowers, and then stopped at Schwartz's Drug Store to buy a couple of six-packs of Michelob beer.

Janice must have expected me. When I drove up her driveway, she slowly walked out of the house to greet me, and after saying hello, made a comment about how big my car was and how much gas it must consume. "Just like you," she said.

It was a comment, meant to ridicule; a slam at me for buying such a large, gas-guzzling car, but I quickly dismissed it and changed the subject.

Janice was dressed in a pretty white blouse with tiny pink and blue checkered designs, very much like Janice, very feminine. After the initial slight, she was polite and warm to me, but not overly so. Although I didn't ask, she told me Roger was playing softball and would be back later on. She invited me in.

I tucked my leather-bound document under my arm, grabbed the beer and flowers from the car, and walked in behind her. Her mother hurried into the kitchen from the living room to see me. "You look wonderful," she said with her usual charming smile.

I opened a beer for Janice and poured it into a glass from the shelf, then offered the same to her mother. "Please, join us," I said. "I have something to show you."

As if she was doing something wrong, her mother said, "I'm really not supposed to, but I'll just have a little." I handed her the flowers and with her twinkling eyes she said, "Oh, how nice. Thank you… I'll put them in a vase."

I poured a glass of beer for myself and the three of us walked into the living room and sat down. Janice's mother motioned for me to sit in her chair, the light blue velvet, high-back chair to the left of the fireplace—a place of honor. I opened my leather-bound document and showed them my bachelor's degree. Janice and her mother read from the document and then raised their glasses in a congratulatory toast.

I scanned the room as we lifted our glasses. Janice was sitting on the couch next to her mother, across from me on the opposite side of the room. I couldn't help remembering that this was the same couch, in the same room, where I had proposed to Janice on Christmas Day, 1966.

I told them about my upcoming teaching position and my summer job as a bartender. We shared a light conversation and few laughs, then I asked Janice if she would like to take a drive to the hotel and say hello to my mother. She had met my mother at the hospital back in '65, after my accident. She said, "No, I don't think so," but then changed her mind. I figured her mother must have encouraged her to go with me while I was out of the room.

When we arrived at the hotel, my mother was very warm and friendly, and was delighted that Janice had come by to pay her a visit. She took a picture of the two of us as I sat on a large sofa with Janice sitting on the armrest to my right, her left arm wrapped around my neck. I started laughing over something and so did Janice; a perfectly timed picture.

"I really have to get back," Janice finally admitted. I figured Roger was in the back of her mind, that he'd be angry or something, so I asked my mother to wait while I drove Janice home.

On the way back, I told Janice we were heading back to Massachusetts that afternoon. I was pretty matter-of-fact about it. I wasn't going to embarrass or humiliate myself, so I kept the conversation friendly and upbeat, my true emotional side well hidden. I needed to leave her with the impression that I would get on with my life, with or without her.

She had my mother's address and phone number. I also gave her Joe Noble's phone number. If she had second thoughts after I left, she could reach me.

I slowly began to accept what had been hitting me in the face for some time. Janice was now Roger's girl, and there was nothing I could do about it.

When we arrived back at Janice's place, I gave her mother a good-bye hug, and then Janice and I walked outside to my car. We held each other and looked into each other's eyes. Neither one of us said a word. It had all been said such a long time ago.

As I headed down her driveway, I saw her in the rearview mirror standing at the top of her driveway, watching me as I slowly went down to the end and turned right onto Brockmeier Road. I was ready to leave. There was no need to pause or delay; nothing was going to change. The rest of my life lay ahead of me...in Massachusetts.

I drove back to the hotel, picked up my mother, checked out and started the trip home. I wanted to get back and finish up the school year with my fourth graders and resume my weekend bartending job at The Cliff, and I was looking forward to the beginning of my new life.

The ride home was uneventful. I don't remember any of it. I knew I would be making one more trip out there. I had one more reason to return. It would be in the late spring of '71.

* * *

I settled back in at Joe's place and returned to my teaching job, and continued with the weekend work at the hotel.

Shortly after the school year ended, Joe and I began working together full time at The Cliff. The hotel staff was busy preparing for the Fourth of July weekend and the crowds that would soon follow. The summer was just around the corner. Joe launched his boat while I was away and it was now tied up in his slip along the pier in Scituate Harbor. The nonstop summer fun in Scituate was about to begin.

265

The Cliff Hotel, as expected, opened the season with some top rock bands playing to a young crowd in the Bamboo Lounge in the lower level of the hotel. I became an instant favorite at the bar. I was quick with a drink and quick with a story. During the day, I worked the outside patio bar and sometimes the service bar and would bring drinks to guests in their rooms. I was all over the place, making money and making friends.

Late one morning, while I was setting up the outside patio bar for the noon-time rush, Carol Channing, the famous actress, walked down from her third-floor room, through the enclosed porch and out through the white double doors onto the beautifully polished flagstone patio. The Cliff was home to many of the world's top entertainers during the summer months. Miss Channing, in the leading role in the stage play "Hello Dolly," was performing at the Cohasset Music Circus just a few miles down the road.

With dignity and grace, she strolled across the patio and appeared in front of me at the bar. I was busy stocking the coolers with beer, counting the cash, laying out napkins and glassware, and enjoying the warm breeze off the ocean. Off to my right, and still in her white, full-length, wraparound bathrobe, was Miss Channing—her hair piled high and done up in curlers. I turned away from my busy routine and greeted her with a smile. "Good morning, Miss Channing."

"Good morning, Mr. Bartender," she said cheerfully. She asked if the bar was open and I said, "We're always open for you, Miss Channing." She asked if I would put together a daiquiri with plenty of freshly squeezed fruit, and added, "I'd like it in a tall glass with a straw." She explained in detail what kinds of fruit she wanted, how much ice, and so on.

"I'd love to accommodate you, Miss Channing, but I don't have any fresh fruit out here," I said, a little embarrassed.

She responded without hesitation. "Well, don't you worry, that's not a problem. I'll just go back in and get some. I'll be right back." She turned, and like a soldier on a mission, walked back across the patio, then up the two steps leading onto the porch, and disappeared through the inner doors to the lobby. Ten minutes later she was back at the bar with her arms cradling enough fruit to satisfy an Egyptian king—oranges, limes, lemons, a few strawberries, and even a banana.

By now the bar was beginning to fill up. A friend of mine, John Egre, who was now living with us at Joe's place, was sitting at the far end of the bar watching as Miss Channing presented me with the fruit. Joe was sitting on a stool next to him. I went right to work cutting and peeling, and squeezing the fruit into a tall mixing glass. I added the Daiquiri mix and the requisite amount of crushed ice, then free-poured some expensive vodka, and placed the metal mixing container down over the glass. Carol Channing was a special guest and I was giving her special attention. I apologized for not including the strawberries or the banana. "I don't have a blender out here," I said. "Electrical service to the bar has not yet been connected. But I will place a strawberry on top. How's that sound?" I followed her instructions, now do this, now do that. She was the center of attention and so was I.

The drink was now ready for a vigorous shake before bring poured it into a tulip-shaped glass with a straw: a masterpiece. Miss Channing acknowledged the others gathered around the bar, nodding and smiling, as I rushed to finish the drink. Customers were waiting, but I continued to put them off. I picked up the drink with both hands, held it out in front of me, began shaking it up, and in a heartbeat, it slipped through my hands and exploded between my feet on the patio floor.

John Egre busted his sides laughing, spraying a mouth full of beer across the bar, and Miss Channing let out an unrestrained howl. She glanced to her right at Joe and John and the others with a deadpan look of disbelief. "I'll be back," she cried out to a gale of laughter. I watched as she walked down to the end of the patio and out on to Glades Road, next to the sea wall. I looked over at Joe and buried my head in my folded arms on the bar and said, as if the world had just ended, "Oh no…after all that work!"

When she reached the sea wall, she turned around and began walking back to the bar. I motioned to Joe and said, "Don't look now but she's coming back! She's not giving up!" I begged forgiveness when she returned. "I'm so sorry, Miss Channing," I said.

Still laughing, as if this were the last performance of a successful season, she told me not to worry. "It's no big deal. I'll just go in and get some more fruit. I'll be right back. Don't you go anywhere!"

I looked over at Joe as if to say, "Can you believe it?" The whole bar was involved now, anxiously awaiting her return. After serving the other customers, and having a good laugh with just about everyone, I went back to work cleaning up the mess on the patio floor.

* * *

It was July 20, 1969. The Apollo astronauts would make history later that night with the first landing on the moon. When she returned with another arm full of fruit, I said, "Carol, (it was Carol now, not Miss Channing) you keep this up and you're going to be the first woman on the moon. I motioned to the sky and, like Jackie Gleason, said, "To the moon, Alice!" The whole bar broke out laughing at my silly playacting, especially Miss Channing. I was enjoying myself and my new-found friend.

I smiled and then quietly, and without fanfare, squeezed the fruit into the large mixing glass and made the drink. All was well. She gently picked it up, raised it in the air as a toast to me, nodded a friendly goodbye to the folks at the bar, and left the patio sipping her long-awaited, and richly deserved, daiquiri.

* * *

The summer of '69 was busy and full of laughs, and I met a lot of people who soon became friends. Labor Day weekend marked the end of the season, and it was wild—loud music, sunshine and swimming, and nonstop drinking. When the long weekend ended, I finished up my responsibilities at the hotel, and directed all of my time and attention to my upcoming grade six teaching assignment.

September was a wonderful beginning to a fresh new set of responsibilities, which brought greater meaning and purpose to my life. I was delighted with myself. Although I was unknown to the students and most of the staff, I settled into a comfortable routine. My students seemed to enjoy me right from the beginning. I tried to make learning fun, and for the most part had no trouble doing that. I taught one reading class and four math classes. When students would become a little restless, which didn't happen often, I would

268

remind them that we both had jobs here. I'll do my job; you have to do the rest. "Remember, your parents are paying me a lot of money to teach you this stuff. I'm not going to let them down and neither are you. Right?"

I was in the middle of teaching my second period math class one day when I glanced up at the clock on the wall to my left...it was a quarter after ten on a cloudless Monday morning. I stopped what I was doing, looked out over the heads of the children in my class and stared at the bulletin board at the back of my room...then quietly muttered, "Well, that's that."

Two days earlier, on Saturday, the 20th of September, Janice had married Roger. The children were wondering what I said and what was going on with me. There was complete silence in the room. I was back in Illinois, lost in my private thoughts. One of my students spoke up. "Mr. Hussey, you all right?"

I told them I was fine. "Just give me a minute," I whispered in a barely audible tone.

I glanced to my right, through the bank of windows showcasing the warm, sun-filled morning and thought, How could two people, once so much in love, have made such a mess out of something so rare? Love must be the only human emotion powerful enough to break through the membrane and enter the soul.

So, for whatever the reason or whatever the circumstance, she had made her decision and I had made mine. She married the wrong guy last Saturday, and I knew it. And maybe, she knew it too.

epilogue

In May of 1971, I was granted a leave of absence from teaching to attend my personal injury trial. Gary met me at the airport in St. Louis and I stayed with him and Amy, and their young son, Gary, Jr., who was now three or four years old. He was a beautiful little boy with curly hair and a happy, playful disposition. The courthouse was only a short distance from their house, so I walked each day, giving me plenty of time to gather my thoughts.

The round of legal depositions had been completed while I was still in school, back in the summer of '68. My attorney had filed a lawsuit on my behalf for $250,000 against the manufacturer of the Chicago Press brake company, Dreis and Krump Industries. The suit was dated August 26, 1968 and filed with the Clerk of Circuit Court, Third Judicial Circuit, Madison County, Illinois—Docket # 65-L615. The complaint alleged that Dreis and Krump could have, at a minimal cost, designed and installed safeguards on their machines which would have eliminated operator injuries.

I was told that Krump Industries had its origins in Germany and had manufactured weapons for the Nazi military during World War II. Krump's attorney was a short, stout man who spoke in a quick, raspy and demanding voice, with rich overtones of sarcasm. He was clearly annoyed at having to waste his time on a case that, in his opinion, had no merit.

I was sitting through one of the lengthy afternoon depositions when he abruptly pointed his finger in the air and said, "This suit isn't worth a damn nickel; not worth the paper it's printed on."

My lawyer, who was sitting across from him and to my left, had been quietly shuffling through his case file. He immediately looked up and, peering over his thin half-glasses, reminded Krump's attorney that he was a busy man as well. He said, a little exasperated, "Please, just get on with your questions. We'll see how much this suit is worth and I think it's worth plenty." They ignored me as their exchange became heated and surprisingly personal. They were talking over one another, barking back and forth like kids in a sandbox. I became disinterested with their posturing and turned in my chair to catch a glimpse of the slow moving Mississippi River. I was sitting across from a tall, open window on the third floor, and I watched as two heavily-laden barges, tied up end-to-end like freight cars, were guided downstream by a double stack, diesel-powered smoking tugboat. I figured they were on their way to New Orleans.

Finished arguing for the moment, Krump's attorney turned, cleared his throat for the stenographer and announced, "We're ready to begin. Is your client ready?"

My attorney nodded in agreement and said, "Yes, we're ready." Krump's attorney fixed his eyes directly on me as he introduced himself to the jury as the attorney for Dreis and Krump. Both attorneys were local guys. Both had established their respective practices years before in downtown Alton, Illinois.

Krump's attorney was a persistent and determined interrogator. He began his remarks with a forced half-smile, trying to seem friendly and sincere. I figured he was setting me up, trying to disarm me. The tough questioning would begin after he was satisfied I would cooperate.

Although I was young and inexperienced with this sort of thing, I was ready for him. I assumed he would attempt to draw me into a compromising position, hoping I'd reveal something to bolster his case, then shove it down my throat at trial. My answers were short, deliberate and cautious. I took my time and frequently turned to H3 for advice. H3 simply told me to tell the truth. "Only answer the question he poses. Don't give him anything extra."

I'm sure my posture and body language gave Krump's attorney the impression I wouldn't be intimidated. If he gave me any shit, I was prepared to give it right back. I figured the jury would see right through this sonofabitch once we got into court, and I could hardly wait for that day.

The round of depositions went on for three days, beginning around ten in the morning and, after an hour-long break for lunch, finishing up around four. On Friday, the last day, we were waiting for Krump's attorney to come back from lunch. He was late. Suddenly, the door swung open wide, and there he was standing against the doorframe about to make his grand entrance, his glassy eyes fixed on H3. Before he had a chance to speak, the stenographer sprang to her feet, asking, in a take-charge voice, "Are we ready to continue?" I figured she must have seen this coming.

He swung the door closed and shuffled his wide girth and rosy cheeks across the room and over to his seat. His white shirt was disheveled at his waistline, like he had attempted to stuff it in before entering. He sat down and continued where he had left off. I grudgingly answered his questions while H3, now fidgeting with his pen and biting on tiny nicotine mints that were supposed to help him stop smoking, objected repeatedly, sometimes motioning with his hand, not even bothering to look up.

They displayed a clear hatred for one another. This was not some courtroom one-upmanship thing, it was deeper than that. It must have been brewing for years, and it annoyed the hell out of me. It was a constant distraction that would flare up and dominate the trial.

When we broke for lunch on the first day of the trial, I called Janice from the pay phone downstairs in the courthouse lobby. She was married now and living in Edwardsville. After their honeymoon, she and Roger had settled into her mother's small house until he could get his construction business off the ground.

I told her I was back in town attending my long-awaited personal injury trial. "I'm calling you from the courthouse in downtown Edwardsville," I said. I asked her some inane question, like, "Do you remember when I was in the hospital and…?" The question was unimportant. The reason for the call was to let her know I was back in town and staying with Gary and Amy, hoping she would show up during the trial. I never asked her directly; perhaps I should have, but I figured it must have been obvious to her. She never came by and neither did her mother.

* * *

During the trial the two opposing attorneys sat across from each other at the same table down front and just a few feet away from the jury. They began barking pointed questions at each other. I was seated to the right of H3, my back to the nearly empty courtroom and across the table from the defense attorney, when H3 slammed his copy of the deposition down on the table and said, "You calling me a liar?"

The defense attorney, grabbing his copy of the deposition and waving it over his head, stood up and roared right back, "You're deliberately misquoting the deposition and misleading the jury and you know it!"

Jumping from his seat and thrusting both arms into the air, the judge announced, "That's it! I want to see all of you in my chambers, immediately!" He dismissed the jury, telling them, "Get some lunch and be back at 2:00 p.m. sharp!"

We entered his chambers through the small door to the left of the bench. He was a straight-talking, no nonsense guy. "What the hell is going on out there? You two had better stop these outbursts. I'm warning both of you. The only reason I'm not calling a mistrial is because you…(meaning me)…have come a great distance and at some considerable expense to be here. However, if there are any more outbursts between the two of you in my courtroom, I'll stop this trial on a dime and send the jury home. You can petition the court to hear it during the fall session. Then someone else can deal with you two! I've just about had it."

He then turned to me and said, "I'm sorry for all this nonsense."

H3 handed me some money and sent me across the street to Schwartz's Drug Store to pick up sandwiches at the lunch counter. "We'll have lunch here and talk about what's coming up," he said.

I thought it was odd for him to be sending me over there. The entire jury would be sitting around that lunch counter, and he must have known that. I figured he was the lawyer and this would be part of his strategy. I didn't think it was a good idea for the jury members to see me carrying all those sandwiches and drinks from Schwartz's back across the street to the courthouse. They might feel less sympathetic toward me because, despite my obvious injuries, I could handle myself with apparent ease, "pain and suffering" notwithstanding.

After lunch, the jury returned to the courthouse and milled around in the hallway upstairs waiting to be called. Several members were seated together along the wooden bench next to the courtroom doors. I overheard one member of the jury, a woman, speaking to another woman about the trial. She was talking about me and what I must have gone through. She wasn't very discreet; she was talking loud enough for me to hear. I thought she was trying to let me know she was in my corner and would probably vote in my favor.

I alerted H3 to what I'd overheard, but it didn't seem to register. He just turned and instructed me, "Go over to the defense attorney, strike up a conversation and appear to be really friendly...put on a smile." This again didn't seem logical to me. Why would I act friendly toward him or toward anybody? I was there to win a lawsuit, not to make friends, or worse, to appear to be having a good time. But he was the lawyer, so I made a weak attempt.

The courtroom doors opened and the jury filed back into court and was seated. We followed the jury and took our seats down front. The bailiff then called for all to rise as the judge entered from his chambers and settled in behind the bench. The session came to order.

The defense tried to explain to the jury that installing safety devices on the press brake machine would be counterproductive to its operation. They argued that "any such device would get in the way and prevent the operator from doing his job."

The attorney then began a calculated move to demonstrate his point. With well-rehearsed theatrics, he stood up and motioned for two men at the back of the courtroom to come forward. They carefully walked down the aisle holding a large piece of sheet steel between them. At his direction, they rested the steel along the jury rail right in front of the first row of jurors, then slowly handed it off to him.

Krump's attorney held the steel with both hands as it rested on the jury rail and began explaining to the jury what would happen if safety switches, requiring both hands to activate, were installed on the machine. Without warning and while he was still talking, he let the steal crash to the floor, startling everyone.

"Do you see ladies and gentlemen of the jury?" he asked. "How could the operator let go of the steel and expect the machine to oper-ate effectively?" I saw right through that. I leaned over to my left and whispered in my lawyer's ear, "That's nonsense. Brackets could be installed to support the steel. It could then be slid into the machine by hand, resting there until the operator activated the machine by pushing two side-by-side safety buttons installed on the face of the machine, away from the action."

For some reason, I wasn't able to get through to him. I don't think he was listening to me. He seemed focused on what had just hap-pened. He leaned to his right and whispered to me, "Did you see that? He just scared the hell out of the jury with that foolish trick. It's go-ing to backfire on him. Just watch and you'll see. You can't scare the jury like that and get away with it."

The defense attorney called me to the stand. I was asked to ex-plain in detail what had happened that night. As I expected, he tried to draw me into a corner, coyly and gently, without causing a back-lash from the jury. He didn't want to blame me outright for causing my own accident. "Were you distracted?" he asked. "What were you going to do after work? It was July 5th .... Had you been out late on the Fourth?" There were several questions—more like statements—all in rapid succession.

He had no interest in my answers. He was making a speech, and making his point without offending me in the eyes of the jury. I was too emotionally involved and nervous to say much. I started to respond, but my lawyer stood up, interrupted me in mid-sentence, pointed his finger at the opposing attorney and launched an objec-tion. "One at a time, your honor, please." So the accusatory questions were presented to me one at a time, but he had made his point with the jury.

Throughout the course of the week-long trial, I kept glancing over at the courtroom door, up the aisle and off to the right, wondering if Janice would suddenly appear. Maybe she wanted to be there. Maybe she didn't. She was the only one at my side during those wretched days and the only one I relied upon. It would have made an enormous difference to me if she had quietly slipped into the courtroom and sat up back. My whole demeanor would have changed.

I answered the questions with a soft, pensive voice, unsure of myself almost from the beginning. The judge asked me several times to "speak up, so we can all hear you."

During his closing arguments, H3 grabbed my right hand, the one with the most damage and loss. He held it up so the jury could get a good look. He spoke of the difficulty I would have for the rest of my life, from making love to driving a car and everything in between. It was so goddamn humiliating for me, but he was the lawyer. Then he grabbed my other hand and did the same. He displayed the anger that was raging inside of me, saying, "This young man was trapped in the jaws of that press brake for nearly ten minutes—a machine with no safety switches or safety devices of any kind. He'll struggle the rest of his life trying to make a living, all because they didn't and wouldn't invest a few extra dollars to install safety switches.

"Ladies and gentlemen of the jury, I sincerely hope you find in favor of him. Maybe then they'll make safety a priority, and save someone else from the agony of such a life-changing injury."

The judge gave the jury their instructions, saying, "Illinois law compels you to reach a unanimous decision. You all must agree." They filed out, one behind the other, through a side door to the right of the jury box. After the bailiff closed the jury room door, I stood and walked up the main aisle and out through the courtroom doors, to the circular hallway and marble staircase. I never said a word to H3. I needed some fresh air and some solitude.

I knew this had not gone well. Now I just wanted it to be over. It had been a hurry-up trial, completely out of my control. I had never liked anyone or anything controlling me or my life. My future was in the hands of others, manipulated by the proceedings, the lawyers— the system.

I wandered around outside, and after a few minutes came back in and headed up the stairs to speak with H3. I was halfway up the staircase when the bailiff stepped out into the upper hallway to announce that the jury was returning.

I walked in and sat down in the usual place, down front and to the right of H3. One by one the jurors entered the courtroom from the side door to my left and took their seats in the jury box. Each of them looked down or straight ahead. I was looking at their faces to get a "read" and none of them offered me eye contact or even a glance—nothing. It reminded me of the courtroom scene in "To Kill a Mockingbird," when Tom Robinson was convicted by a jury that filed in and sat down with their heads hung low, all of them knowing he was innocent but too compromised to acquit. This was a lost cause.

After they were all seated, the bailiff asked the court to rise. We all stood as the judge turned to the jury and asked the foreman if they had reached a verdict.

"We have your honor," said the foreman.

The judge responded, "And what say you?"

"We the jury, find in favor of the defendant, your honor."

It happened so fast. I was unprepared and confused. I had lost. Even though I was expecting this, it startled me. I didn't really know for sure that I had lost until my lawyer flopped down in his chair and rested his head on the table. I paused, momentarily glancing across at the faces of the jury, then sat down slowly and wondered to myself, Now what?'

H3 began to rise slowly, and with a little dramatic flair, he cleared his throat, stood ramrod straight and addressed the judge. "Your Honor," he said in a calm but firm, matter-of-fact tone. "If you please, your honor, I'd like the court to poll the jury." I didn't know what that meant, but I figured he was up to something. Maybe he could somehow get this reversed.

The judge agreed to the poll, and asked each member of the jury, one-by-one, to stand when called and affirm the verdict. "Did you find in favor of the defendant?" H3 asked. Each stood when their number was called and said, "Yes, your honor." They found no fault with the manufacturer, Dreis and Krump. Not one member of the jury found in my favor. No one would "hang the jury." No one wanted to return on Monday.

The woman I thought I could count on, the one in the waiting area who spoke so loudly and openly on my behalf, quickly looked down when I glanced over at her. All I needed was for one person to say they weren't sure or they needed more time. But not one of them spoke up.

So that was that, I thought. I signed some papers and had a pleasant conversation with the judge. He seemed genuinely sympathetic. He took me aside and said, "You seem like a nice young man and you handled yourself very well in here. I wish you the best in the future."

"Thank you, your honor," I responded. Then I turned to H3, who was still sitting, mulling over the verdict, seemingly bewildered. I said goodbye and he said something about an appeal. I wasn't listening.

I walked out of the courtroom, down the marble stairs and across the street to Vanzo's. By now it was nearly four in the afternoon. I ordered a beer and called Amy from the pay phone to see if Gary was home. It wasn't long before he came through the door and sat down with me for a drink.

I told him what had happened. I also told him that I felt betrayed by that jury. I rationalized the verdict by saying, "I'm not a local guy. I don't live around here anymore. If I did, I think they would have returned a different verdict." He agreed, but it didn't matter. It was over.

I borrowed Gary's car and drove over to Janice's mother's house to say hello and tell her how it all turned out. I was sure she'd love to see me and hear all about what happened at trial. She invited me in and I wrapped my arms around her and gave her a kiss on the cheek. It was so good to see her. She was standing over the ironing board in the kitchen next to the folding pantry doors, ironing some of Wally's shirts. I didn't say very much about the trial itself, except that it didn't go my way.

She was visibly angry. I had never seen her angry. Her eyes widened and her lips tightened as she said, "I'll never vote for that judge again!"

She asked me how I was and I told her I was fine, no big deal. "I can't stay very long though," I said. "I really don't want to be here when Wally comes home." As much as I cared for her and Janice, I would have been embarrassed to be seen by him or anyone else after all those years, like someone who just can't ever give it up. And I didn't want to see Janice, either. I wouldn't know what to say. I kissed Janice's mother once again, then turned and left through the screen door on the back porch.

afterword

I haven't seen it all, but I've seen enough to know that patience, keeping your word, honesty, integrity, setting standards for yourself, saving your money, and always trying to better yourself are worthy goals, and you can benefit greatly by listening to your inner voice, and following your intuition—your heart.

I'm also reminded of the words from Shakespeare, who offered advice, through the voice of the fool in *King Lear*, to be modest and to take caution with your tongue:

Have more than thou showest,
Speak less than thou knowest,

And thou shall have more
Than two tens to a score

I invite you to read *IF* by Rudyard Kipling, and The *Road Less Traveled* by Robert Frost. These two poems inspired and encouraged me at an early age to set my own course and begin my own journey, independent and free.

And when times were tough, I was comforted by my faith in the future—believing in the promise of America and knowing full well that nothing lasts forever.

I have found that one success, no matter how small, will build upon itself. So I encourage you to take the first step, the first class, the first lesson, the first job, and begin your own journey. Don't ever stop trying, even if you have doubts...especially if you have doubts.

Always enjoy your friends as they enjoy you, but never allow them to interfere with the goals you've set for yourself. During a reflective moment in the movie *Million Dollar Baby,* Morgan Freeman's character says, "…and he gave his all, for a dream that only he could see." That scene hit me personally.

* * *

Never forget that much of the hard work has already been done for us. The fertile soil of freedom has been nurtured by generations of Americans willing to sacrifice everything. From Bunker Hill, to Omaha Beach, to Vietnam and beyond—the broken hearts, the spilled blood and the endless tears…the price paid in full.

If you're willing to work and work and work some more, you'll put that hard-fought, God-given freedom to good use. And as you gain confidence, set your sights on the impossible. Then watch with a smile as your dreams race across the endless wonders of a midnight sky.

Success in life is not necessarily about winning or losing; it's the journey, and the many wonderful people you meet along the way. It's the desire to achieve something greater than personal ambition…an attempt to make a difference. To leave the world a better place because you dared, you tried, you set an example.

Several years ago, I broke open a fortune cookie and read the message tucked inside: "Life is an exciting adventure or it's nothing at all." I folded it and tucked it in my wallet in case I ever needed reminding.

* * *

My son Gregory, returned from Iraq a year after I began writing this book. While on convoy from western Anbar to Fallujah, he sustained some loss of hearing when an Improvised Explosive Device (IED) detonated between his vehicle and the one behind him. Three seconds earlier and his vehicle would have been destroyed.

His unit made it out of Fallujah to the Green Zone in Baghdad, where they boarded a U.S. military flight to Kuwait and from there across Europe en route to America. Twenty-two hours later, they landed in Maine for a brief welcoming home ceremony, then on to Ft. Hood, Texas for the official homecoming which was held on post at the Stryker Gym. I was in the gym that day when he and his fellow soldiers, came running in formation through a cloud of smoke and blaring patriotic music, to an overjoyed crowd of family and friends.

He deployed once again to Iraq for a second year-long tour, where he volunteered to serve as the turret gunner on an eleven-man border patrol team—one of many such teams strung along the border with Iran. He was awarded the Bronze Star for Meritorious Service during time of war.

Gregory has most recently completed the Army Ranger School at Ft. Benning, Georgia—two months of the most demanding and rigorous training imaginable. When he returned home, having lost twenty-three pounds, he regained his muscle mass and stamina, and went back to Ft. Benning to complete the Army's Paratrooper School. He has recently taken over command of a unit attached to the U.S. Army's 2nd Cavalry Brigade in Vilsec, Germany, and is now training and otherwise preparing his soldiers for a yearlong mission into Afghanistan.

* * *

As captain of her high school gymnastics team, my daughter Jennifer became the 1992 Massachusetts State Champion in the Balance Beam. She is also an accomplished downhill skier and competed nationally in figure skating as a member of the synchronized team from the Skating Club of Boston. She also performed in the Boston Ballet's *Nutcracker* for five consecutive seasons during the '80s and early 90s.

While in college at Salve Regina University in Newport, Rhode Island, Jennifer began a year-long intensive training program in preparation for a spot on the U.S. Olympic Luge Team. During the 1998 Olympic trials, held at Lake Placid, New York, she was injured while flying down the ice laden track at speeds approaching eighty miles an hour. It happened on the final turn of her last run and wound up in the hospital with lacerations on her face and neck. She quickly recovered and was game to continue. She did continue and eventually ranked 16th in the overall competition but missed the cut. The Team went on to compete that year in Nagano, Japan.

She is married now and living in lower Manhattan, New York. She earned her Master's degree in finance and has found success in the financial capital of the world.

* * *

Looking back on my college years, my bachelor's degree from Southern Illinois University became my "ticket to ride," my stepping-stone to the future, a future limited only by my imagination, my intelligence and my personal ambition. It marked the culmination of a truly remarkable adventure, one filled with nonstop academic demands, deeply personal experiences and equally memorable, rich and lasting relationships—a nearly impossible dream that somehow worked out. I had met the challenge and passed the grade and was awarded my leather-bound document. I could now try my hand at anything, and that's what I've done.

As a classroom teacher, I readily admit to enjoying a fair amount of success from a series of student-centered programs, which not only enhanced the learning experience of my students, but also gave greater meaning and purpose to my life. It was a perfect place for me at that time in my life. I was doing what I loved and loved what I was doing.

During my first year of teaching, I met Brenda, a charming and strikingly attractive second grade teacher assigned to a classroom in a separate wing of the same school building. We enjoyed a wonderful seven month relationship and eventually were married. Shortly thereafter we bought our first home, and started our own family. By now, I had come full circle and was now quite content with myself.

I even signed up at a local civilian flight school and began a series of flying lessons—something I had wanted to do since I was a young boy. I actually flew a few of my own "touch 'n goes," mostly in Cessna 150's and 172's, flying out of Marshfield Airport and Wiggins Airfield in Norwood. I remember taking off from Wiggins one Saturday afternoon and cruising along at 3000 feet when I strayed into the flight path of an incoming 747 on a final approach from Europe. The tower alerted the 747: "Traffic at twelve o'clock." That was me. I banked a hard right and dropped a thousand feet in the blink an eye.

The dependent relationship with Janice and the tough times that followed were behind me now. I had let that go, now focusing on my family and my future, and like a horse with blinders, steadied my eyes on what was in front of me.

* * *

After twelve years of teaching in a fully tenured position, I decided to take another swing at the ball. I was living the promise of a country rich with opportunities and was ready for another challenge, another adventure. I wondered how high I could reach or how far I could go.

In the summer of 1976, I stumbled my way into the world of business, the demanding and unpredictable world of construction. It wasn't long before I realized the full nature of what I'd gotten myself into, and I was ill-prepared for most of it: Union bosses, thieves, extortionists, ex-cons, payoffs, and etc. Adding more chaos to an already chaotic enterprise, I was constantly engaged in conflicts with the Environmental Protection Agency (EPA), the Internal Revenue Service (IRS), and the Massachusetts Department of Revenue (DOR). Mixed in were episodes of stolen tools and equipment, job sites sabotaged or engulfed in flames, a flurry of suits and countersuits, unimaginable emergencies with manned 100 foot, split-boom cranes, hydraulic lifts and staging platforms.

My life was threatened more than once as I worked on several major waterfront projects along Boston Harbor during a renaissance of redevelopment lasting ten years or more—The World Trade Center, The Boston Design Center, The Charlestown Navy Yard, The Black Falcon Terminal, and Hoosac Pier, to name a few.

I filed for bankruptcy protection on a Friday with my original corporation, and continued in the same business under a different corporate name on the following Monday. I brought each and every payable account into the new corporation and explained to them, "I didn't add you to the bankruptcy list. I owe you your money and I'll pay you every cent. You'll just have to give me time." There was one account, however, I did document. It became the reason for the bankruptcy which was resolved during the subsequent proceedings. I kept

285

five people on the payroll and laid-off everyone else, and thirty-four months later I lived up to my promise and paid everyone off— everyone, including the IRS and the DOR who were also willing to wait, as long as I "remained current."

After thirteen years, I decided to sell my businesses and run for public office. At this point in my life I felt I'd seen and done enough to assess legislative proposals and make reasonable decisions in the best interest of the public. So, in 1989 I entered the race for Massachusetts State Senate from the Norfolk and Plymouth District, which included the eight towns, strung along the coast, south of Boston.

I had cut my teeth in politics as a volunteer on the Lucile "Cile" Hicks for Senate campaign in the spring of 1989. I had literally no idea how to run or organize a political campaign, so I worked and watched as her campaign became the "table setter" for the 1990 November cycle. It was an exciting, full-blown and well organized campaign, and I witnessed it all from the inside.

There were seven of us in that 1990 election cycle to replace Senator William Golden—four Democrats and three Republicans. The results of that campaign are well known in Massachusetts circles.

Primary election night, which was held in early September, surprised many of the pundits. Robert Hedlund, the young, brash, truck-repair businessman from Weymouth had won by three votes, which immediately triggered a recount. Following the recount, Robert Hedlund had increased his lead and became the Republican nominee. Robert Ambler, also of Weymouth, became the Democrat nominee. After losing the Primary, I gathered up what was left of my campaign and, along with my campaign staff and volunteers, joined forces with Hedlund. He coasted to victory on election night in November of 1990.

It was another adventure. Another exciting wild ride… no brass ring and no regrets. It was an experience that could never have been taught or understood in a classroom. I didn't win the election, I didn't change the world and I didn't go broke in the process. I knew however, that I, and those who joined with me, had made a difference.

* * *

I now have the high honor and great responsibility commensurate with vying for a seat in the Congress of the United States. The Massachusetts 10th Congressional District stretches along the coast from Quincy to Plymouth, and continues south to Cape Cod and the Islands.

In my opinion, the mission is clear and the cause is just. America, the America I've known from my childhood, with all of its political machinations, is currently facing a prolonged period of extraordinary and unprecedented instability. I cannot sit by and watch this federal government unravel, ignore and cast aside the principles laid down by our ancestors—our founding fathers and the women who courageously supported them.

As of this writing, I'm entering the ninth month of this campaign. I must admit, however, that just over the horizon lies the moment of greatest decision. The question I need to answer is simply, do I go forward or come to terms with what is already pressing heavily on my mind. My age and the toll it's beginning to take are serious factors, and of greater concern to my family and me is the realization that my son is preparing for a yearlong deployment to Afghanistan as part of the announced U.S. Military Surge.

Since leaving high school in 1959, I've never quit or given up on anything, so this decision is especially meaningful to me.

To join with my son in a combined effort to support and defend the interests of my country continues to pull me into this race. Perhaps, however, the time has come to take life more in stride. Perhaps I can make a difference in other, less demanding, ways. Perhaps I just need to take some time away to reflect on the best use of my time. As an aircraft begins its roll down the runway, passing various markers before takeoff, this decision must be made and made soon.

My son called home last week from his post in Germany to ask me how the campaign was going and to suggest I read the latest Drudge Report and something from Charles Krauthammer. "Dad," he continued, "I know you're proud of me, as I am proud of the men and women under my command, and believe me Dad, I'm proud of you too. We'll fight this enemy together. You fight 'em in Congress and we'll fight 'em on the ground...you're part of our team. Everyone says to say hello to the next Congressman from Massachusetts!''

I thanked him for his call and before hanging up, signed off with my familiar and personal, ''I love you, boy!''

He quietly responded, ''Love you too, Dad.''

acknowledgements

My deepest thanks and respect go to my wife Brenda. I will always be grateful to her for her strength, her patience and her encouragement as I sat down and began to chronicle events in my earlier life, long before we met, that impacted me profoundly—events that compelled me to face the future with optimism and courage or become a miserable failure.

Further, I wish to thank my brother Peter who, after reading a draft of this book, called with a heavy heart to tell me how pleased he was that I had written it all down. With all the hardship he has endured from his childhood until now, I can say without hesitation, he is truly a remarkably courageous man.

Thank you also to Audrey Beth Stein of the Cambridge Center for Adult Education in Boston for her advice during the early days.

And to Faye Rapoport DesPres of Waltham, Massachusetts and Joan Schweighardt of Albuquerque, New Mexico for their editing services and their friendship.

Also, to Kat Massaro of Barking Kat Design, Stony Point, New York for her endless patience with me.

And to Karyn Donahue from Eastern Nazarene College in Quincy, Massachusetts for support and encouragement in the early days.

And to Steve Jankowski, Director of Alumni Affairs at Southern Illinois University Edwardsville (S.I.U.E.). Stephen Kerber, University Archivist and Bill Brinson University Photographer, for assisting with my research.

And to the good people at the *Edwardsville Intelligencer Newspaper*, Edwardsville, Illinois who took the time to stop what they were doing to draft a letter giving permission to use some of their material.

Also, to Carol Frisse, Director of the Madison County Historical Museum and Archival Library, Edwardsville, Illinois. Carol took a personal interest in my project and spent several hours combing through publications and files for relevant information.

And to Bruce Donahue, who provided detailed background regarding "Vanzo's," a popular watering hole where businessmen, politicians, and courthouse dignitaries gathered in the back smoke-filled rooms, plotting the course of history in Madison County, Illinois.

And to the many others, too numerous to mention, who inspired me to tell this story.